THE PRESERVATION CHALLENGE

A Guide to Conserving Library Materials

by Carolyn Clark Morrow

with Gay Walker
Introduction by Pamela W. Darling

Knowledge Industry Publications, Inc.
White Plains, NY and London

Professional Librarian Series

The Preservation Challenge: A Guide to Conserving Library Materials

Library of Congress Cataloging in Publication Data

Morrow, Carolyn Clark.
    The preservation challenge.

    (Professional librarian series)
    Bibliography: p.
    Includes index.
    1. Library materials--Conservation and restoration--
Handbooks, manuals, etc.   I. Walker, Gay. II. Title.
III. Series.
Z701.M547   1982   025.7   82-18726
ISBN 0-86729-028-5
ISBN 0-86729-027-7 (pbk.)

This book has been printed on acid-free paper.

Printed in the United States of America

10   9   8   7   6   5   4   3   2   1

Table of Contents

List of Tables and Figures

List of Illustrations

I

Introduction

by Pamela W. Darling

People die. We accept it as inevitable. Pets and houseplants share our lives for a few years but we recognize their mortality, as we know that the favorite old car, the washing machine, the comfortable shoes will eventually have to be replaced. Buildings, institutions, societies, even civilizations flourish, and vanish. Surrounded by evidence of impermanence, trivial and cosmic, we cling to the faith that knowledge, wisdom, truth will endure, bridging the centuries, nurturing cultural progress, sustaining humanity through the ages.

In ancient times this belief was manifest in reverence for the tablet or scroll or parchment on which were recorded the laws that brought order to society or the poems that flowed from its heart. In our era, the talisman has been the book—quintessential medium of communication from one age to the next; compact, portable source of information or inspiration; next in priority after food and water for those stranded on the proverbial desert island.

It is but a small step from the conviction that truth is eternal to the assumption that books, and the related media on which facts and ideas are recorded, will last forever. Do not cave paintings, cuneiform tablets and papyrus rolls speak to us still of peoples otherwise lost to history? The recorded word—etched in stone, inscribed on paper, encoded on magnetic tape—has for centuries served as mankind's bid for immortality, an adroit end run around the inevitability of death, both the assertion and the proof that humanity surpasses the "nasty, brutish and short" life of uncivilized creatures. The survival of thoughts beyond the life of the thinker gives significance to the human experience, and so we are comfortable in believing that the materials on which we record those thoughts will live on after us.

But it has never been true. For every cave painting and laboriously copied manuscript that has survived, countless thousands—even millions—have long since vanished without a trace. The great library at Alexandria was engulfed in flames; the sacred texts of a thousand religions have disappeared along with their adherents; the engineering drawings, however primitive, that preceded the construction of Stonehenge and the Great Pyramids have disappeared. Our easy, comforting assumption that the records of our own civilization are somehow safe from the forces of annihilation is false. Pages crack and shatter, bindings decay, photographs fade, free electrons bounce in and out of electronic media to garble and destroy the message.

What should we do in response to this awesome realization? Can we do anything? This book, *The Preservation Challenge,* itself doomed to eventual disappearance, presents the case for "library preservation." It reviews the physical causes of deterioration, summarizes what has been learned thus far about controlling or even reversing the process, describes procedural and organizational strategies for prolonging the life of record materials. It offers no guarantees. Our civilization, like those before it, is likely to pass from the world some day. Yet we cannot sink back into fatalism. *The Preservation Challenge* asserts that librarians and others who collect and maintain society's records can delay the perhaps-inevitable decline, drawing from vast stores of accumulated knowledge some techniques for retarding the natural forces of decay.

THE PRICE OF PROGRESS

Libraries have long been recognized as institutions responsible for preserving the information, the intellectual heritage, of society. But for many years that responsibility has been viewed chiefly in terms of assembling and providing access to collections of materials. Such attention as was directed toward the physical aspects of collection management revolved around shelving, labelling and those packaging techniques—binding, boxing, placing in folders—necessary for convenient handling of floppy or odd-sized items. In the past, aggressive programs for the physical care, protection and remedial treatment of library materials did not seem particularly necessary. Several factors, arising out of our passage from an agricultural through an industrial into an information era, have combined to alter that situation dramatically.

The mechanization of printing and the spread of literacy during the 19th century brought about a sharp increase in the reading public and the materials produced for its members to read. No longer were books the exclusive domain of a studious clergy or the leisured elite, in whose monasteries, stately homes or private university libraries they rested on oft-dusted shelves, to be used occasionally by well-mannered visitors or earnest young scholars. As education became compulsory, the popular press was born, and the public library movement grew, both the variety and the quantity of materials being added to all kinds of libraries rapidly increased. The ways in which those materials were used underwent corresponding changes.

Simultaneously, to meet the voracious appetites of larger and faster printing presses, paper manufacturing was transformed. One result of mass production was the creation of papers whose physical and chemical components have proven to be highly unstable. Their susceptibility to deterioration has been steadily aggravated by changes in storage conditions. Frequent temperature/humidity cycling brought on by increasingly complex central heating (and later air-conditioning) systems accelerated the natural aging processes in paper, leather, cloth, glue and the heterogeneous ingredients of proliferating new media. Cost-saving fluorescent lights introduced dangerously high levels of ultraviolet radiation into previously dim-lit stacks. Countless industrial plants and automobiles pumped tons of dirt and damaging chemicals into the air.

"Books" or "record materials" began to give way to "information media" in the professional parlance, and the growing threat to their physical existence became more apparent as society's need for the information they embodied grew. Format conversion to speed dissemination, simplify storage and—increasingly—to salvage information from decaying originals, became common. Photocopying, microfilming, computer data bases, video and optical disc recording—ad hoc responses to a multitude of information needs—offer important new tools for the preservation task, but at the same time add to library collections many new forms, each with its own particular care and treatment requirements.

The results of these accumulating changes show themselves with growing frequency in the stacks and reading rooms of libraries and archival repositories everywhere. Manuscript inks fade, bindings fall apart when opened, paper crumbles on the shelf, photographic images disappear, sound recordings crackle and screech, discs and tapes give back gibberish on the terminal screen.

RESISTING THE "INEVITABLE"

The American library profession has, perhaps slowly but steadily, responded to the mushrooming crisis. Wide-ranging research, regional and national planning, and the pioneering development of local programs to attack various facets of the preservation problem have marked the growing professional awareness that selection, acquisition, cataloging and reference are no longer enough if the library is to maintain its role as preserver of society's records.

Not too many years ago the terms "preservation" and "conservation," if they did not conjure up images of endangered species, polluted rivers or historic houses, suggested the world of rare books and precious manuscripts. There were only a few library conservators, who worked on these scarce or unique objects as the museum conservator worked on one-of-a-kind paintings, sculptures, native baskets or dinosaur bones. Since most library materials are not unique, since most library patrons come seeking information rather than an encounter with a cultural artifact, since the physical state of materials in the general collections is incidental to the value of the intellectual content, preservation activities were typically assigned—with the notable exception of binding—to "special collections" staff. All that is changing in this penultimate decade of the 20th century, as non-special collections visibly crumble, taking their contents with them into the dust bin.

THE MUSEUM CONNECTION

The growing field of library preservation owes much to its older counterpart in the museum field. Basic theory about the processes and control of deterioration, and specific practices such as treatment of paper, cloth and leather objects, are directly transferable. But there are major differences between the two. While museum objects are meant to be observed, library materials, almost by definition, are collected in order to be used. Thus many mounting techniques, protective storage measures and restricted access policies appropriate for museum objects have little application in libraries.

Use of books, and some other library materials, involves not only handling but also moving the parts in relation to one another (opening covers, turning pages, winding film). This brings a special set of structural and kinetic engineering questions into storage and treatment processes. The sheer number of items in library collections and their average unit value, in contrast to the number and value of items in most museum collections, make extensive individual conservation treatment impractical and economically unjustifiable.

The nature of museum objects and the social function of museums—to preserve cultural and historic objects in their original state so that the artist's original conception or the craftsman's technique can be studied and appreciated by future generations—bring a number of ethical dilemmas into the treatment process. Materials and techniques that are faithful to the original may not be permanent or durable; replacing a missing piece or touching up a worn spot to restore structural stability or aesthetic effect may conceal vital evidence of the history or provenance of the piece. There are categories of library materials—those whose value as artifacts equals or exceeds the value of their information content—for which the museum conservator's "Code of Ethics"* must be meticulously observed. But for many, perhaps most, ensuring the survival of the message must take precedence over preserving the original media. This need in itself raises ethical issues in the form of selection criteria and treatment priorities.

THE EXTRA CHALLENGE

Library preservation therefore has an additional complex dimension, which manifests itself in substantial attention to administrative matters. Paralleling the development of laboratory techniques for the physical care of individual items has been the creation of a body of theory and practice which focuses on the care of whole collections. The two converge in the search for viable methods of mass treatment (cold storage, mass deacidification, "phased" preservation). But preservation administration also encompasses wide-ranging, non-laboratory policy and procedural questions, such as patron acceptance of alternate formats, the enhancement of bibliographic control mechanisms to support cooperative preservation efforts, the impact of shifting collection development priorities and resource-sharing agreements on local preservation responsibilities.

"Code of Ethics and Standards of Practice," in the *AIC Directory* (Washington, DC: American Institute for Conservation of Historic and Artistic Works, 1980), pp. 9-22 (or latest edition).

Books and other media are generally produced in quantity, and there is a large measure of duplication among library collections. At the same time, the tradition of inter-institutional sharing of resources is strong (notwithstanding the recent phenomenon of fees for interlibrary loan service), so that patrons of any library have at least indirect access to the holdings of almost all others. These two factors lead to a widely accepted principle: that the responsibility for preserving those items held by more than one library can be shared. By dividing the work, at least one copy of many more titles can be saved, and scarce human and financial resources will not be squandered on duplicate efforts. The principle is sound, but the challenge of implementing it has yet to be met.

The usual impediments to cooperation present themselves: the difficulties in getting to know and trust colleagues in other institutions, the delays and complexities of *inter*institutional information exchange overlayed on the maze of *intra*institutional communication, the challenge to authority implicit in collective decision-making whenever it affects local policy or procedure.

Beyond these, cooperative sharing of preservation work is further hindered by factors resulting from the comparative youth of the field. Local preservation programs are not, in most institutions, well-developed, nor are staff in many libraries well-versed in the subject. Consequently, collective activities often begin with a pooling of weakness and ignorance ("Who knows what to do about mold?", "Does anyone know of a good binder?", "How do we start a preservation microfilming program?", "How much should be budgeted for preservation?"). Some, unfortunately, end at the same point; but with patience and creativity, others have found the way to successful tugging at joint bootstraps. Sharing insights and experiences gained from local attention to this or that aspect of preservation can shorten the time-consuming process of developing procedures for the care and treatment of a variety of materials.

Many of the tools and resources necessary for efficient cooperative preservation work, however, are still (in 1982) primitive or lacking altogether. These include techniques and regional facilities for a variety of mass treatments, operational mechanisms for agreeing on who *will* preserve what, and bibliographic systems capable of disseminating information about who *has* preserved what.

COMMITMENT & LEADERSHIP: THE "BOSS" FACTOR

The most crucial factor is of a very different nature, and that is the extreme variation in administrative commitment to preservation found in any cross-section of libraries. The effects of this disparity are plain enough: where commitment is lacking, adequate human and financial resources are not allocated to preservation work, local programs are slow to develop, and the institution is a poor partner in cooperative efforts. The converse is of course true, with the result that the field of library preservation in the early years was populated by a few pioneering leaders and a lot of straggling followers. The commitment issue, in fact, may be the pivotal point, deserving of closer examination.

Several elements must come together if the policy-making, resource-allocating powers within a library or archival institution are to make a substantial commitment to preservation. First, awareness of the problem: recognizing that deterioration is going on, that its rate seems to be accelerating, that higher and higher percentages of the collections are being affected. Second, acknowledging the significance of the problem: identifying the effects of the physical erosion of the collections on the institution's ability to fulfill its service goals now and in the future. Third, believing that something can actually be done to solve the problem.

The first is straightforward. Few professionals remain ignorant of the existence of the problem, thanks to a widening stream of articles in the general literature, proliferating workshops and seminars, and speeches at local, regional and national conferences. The move from awareness to concern is not too difficult, though some drop out along the way, believing (rightly or wrongly) that their collections are not affected—"because we don't have many rare books" or "we're not a research library" or "we're not a museum; our patrons want information, not artifacts" or "our collection is new and hasn't had time to deteriorate." Closer analysis generally proves such convictions to be ill-founded. Deterioration is blind to type-of-library distinctions, and few collections consist solely of materials to be discarded after a few years. Thus the profession as a whole is steadily growing in its understanding of the nature and significance of the preservation problem.

But what of the third element, believing that something can be done about it? This is the hard stretch on the road to commitment, harder in proportion to awareness of the immensity of the problem. As we feel hopeless before the inevitability of death and taxes, so we are tempted—after a brief period of hand-wringing and furrowing of the brow—to turn helplessly away from the challenge, assuaging our consciences with the rationalization that it is better to put our too-scarce resources into activities with greater chance of success. Horrifying statistics about the millions of deteriorating items and the high unit costs for this or that type of care may lead even the most courageous administrator to decide that his/her institution "cannot afford" to give priority to preservation. The truth is that we cannot afford *not* to do something about the problem, but only a few will be able to make that leap until we all have a much clearer idea of what the "something" is.

GROWING COMPETENCE AND RESPONSIBILITY

That this book can be written now is evidence that the final hurdle is breaking down. The next two chapters discuss in detail the causes of the problem, presenting much to discourage and depress the reader. But the remainder of the book describes a broad array of "somethings" that can and are being done in many different institutional settings: environmental control, "care"-ful handling, improved materials and techniques for repair and binding, advances in conservation treatment, salvaging information from disintegrating media, methods and criteria for establishing preservation priorities and selecting appropriate treatment options. Case histories illustrate organizational alternatives for integrating expanding preservation programs into existing administrative structures, processing workflows and service functions. The final chapter catalogs the professional resources and educational opportunities that enable us to transform commitment into competence, while chapter footnotes and a bibliography provide access to the proliferating published literature through which expertise is shared and the theory and practice of the field are further advanced.

The Preservation Challenge is more than a call to action. It offers concrete tools for responding to the physical needs of our collections, and a conceptual framework in which to wield them. It stands as proof that we can delay the processes now undermining centuries-old collections, that there is hope for preserving the best of our intellectual inheritance for future generations. No, not everything can be saved; we shall never overcome the natural forces of deterioration completely. But we are not without power to control, to channel, to retard those forces; we can choose what will survive and what will perish just as we chose what was added to our collections in the first place. And with that power and ability to choose comes inescapable responsibility.

Preservation can no longer be dismissed as a luxury program for a few elite research libraries. It is central to the mission of *every* library and record repository. Familiarity with its theory and practice is as essential to successful professional performance as is mastery of the principles of bibliographic control, the intellectual framework of strategies for manual and automated searching, or the basic concepts of contemporary management and fiscal administration.

The preservation responsibility is shared by every member of the staff. Decisions made by people who may not go near the collections from one month to the next—decisions concerning acquisitions, access or weeding policies; staff assignments and continuing education priorities; negotiations with building maintenance personnel—may have even greater impact on the survival of the collections than the actions of those who handle materials every day.

The profession has a long way to go in solving the preservation problem, but ignorance is no longer a respectable excuse for not joining in the effort. Responsibility to society, present and to come, compels us to careful study of the questions raised on the following pages, to thoughtful application and extension of the partial solutions presented here. If enough people commit themselves to this vital task, the information in this volume will be superseded before the book itself needs preservation treatment.

II

Deterioration of Organic Material

Library materials contain a great variety of substances, the vast majority of which are organic and thus subject to deterioration. Recall that organic materials are those that originated as plant or animal matter, including many synthetic materials. In a scientific sense, deterioration is the transition from one energy state to another. In a practical sense, deterioration means a decrease in the ability of a material to fulfill its intended function.

Library materials transmit information to a user. Thus deterioration can be any action (physical, chemical or biological) that interferes with that transfer. Deterioration, an irreversible process, must not be allowed to progress beyond the point where the intellectual content cannot be reformatted, or converted to a different medium, when appropriate.

Deterioration of library materials results from the action of agents present in the library environment. In most cases the agents promote degradation by reacting with the substances that comprise library materials. The specific location and climate where a library is located determines which potential agents are present to shorten the useful life of materials. Library materials in the United States are located in every type of climate except tropical rain forest and polar. Collections in the desert and steppe climates of the American west will have different environmental challenges than collections in the humid subtropical climates of the southeast or the humid marine climate of northern California, Oregon and Washington.

The *intensity* of the environmental agents is similarly dependent on the prevailing climate of the region in combination with a specific location. For example, in the desert, dirt acts as an abrasive on the surface of library materials. In the more humid central plains, dirt acts as an abrasive and also provides nutrients for mold growth. In Chicago, the "Windy City," dirt carrying the contaminants of urban air settles on library materials, abrades the surface, provides nutrients for mold growth and promotes acid deterioration of leather and paper.

Environmental agents promote deterioration in three major ways—chemical, physical and biological. A specific agent, however, is capable of multiple effects. For example, water (moisture) may physically damage hygroscopic (moisture-sensitive) materials such as paper and vellum by expanding them; it may also be a reagent in chemical reactions within a material; or it may provide essential moisture for fungal growth. Although fungi primarily cause biological deterioration, the end result is material that is *physically* weakened.

Deterioration of library materials is a complex problem. Not only is there a great potential for deterioration owing to the very nature of library materials, but there are a number of diverse deterioration agents—acting alone or in combination and exerting multiple effects. The challenge to the library profession is to understand deterioration well enough to control it so that library materials fulfill their function for as long as they are needed.

AGENTS OF DETERIORATION

Light

Of all the chemical and physical agents of deterioration, light is the most potent. Light is the form of radiation that we can see; radiation is measured in wavelengths. Wavelengths of ultraviolet, visible and infrared radiation are potential deteriorative agents within a library environment. The shorter the wavelength, the more potent the effect of the radiation. Thus, the short, high energy wavelengths of ultraviolet (UV) radiation will cause far more damage than infrared (IR) radiation. Fortunately, the ozone layer above the earth prevents radiation with wavelengths shorter than ultraviolet from striking the earth. Glass windows filter wavelengths of 300 to 325 nanometers (25% of the UV radiation), as well as much of the infrared radiation.

Radiation is a form of energy that promotes deterioration by activating chemical reactions. The minimum energy a molecule must receive in order to react is "activation energy." Activation energy is specific to different materials, and reaction will not occur if the activation energy for a material is not reached. Light is a very effective source of activation energy.

Photochemical degradation, or the deteriorative effects of light on organic materials, leads to discoloration and embrittlement. Deteriorative reactions proceed when the material absorbs light energy so that its molecules can react with oxygen. Material thus "radiated" is susceptible to oxidation long after the light source is removed. The activation energy was sufficient to start the reaction and it can proceed on its own—even in complete darkness.[1]

The effects of exposure to light, however, are not immediately apparent. Organic materials exposed to radiation first enter an induction period where there appears to be no effect. Actually, light is being absorbed, and if the activation energy for a specific material is reached, chemical reactions that were initiated can proceed to completion. Even brief exposures to light will promote deterioration.

Since it is obviously impossible to keep light away from library materials, some deterioration is inevitable. The rule of reciprocity states that by controlling exposure to light we can control the *rate* of deterioration. This can be done either by controlling the type and amount of light (the intensity) or by controlling how long an object is exposed to light. This principle is particularly important in the exhibition of rare and unique materials. It can be summarized by the following formula:

$$\text{Total exposure} = \text{Time} \times \text{Intensity}$$

There are three sources of illumination common to libraries—natural light coming in through windows and skylights, tubular fluorescent lamps and incandescent bulbs.

Incandescent light is produced by passing electric current through a coiled tungsten filament inside of a glass bulb. Since most of the electricity passing through the filament is converted to heat (94% for a 100-watt bulb), incandescent lighting is not energy efficient for commercial applications. Incandescent bulbs do not, however, emit the shorter wavelength UV radiation and thus do not promote photochemical degradation.

Fluorescent lamps produce light by an electric current passing through mercury vapor trapped in a glass tube. Fluorescent tubes require a control unit between them and the electrical current; the tubes do not generate heat, but the control units do. Tubes are coated on the inside with phosphor powders capable of fluorescing, that is, absorbing radiation and re-emitting it at a longer wavelength. Mercury atoms excited by the electric current emit UV radiation in specific wavelengths (mostly 253.7 nanometers). The UV radiation does not produce "visible" light, however, until it strikes the phosphor coating. The selection of phosphors will not only determine the "color" and "quality" of the light produced but will significantly affect the *quantity* of UV radiation emitted from the lamp and thus its ability to promote photochemical deterioration.

Daylight coming through windows has a much higher proportion of UV radiation to visible radiation than do fluorescent lights. Even on a cloudy day, the UV radiation in natural light will cause more photochemical deterioration than will fluorescent lights. Table II.1 rates light sources commonly found in museums and libraries in terms of probable damage per footcandle. It is a useful way of comparing the damage hazard of different sources of light. Six different light sources are compared to zenith skylight (100% damage). Skylights are more damaging than sunlight through vertical windows, cool white fluorescent light (CWX) is more damaging than white fluorescent light (WWX) and incandescent light is least damaging. The last column shows the probable rate of damage when the UV radiation is filtered out.

Architects, lighting engineers and building planners do not typically consider photochemical deterioration when designing lighting systems for libraries—except perhaps for exhibit cases in rare book rooms. They are primarily concerned with the initial and operating costs of the system and the function of the areas to be lighted (i.e., open stack versus closed stacks, carrels versus general reading areas and technical services versus restrooms

Table II.1 Probable Damage per Footcandle (D/fc)*

| | D/fc (Percent) | |
Light Source	Unfiltered	Filtered
Clear zenith sky light	100.0	8.5
Overcast skylight	31.7	5.1
Sunlight	16.5	4.0
Fluorescent (CWX)	11.5	3.1
Flourescent (WWX)	9.2	1.8
Flourescent (daylight)	8.4	5.1
Incandescent	2.8	1.3

*Expressed as a percentage when clear zenith skylight is 100% damage. Percentages are for unfiltered and UV filtered light.

Source: Adapted from the *Illuminating Engineering Society Lighting Handbook* (New York: Illuminating Engineering Society, 1972), pp. 12-24.

and lobbies). The quality and uniformity of the light are also important considerations. It is generally understood that greater intensities of light (more than 35 footcandles) are not necessary or desirable in libraries and contribute to eye fatigue. This is fortunate because greater intensities of daylight or fluorescent light will increase the rate of photochemical deterioration.

Heat

Heat, like light, is a form of energy that promotes deterioration. Temperature is a measure of the intensity of heat energy.

Heat is a source of activation energy. Even at low temperatures some molecules have sufficient energy to react, although the *rate* of their reaction is greatly reduced. The Arrhenius law states that the rate of chemical reactions will change logarithmically as a function of temperature. The higher the temperature, the faster the library materials will deteriorate. The usual rule of thumb is that for every 10° C (18° F) rise in temperature, the rate of chemical reaction doubles. However, the rate of chemical reactions in *cellulose* (paper and cloth) doubles for each 5° C (9° F) rise in temperature.[2]

Just as libraries cannot keep materials in constant, total darkness, they cannot store materials permanently at extremely low temperatures. Thus deterioration from the effect of heat is inevitable. Libraries, however, can *significantly reduce the rate of deterioration* by lowering temperatures. Library materials stored at 70° F will deteriorate approximately half as fast as library materials stored at 79° F. Any material composed of organic materials that are easily oxidized should be stored at as low a temperature as is practical. This will reduce the heat-induced energy of the molecules and slow down the degradation process.

Heat also affects deterioration by increasing physical processes such as the movement of water and air through solids. The results are desiccation (drying), embrittlement and distortion (warping).

Fluctuations in temperature are undesirable because many library materials are made up of several component materials that absorb heat and expand at different rates, for example, the parts of a bookbinding or the gelatin emulsion of photographic film. Rapid and frequent changes in temperature will cause stress that leads to structural breakdown. This is especially significant when combined with the ability of organic materials to absorb and release moisture in response to changes in temperature.

Heat is an insidious agent of deterioration. We cannot *see* library materials expanding and contracting nor can we *see* chemical reactions occurring. The results, however, are all too obvious—brittle paper, cracked and warped leather bindings and flaking photographic images.

Humidity

Separating heat and humidity as agents of deterioration is rather arbitrary since their effects are largely interactive. The ability of air to hold moisture is dependent on temperature since warmer air can support more moisture. Because of this dependence, humidity is usually expressed as a percentage of the maximum amount of water the air could hold at a particular temperature. This is termed the relative humidity (RH).

$$\text{RH} = \frac{\text{Amount of water in a given quantity of air}}{\text{Maximum amount of water that the air can hold at that temperature}} \times 100\%$$

In a sealed container, such as an exhibit case or shipping container, the amount of water vapor in the air remains constant so that condensation can easily form if the temperature is raised or alternatively lowered and raised.

Water acts as a physical agent of deterioration by causing hygroscopic materials to undergo dimensional changes. When RH drops, moisture is released; when RH increases, moisture is reabsorbed. This process of expansion and contraction can cause library materials to break apart physically. This kind of physical stress is exacerbated by the fact that different component materials absorb moisture at different rates and in different amounts.

For example, if a hygroscopic material such as vellum or paper is restrained (in a frame or binding), cycling of RH will cause warping, cockling and tearing. On the other hand, water is necessary to prevent desiccation and embrittlement. For most organic materials, there is an optimum moisture content for the maintenance of useful physical properties.

Water is also a chemical agent of deterioration. Fading of dyes in leather, paper and cloth occurs more rapidly at higher humidities. Water is necessary in the acid hydrolysis of paper, and it facilitates the action of industrial and urban air pollutants on organic materials.

Library materials are ordinarily exposed simultaneously to the effects of light, heat

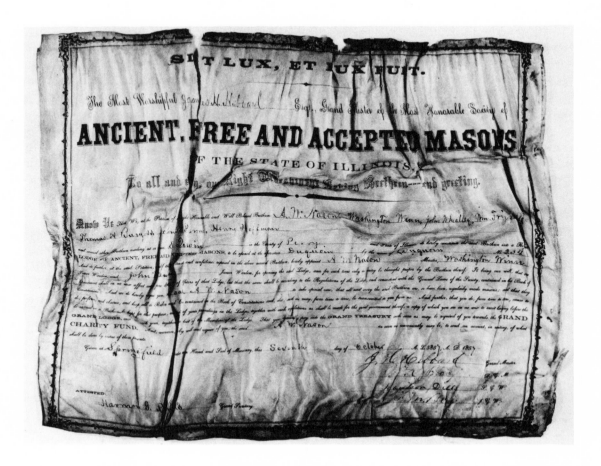

Parchment document that was framed and subjected to fluctuating temperature and humidity.

and moisture. By controlling the *intensity* of these deteriorative agents, libraries can reduce deterioration and promote preservation of their collections.

Gaseous Air Pollutants

The burning of fossil fuels (coal, petroleum, oil and natural gas) causes concentrations of gaseous air pollutants in cities and industrial areas. It is these concentrations of man-made pollutants that promotes the deterioration of cultural property in libraries and museums. Of these pollutants, sulfur dioxide is a major deteriorative agent.

When fossil fuels are burned, sulfur impurities combine with oxygen to form sulfur dioxide (SO_2). Since SO_2 is readily absorbed on surfaces, fortunately, the concentration indoors is only one-half of what it is outdoors. However, in urban and industrial areas, that one-half is still a significant concentration. Sulfur dioxide quickly combines with more oxygen to form sulfur trioxide (SO_3), which combines with omni-present moisture in the air to form sulfuric acid (H_2SO_4). Sulfuric acid is a strong corrosive chemical that degrades surfaces. The most obvious effect in libraries is leather deterioration—a powdery, weakened condition termed "red rot."

Sulfur dioxide is also a hazard to cellulose materials (paper and cloth). The oxidation of sulfur dioxide to sulfuric acid is aided by impurities in the materials, such as traces of iron, alum sizing and residual lignin. The impurities act as catalysts to chemical reaction. The most familiar effect in libraries is the brown, brittle edges of books caused by sulfur dioxide penetrating the pages and reacting with the impurities to form sulfuric acid.

Besides the acidic effects of sulfur dioxide present in urban areas, photochemical oxidants such as ozone are strong deteriorative agents. Ozone acts as a powerful destroyer of organic materials by breaking the double bonds on carbon chains. The ozone problem, which was first identified in Los Angeles, has spread to all urban areas. It is a particular syndrome of the sunbelt.

Most of the nitrogen oxides present in urban areas are harmless; however, nitrogen dioxide will combine with oxygen and water to form nitric acid. Nitric acid has strong acidic as well as oxidant effects and attacks the dyes in ink, cloth, leather and paper.

Not all gaseous pollutants are produced out of doors. Organic acid vapors are given off inside of buildings, particularly by wood. Ozones are produced by certain electrical and lighting equipment used in buildings. Degradation of polyvinyl chlorides by heat and light produces hydrogen chloride, which reacts to form hydrochloric acid.

In recent years there has been considerable effort made to reduce and control urban concentrations of sulfur dioxide and other pollutants. The effects of acid rain (sulfur dioxide dissolved in water droplets) on buildings and statues and on vegetation and lakes in rural areas downwind of cities has elicited a public outcry. Gaseous air pollution is now measured and regulated to levels acceptable for humans. Like all regulations, however, abuses occur, and control in individual situations is difficult. Even low concentrations of pollutants are significant to libraries when the *cumulative* effect is considered.

Particulate Matter

Dust, dirt, sand and smoke constitute a considerable hazard for library materials by soiling and abrading, by facilitating the action of water and biological agents and by carrying and combining with gaseous pollutants.

The largest particulates are formed by direct mechanical action—dust formed by grinding processes or by fine sand or dirt shot directly into the air. The smallest particulates are formed by chemical processes or from incomplete combustion of fuels. These small particles remain suspended in the air until they become trapped on a surface.

Particulates are hygroscopic. A film of dust or dirt will maintain a higher moisture level on the surface of an object and will provide a medium conducive to the growth of fungus. In the presence of moisture, certain particulates undergo acid chemical reactions and promote degradation of library materials. Since dust and dirt are solid particles of varying size and hardness, they exert an abrasive action on moving parts, for example, when reshelving books or reading microfilms.

Particulate matter in urban areas can be reduced by adherence to air quality and emission control standards and by ventilation and filtration systems in library buildings. Although often viewed simply as a nuisance in libraries, dirt and dust are significant deteriorative agents.

Fungi

Fungi are a large and heterogeneous group of plant organisms; "mold" and "mildew" refer to small, nonparasitic fungi. Fungal growth in libraries usually appears either as a fuzzy gray coating or as colorful patterns and blotches. Fungi act as biological agents of deterioration to ingest organic materials and cause weakening and decomposition. The by-products of growth are unsightly and difficult or impossible to remove.

Spores necessary for the reproduction of fungi are found everywhere. Growth occurs when conditions are favorable, which can be complete darkness as well as light, although exposure to UV rays in sunlight will kill many fungi.

Library materials constitute unlimited nutrients for mold growth; only moisture and temperature are added requirements. Since the range of optimum temperatures for growth is 59°-86° F (15°-30° C), the moisture content in a library is the critical growth factor. Optimum moisture for fungal growth is usually 80%-100% RH, but during long-term storage fungi will grow (albeit more slowly) at RH as low as 60%. Of course, rapid multiplication and dissemination occurs when conditions are just right. For example, a rapid rise in temperature of even a few degrees will raise the surface moisture on library materials considerably and will facilitate mold growth.[3] When equilibrium moisture is again reached between the ambient air and the object, growth slows or stops—until the next time. Dust and dirt, being hygroscopic, will further attract moisture to surfaces. In a moist environment, water in the pores of paper provides just the right atmosphere for fungal growth.

Fungi are very patient. They are very resistant to unfavorable conditions and will simply wait until conditions are right to resume growth. Spores on herbarium specimens have been known to remain viable for as long as 25 years. Fungi are an ever-present danger to library materials.

Insects

Insects introduced into a library will find a veritable feast. Uncontrolled, they will rapidly ingest paper, cloth, leather, parchment and vellum, and glue and paste. Detection is difficult since it depends on identifying damage, and many insects are nocturnal or do their work in infrequently visited spots. Some insects eat only on the surface, softening and weakening it, while others form elaborate tunnels. Others eat only the glue and paste.

The so-called "bookworm" is actually many species of beetles that ingest cellulosic and proteinaceous materials during the larval stage. Many other insects are also common to libraries. Cockroaches will eat paper and books and leave unsightly droppings similar to fly specks. Because they are so large, their damage resembles that of gnawing mice. They are particularly resistent to insecticides. Silverfish are pale, primitive insects that feed on the surface of paper and are active at night. Termites form colonies like ants and feed primarily on cellulose. They are frequently found on the bottom of boxes because they like moist, dark environments.

Movement of library materials between floors, especially from the basement to upper floors, can increase the hazards of infestation—especially if cleaning and treatment schedules are not strictly followed. Fortunately, most libraries have eradicated insect pests; the main threat is from incoming retrospective collections, collections previously stored in attics or basements, or materials purchased from tropical climates where insect problems are almost insurmountable—even among new stock.

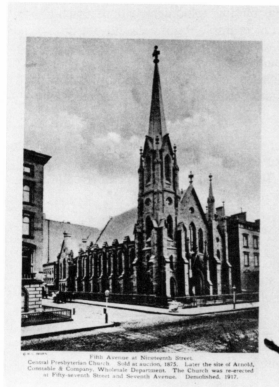

Fifth Avenue at Nineteenth Street.
Central Presbyterian Church. Sold at auction, 1875. Later the site of Arnold, Constable & Company, Wholesale Department. The Church was re-erected at Fifty-seventh Street and Seventh Avenue. Demolished, 1917.

An Old New York School

By Eveline Warner Brainerd

It was in midsummer of 1816 that a young and, if her middle age told truly of her youth, a beautiful English woman opened a little school in what was then the upper part of the city of New York. Some twenty years before, there had come to seek their fortune in the growing town on Manhattan Island, a sturdy Kentish family named Boorman. Active citizens of their new home they proved, and two of the children, Esther and James, we know had more than common weight and influence. Early in life Esther Boorman Smith found herself with two little daughters to support, and with few enough occupations to choose from. Not even women teachers were needed as they are to-day, for the public free school was still an experiment and but two existed in the city. Small private schools there were a-plenty, for the most part short-lived ventures, and though often carried on by women, most of the instructors were men. Indeed, in this very year was opened a most promising school under the patronage of Drs. Gardiner Spring and J. B. Romeyne and George Griffin, Esq., two of the most influential clergymen and one of the most noted lawyers of the time. However, 1816 was a good year in the new land, and so there appeared in the "Evening Post" for July 11 the following advertisement: "Mrs. E. Smith's establishment for the board and tuition of young ladies, No. 3 Hudson Square, is now in readiness for the reception of pupils as boarders or day boarders. The different branches of education by the most approved masters. Further information may be had on application to Mrs. S., and those to whom she is unknown are respectfully referred to the following gentlemen: the Rev. Dr. Mason, Samuel Boyd, Esq., Dr. J. H. Rogers, and Peter Radcliff, Esq."

Esther Smith is described in later years as not only a very beautiful woman, but of great charm of

[371]

"Bookworm" damage to a volume (center, foreground).

People

Human beings are oft-cited agents of deterioration, with librarians and bookbinders at the top of the list.

Librarians, as policy-makers, are directly responsible for the overall preservation and conservation of their collections. Furthermore, by their example, library patrons learn how to treat library material. Librarians determine standards for environmental control, choose services such as binding and reprography, and set policies for shelving and circulation. By inattention to preservation and conservation concerns, they may inadvertently act as agents of deterioration.

Library materials are meant to be used. Thus, simple wear and tear is largely unavoidable. Materials become soiled and abraded, protective coverings for books (bookbindings) wear out and film and plastic-based materials become scratched. Wear and tear is a fact with which librarians must live and for which they must plan.

Well-meaning but inappropriate treatment can cause deterioration and structural breakdown. Library materials are *physical* as well as bibliographic items whose structures must fit their intended purpose and expected use. For example, books should not be bound so that they are difficult and/or impossible to read. They should not be mended with unsound, impermanent materials that cause damage either immediately or in the future. Film materials should not be improperly sliced or incorrectly wound on their reels. Inappropriate treatment is not just a nuisance; it can obscure or destroy information and certainly wastes money.

Library materials also deteriorate as a result of improper use. Library staff and patrons may cause inadvertent damage by misuse of library materials. To most library patrons, library materials are merely merchandise. To many library staff members, library materials represent tasks to be dealt with as expediently as possible.

There is also deterioration from deliberate abuse. Careless and selfish behavior will occur in the library setting despite priorities of service to patrons. Since libraries traditionally make materials widely available with very few restrictions, they will never be able to eliminate vandalism and abuse completely. Clearly stated policies for use and circulation, alert staffs and swift retribution for offenders may offer some deterrent to deliberate abuse.

Fortunately, people can be seen and talked to and, in most cases, reasoned with. They can read instructions and follow policies. They can also choose *not* to read or listen. Their potential as agents of deterioration is almost unlimited.

Disasters

Disasters are an ever-present threat to library collections. No library is immune to the devastation that can occur as a result of natural or man-made disasters.

Library materials constitute a highly combustible, compact fuel that can totally combust. Fires can result in total destruction of a collection. Nearby items not directly engulfed in flames can be irreparably charred or destroyed by soot and smoke. Heat from a fire causes bindings to shrink and warp and plastic-base materials to melt. Water used to fight a fire can cause widespread damage—from the water itself, as well as from the force of high pressure hoses. A building that has burned cannot be entered immediately, which delays salvage efforts and results in further damage.

In addition to fire and heat, water from fire-fighting, floods, tornadoes, high winds and rain, melting snow, roof leaks, burst water plumbing, and so on, is a serious agent of deterioration. Library materials will absorb water, swell, distort and become extremely vulnerable to physical damage. Great strain is placed on structures such as hinges and sewing. Because the cloth and leather coverings of bookbindings absorb less water than the paper book block and the cover boards, bindings often seriously warp and the shape of the spine becomes concave instead of convex. Dyes and inks may bleed and book pages stick together. Leather and vellum produced prior to 1700 will fare well if dried carefully under controlled conditions, but modern leather once soaked may become brown sludge or shrink seriously. Books with coated paper will "block" or the text leaves will stick together in one clump if allowed to begin drying after they have been saturated. The film emulsions of photographic materials will absorb water; without attention, it takes only three days for the emulsion to separate from the film base. The dye layers of color photographic materials will separate within 48 hours. (Immediate reprocessing of photographic materials is essential if they are to be saved.)

Dirt and debris carried by flood waters can become imbedded in materials and greatly complicate salvage and restoration. Wet books will swell and jam themselves onto shelves within eight hours if there is not sufficient room at the end of each shelf to accommodate swelling.[4] Once jammed, they are very difficult to remove, or worse, they may pop off the shelf and onto the floor where there may be mud and dirt and where they are susceptible to further damage.

Water-damaged book with warped binding.

Disasters, by their very nature, cause disruption and panic. Salvage efforts can be delayed by smoke or heat from a recent fire, continuing bad weather or the danger of loose electrical wires. Without an existing disaster preparedness plan, a library staff will be unprepared to act quickly to organize salvage efforts. There also may be bureaucratic delays in obtaining the necessary supplies and equipment. Regardless of the reasons, delay causes further damage to a collection.

The most critical problem associated with delay is the danger of widespread mold growth. Omnipresent mold spores will proliferate on damp materials within 48 to 72 hours—depending on the temperature, relative humidity and presence of dormant mold spores.

A disaster situation usually encourages people to act quickly, often without thinking. If salvage efforts are not coordinated by a person knowledgeable about the vulnerability of wet materials, further damage may ensue. Books and paper will absorb 60% to 80% of their weight in water. Wet paper is not only heavy, it is weak and tends to stick together by surface tension. Attempts to "straighten" wet paper or books will inevitably result in torn and stretched paper. More problems are caused as wet materials begin to dry. Coated paper will irreversibly stick in a clump, and during uneven drying, capillary action will pull water soluble adhesives/dirt/dyes through paper and cause "tide marks."

The salvage and restoration of water-damaged library materials is a frustrating, time-consuming and expensive operation. Fortunately, freezing and vacuum-drying techniques (see Chapter VIII) have developed that enable libraries to salvage most materials if appropriate action is taken immediately. Many libraries have recognized the importance of disaster prevention and preparedness and have taken steps to plan for a possible disaster.

INTERACTIVE EFFECTS

Although agents of deterioration can be discussed separately, library materials are, more often than not, subjected to the simultaneous effects of several agents. The greatest potential for destruction lies in the interactive effects that promote chemical, physical and biological deterioration. In most cases, the action of one deteriorative agent is intensified and hastened by the presence of one or more other agents.[5]

Several agents are essential to the activity of other agents. For example, light produces ozone and gaseous pollutants produce particulate matter. High humidity is essential for fungal growth and encourages infestation by insects. Moisture intensifies photochemical degradation and is a necessary catalyst for deteriorative chemical reactions precipitated by heat, light and gaseous pollutants. Low humidity, on the other hand, intensifies the resultant brittleness and desiccation from those chemical reactions. Heat, like humidity, promotes fungal growth and insect infestation. It hastens chemical reactions activated by light and gaseous pollutants.

Fluctuating temperature and humidity intensifies physical deterioration because it causes materials to expand and contract alternately. Even if the absolute humidity in the air remains constant, fluctuations in temperature will cause the relative humidity to vary considerably, affecting the amount of water absorbed or released. Hygroscopic materials may literally break themselves apart under such conditions.

Particulate matter and people have many interactive effects. Dust and dirt absorb water and gaseous pollutants before the particles stick to library materials. Dust already on materials will attract mosisture and provide nutrients for insects and fungi. Dirt intensifies the damage caused by people, and people bring dirt into libraries. They also bring in food, which attracts insects. Library materials embrittled by chemical reactions, heat and low humidity are more subject to damage by people.

Deterioration is complicated because there are so many variables; it is important because the results are irreversible. Library materials that have become weakened or degraded by the action of deteriorative agents may not be able to be strengthened again. Libraries seek to control deterioration so that they can extend the useful life of materials and protect their investment. For some materials, the object is to extend life indefinitely. But for most libraries, efforts made to retard deterioration will be based on what is practical, cost-effective and appropriate to the needs ʋf the collection and the mission of the library.

FOOTNOTES

1. Thomas B. Brill, *Light: Its Interaction With Art and Antiquities* (New York: Plenum Press, 1980), p. 187.

2. Garry Thomson, *The Museum Environment* (London: Butterworths and Co. Publishers, Ltd., 1978), p. 185.

3. Carl J. Wessel, "Deterioration of library materials," in *Encyclopedia of Library and Information Science, Volume 7,* eds. A. Kent and H. Lancour (New York: Marcel Dekker, 1972), p. 87.

4. Peter Waters, *Procedures for Salvage of Water-Damaged Library Materials* (Washington, DC: Library of Congress, 1975), p. 3.

5. Glenn A. Greathouse and Carl J. Wessel, *Deterioration of Materials: Causes and Preventative Techniques* (New York: Reinhold Publishing Corp., 1954).

III

Library Materials:
Their Composition and Preservation

The preservation task facing libraries is complicated by the diverse nature of library materials, both in composition and structure. Furthermore, new materials and formats continuously emerge that increase the range of possibilities. Fortunately, librarians, manufacturers and publishers are becoming more aware of preservation concerns and are moving slowly toward the resolution of many preservation issues.

PAPER

Evolution of Papermaking Technology

Until the 19th century, paper was made almost exclusively from cotton or linen rags. High-quality, clean rags were in great demand, and every scrap of material was saved. As early as 1666, for example, the English Parliament banned the use of cotton and linen for burial cloths—to conserve rags and also to encourage wool production.

In 1719, French scientist and naturalist Réné Réaumur suggested wood as a source of papermaking fiber after observing that wasps made very fine "paper" from wood. In the late 18th century, Jacob Schaeffer, a Bavarian scientist, experimented with and made paper from bark, straw, cabbage stalks, corn husks, potatoes, pine cones and moss, as well as wood. In 1801 in England, Matthias Koops set up a company for the making of paper from straw and produced the first commercial paper from vegetable fiber.

Regardless of the source of fiber, all paper was made by hand until the invention of papermaking machines in the early 19th century. Western handmade paper was made by dipping a mold into a vat of beaten or macerated cloth fibers suspended in water. Traditionally, the mold was a rectangular screen made of horizontal wires, which were laced together by vertical wires and attached to a rigid wooden frame.

An individual sheet of paper was formed by plunging the mold at a near vertical angle into a vat of suspended paper fibers and removing it perfectly horizontally. As the mold was lifted from the vat, the vatman would shake the mold to ensure even distribution of the fibers in both directions. A wooden frame called a "deckle" kept the wet fibrous mass from flowing over the edges of the mold. Excess water was drained from the mold, the deckle removed and the water-logged sheet of paper "couched" (transferred with a rocking motion) onto a wool felt. Another felt was placed over the sheet and the process could begin again. Later the pile of wet paper was further pressed, hung to dry and cured or conditioned.

At the end of the 18th century and the beginning of the 19th century, Nicholas-Louis Robert in France and the Fourdrinier brothers in England (among others) were instrumental in developing the papermaking machine. The first machines were very simple. Paper was formed on a continuous woven wire cloth or screen that captured the mascerated fibers or pulp and allowed excess water to be drained or suctioned off. Much of the work after the sheet was formed was still done by hand.

The first paper made on machines was high quality since it was still made from rag pulp. The major difference was that machine-made paper could be much wider (30-60 inches) and any length.

The development and acceptance of the papermaking machine in Europe and the United States was rapid. Thomas Gilpin started the first successful machine papermaking mill in 1817 on the Brandywine Creek north of Wilmington, DE. By the 1830s, machine-made paper was well established. With the increased demand for printed works, the need for more plentiful and cheaper sources of fiber became even more critical.

Despite the early success of Schaeffer in the late 18th century, wood was not investigated seriously as a source of fiber until the 1840s in Germany. The first mechanical wood pulp was made in 1849 by Friedrich Keller, who ground wood blocks against a revolving wet grindstone. The wood fiber was mixed with 40% rag fiber to give it strength. By the 1860s, ground wood pulp was being produced commercially in the United States.

The groundwood process produced cheap fiber for papermaking; however, lignin (noncarbohydrate portion of the cell wall of plant material), resins and other impurities remained with the fiber in the pulp. Some purification of the fiber was necessary to produce a more durable paper. Pulp produced by chemical processes was developed by the 1850s and proved to be a superior method for producing fiber.

Papermaking in the 19th century was influenced by the industrial revolution and the rapid expansion of a literate public. New technology was necessary if enough paper was to be produced to meet the demand. Many of the technological improvements, however, resulted in paper that was destined to deteriorate rapidly. The discovery of chlorine bleaching made possible the use of dirty, weak rags that had been unsuitable for papermaking in the 18th century. Overbeating of the pulp in new machines produced shorter fibers, which could be used because of the refinements of papermaking machines—together the result was weaker paper. The use of wood pulp (especially ground wood with its high lignin content) and improperly processed chemical wood pulp produced paper with inherent impurities. As a finale, alum-rosin "size" with its constituent of sulfuric acid became widely used as a replacement for the more expensive gelatin size. (Size is needed to add body to the paper and to prevent the "feathering" of ink.) The first half of the 20th century was an expansion of the technology of the late 19th century with continued emphasis on high production and low cost.

Composition and Manufacture of Modern Paper

Paper, regardless of the source of the pulp or the manufacturing method, is made up of a thin matting of intertwined cellulose fibers. Differences in the properties of paper are the result of the source and pureness of the fiber, the methods of producing and beating or refining the pulp, additives to the pulp, and coatings or finishes applied to the paper after it is formed. All these factors affect the permanence (chemical stability) and durability (physical strength) of a particular paper.

The major sources of cellulose fiber for paper constituting library materials are cotton fiber, cotton linters (short fibers adhering to cottonseed after ginning), cotton or linen cuttings from new fabrics (rags) and wood (mainly spruce). Many papers are composed of a combination of these fibers. Cotton pulp, a source of pure, stable cellulose fiber, yields high-quality papers. Wood, however, is the major source of modern papermaking fiber.

Wood pulp is produced by two main processes—grinding and cooking in chemicals. Both mechanical and chemical wood pulp contain residual impurities and lignin that should be removed by washing, bleaching and chemical extraction. Lignin, the binding agent between wood fibers, is a complex group of related materials that is very difficult to remove completely from pulp. Lignin left in paper, for example, turns brown when exposed to heat or chemical reaction. Groundwood pulp is used where permanence and durability are of minor importance because it contains most of the constituents of wood plus all of the lignin. Pulp produced by chemical treatment of wood chips has the *potential* for producing strong papers, providing impurities and residual chemicals are eliminated from the finished pulp.[1]

In the paper mill, pulp is beaten or "refined" prior to sheet formation. During beating, the cellulose fibers are shortened, hydrated (swollen with water) and fibrillated (frayed). Fibrillation increases the surface area of the fibers and enhances hydrogen bonding. Paper is held together by hydrogen bonding between cellulose molecules and intertwining of fibers and *not* by sizing or additives. Thus, the length of the fibers and the amount of fibrillation affect the durability of the paper. Sizing and other additives may be added during refining of the pulp, later before the sheet is formed or after the sheet is formed. Sizing with starch, animal glue, rosin or synthetics is the most common additive. Loading materials such as clay or calcium carbonate improve opacity and printability.

The modern papermaking machine is an enormous, complicated mechanism geared to high production, speed and uniformity. It can produce a reel of paper 80 to 360 inches wide and of indeterminate length. Paper can be produced at 500 to 3500 feet per minute.

The process of forming the sheet starts when diluted pulp (99.5% water) is fed onto a continuous moving wire through a mechanism called the "headbox." The headbox regulates the consistency and flow of the pulp, which is vital to the uniformity of the web (sheet) of paper. As the pulp moves along the wire, water drains out through the mesh and the wire is given a sideways shake to help interweave the fibers. Because the pulp is moving at high speeds in one direction, the vast majority of the fibers will align themselves in the direction of the flow. The machine or grain direction of the finished paper is an important property since paper bends, flexes and tears more easily *with* the grain. At the end of the moving wire, more water is removed by suction, and a "dandy roll" makes a watermark (and sometimes fake chain and laid lines). A "couch roll" covered with woolen felt lifts the paper web from the wire and transfers it to the "press rolls." Pressing removes more water and helps consolidate the sheet.

Paper passes from the press section to the dryer section containing 60%-65% water. In the dryer section the web of paper is passed over and under steam-heated hollow cylinders to reduce water content to 5%-10%. Frequently, drying is interrupted by surface sizing or coating operations. The paper web is finished by passing through "calendar rolls" that increase smoothness and gloss on the surface of the sheet. Various finishes can also be given to the paper during "supercalendaring." Finally, the completed web of paper is wound on a reel.

Quality of Modern Papers

Since the introduction of machine-made paper and wood pulp, papermakers have not consciously chosen to manufacture impermanent paper, nor have publishers deliberately chosen paper stock that was destined to deteriorate rapidly. Both have simply been responding to pressure to produce more and more paper products and books. By the time the ramifications of producing and using impermanent paper were well demonstrated, and librarians and public officials had raised an outcry, the pulp and paper industry was firmly entrenched in production of paper with a high acid content.

The fact that outrage against impermanent paper had little immediate impact is hardly surprising. The technology of producing permanent (acid-free) paper on a large scale was not even possible until the 1960s. Also, book paper comprises only about 1% of the paper industry, and hard cover books are an even smaller portion. The profits of the papermaking industry are based on the enormous productivity of the machines, and system conversions from acid processes to alkaline are time-consuming and costly.[2]

Publishers, through their production managers, suppliers and printers, choose paper used for books and are responsible for the quality of the paper used. There are many factors that influence choice, including cost, printability and availability. For the vast majority of publications reaching libraries, however, permanence has *not* been a factor in paper choice. Fortunately, since 1960, the situation has vastly improved. The causes of paper deterioration have been clearly elucidated, synthetic alkaline sizes are available to replace acidic alum-rosin size and standards and specifications for permanent and durable book paper have been developed and disseminated. Cooperation and dialogue among librarians, publishers and papermakers have increased. More important, however, the cost benefits of alkaline papermaking processes have been demonstrated, and more and more mills are "going alkaline."

Why Paper Deteriorates

The reasons why paper deteriorates are well known today, but this has not always been the case. Because paper made from rags, the old way, was in better condition than paper made from wood pulp, investigators pointed to *fiber* content as the indicator of permanence. During the 1930s and 1940s it was assumed that an "all rag" paper would ensure permanence—despite evidence to the contrary. The National Bureau of Standards (NBS) stated in 1935 that paper permanence could not be guaranteed by specifications of a particular fiber but was based on purity, strength (durability) and stability. It was not until 1959, when William J. Barrow published the results of his research, that the causes of paper deterioration were elucidated and accepted.* Central to his research was the assumption that a prediction of stability could be extrapolated from accelerated aging tests using heat (72 hours at 100°C = 25 years). This technique was devised by NBS in conjunction with its own research.

Barrow concluded that acid from chlorine bleach, unpurified wood pulp and alum-rosin sizing were the major causes of paper deterioration. He also maintained that a competitively priced stable paper could be produced from purified chemical wood fibers.

Without a cheap alkaline size to use in place of alum-rosin size, it was not possible to produce permanent (alkaline) paper on a commercial scale. Fortuitously, just as Barrow's experimental papers were being manufactured, the first commercially successful alkaline size came on the market. Test runs of alkaline paper produced in 1959 at the Standard Paper Manufacturing Co. in Richmond, VA, produced paper that exceeded Barrow's "tentative specifications" for permanent and durable paper. Since 1960, the manufacture of acid-free book paper has been gradually increasing. In 1980, approximately 25% of the book paper manufactured in the United States was acid free.

Recommended standards for permanent and durable paper now include specifications for purified chemical wood fiber, an alkaline pH (usually 7.5-8.5), requirements for folding endurance and tear resistance and an alkaline reserve (usually 2%-3%) left in the paper to resist acidic elements in the environment.[3,4] These standards are discussed in more detail, below.

---

*William J. Barrow (1904-1967) pioneered research into the deterioration of paper, techniques for deacidification and lamination, and specifications for permanent/durable paper. His research was conducted at the W.J. Barrow Research Laboratory in Richmond, VA, and funded by the Council on Library Resources.

Testing and Standards

The paper that finds its way into libraries is a very small part of the total yearly production of the paper and paperboard industry. Even among manufacturers of book papers, only a small percentage of the output becomes part of the resources of libraries. In the supply and demand world of commercial papermaking, libraries have a very faint voice. Thus, it is vital that libraries agree on standards for paper to be included in collections of permanent research value. The presence of standards does not automatically ensure that publishers will choose permanent and durable paper; without standards, however, publishers do not even have the option.

Standards are based on objective tests of the chemical and physical properties of paper. Independent paper-testing laboratories provide specialized testing—usually to determine if a particular paper meets federal or commercial specifications. Standards have been developed by the American Society for Testing and Materials (ASTM), the American National Standards Institute (ANSI), the Technical Association of the Pulp and Paper Industry (TAPPI) and the International Standards Organization (ISO). Since paper is extremely hygroscopic, the moisture content of the paper at the time of testing is critical to the test results. Testing is usually conducted at 50% RH (relative humidity) and 73 °F. Tests must also indicate the machine direction (grain) of the paper.

Fiber analysis tests determine the type of raw material, the pulping process (chemical, mechanical, alkaline or acid), chemical treatments of the pulp such as bleaching, and additives to the pulp. They can also measure fiber length and the degree of fibrillation and check for the presence of groundwood and lignin. The results of fiber analysis tests are significant predictors of the future permanence and durability of a particular paper.

Besides fiber analysis, basic tests to predict paper permanence include pH (acidity or alkalinity) and accelerated aging tests. The pH of paper, as measured on a logarithmic scale from 0 to 14 where 7 is neutral, is the most significant predictor of paper permanence. Aging in an oven at 100 °C for 72 hours is approximately equivalent to 25 years of normal aging. Although there has been much controversy over the accuracy of accelerated aging tests, recent research implies that the correlation, while not exact, is accurate enough for long-term predictions of paper permanence or impermanence.[5]

The durability or strength of paper is determined by tests of fiber length and thickness, sheet formation or the distribution of bonds between fibers, and hydrogen bonding between fibrils. In addition, quantitative tests provide data that can be used to compare papers or specify limits. For example, "folding endurance" measures the number of times a paper strip can be folded back and forth until rupture occurs; "tensile strength" measures the force required to pull a strip of paper apart; "bursting strength" measures the force required to burst paper; and "internal tear" measures the force required to tear a given number of sheets of paper.

A number of tests measure optical qualities such as color, brightness and opacity, and physical qualities such as caliper (thickness), smoothness, porosity, degree of sizing and dimensional stability. These tests are not important in terms of permanence or durability but reflect the "printability" of a paper. Optical properties are important to librarians as well as printers, however; a paper that starts out white and bright will become dull and brown if it does not also have properties of permanence at the time of manufacture.

Preservation Issues

Deteriorating paper represents an enormous and complex preservation and conservation challenge for librarians. The reasons *why* paper deteriorates are well known; it remains for libraries to quantify the problem and to develop the rationale, procedures and technology for multiple solutions.

The first step in combatting deterioration is to control and/or remove deteriorating elements in the environment. Libraries can thus eliminate needless deterioration and retard the deterioration that is inevitable over time. Second, libraries must devise a system for the reevaluation, replacement or reformatting of those materials already in an advanced state of deterioration. "Brittle books" constitute large portions of older, urban collections but are found in all libraries. The critical years of publication are roughly 1850 to 1950. Third,

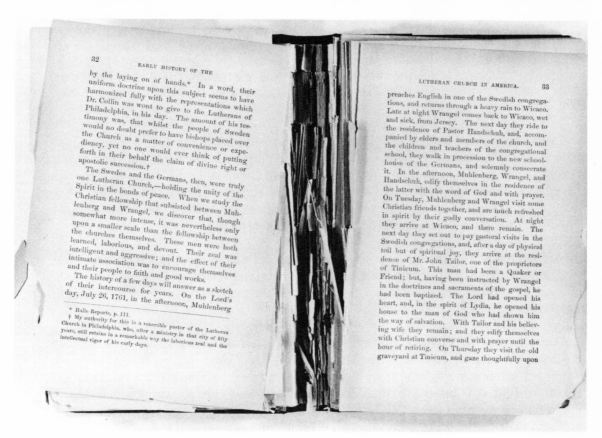

"Brittle book" exhibiting deteriorated paper.

libraries should take advantage of the technology available for stabilizing paper subject to acid deterioration. The process of deacidification and buffering neutralizes acids present in the paper and leaves an alkaline reserve as a buffer against future acid attack. Unfortunately, deacidification will *not* restore strength to paper already weak and brittle from acid deterioration, and present methods of strengthening paper are unfeasible on a large scale. Mass deacidification methods currently available are costly, and services are difficult to procure. Hand methods of deacidification are so time-consuming that they can only be justified for rare or unique materials.

Finally, libraries should learn from the past and aggressively promote the use of permanent and durable book paper. This issue has received long discussion in the library world. Most recently, the Council on Library Resources Committee on Production Guidelines for Book Longevity has been working toward encouraging publishers to stock permanent and durable paper for use on appropriate titles. An ANSI Z39 Committee, ''Paper Quality for Library Books,'' has been formed to produce a standard for publishers to follow.

LEATHER, PARCHMENT AND VELLUM

Properties and Manufacture

Most bookbinding leather is goat- or calfskin, although sheep- and pigskin are also used. Leather consists of bundles of collagen (protein) fibers that interweave in a three-dimensional manner. Unlike the two-dimensional weave of cloth, the fibrous weave of leather results in an exceptionally strong and flexible material that can be molded over different shapes.

Leather is tanned to make it pliable, soft and resistant to putrefaction. Vegetable tanning converts skin to leather by the use of plant tannins (primarily tree bark) and synthetic tannins. The purpose of tanning is to produce stable chemical bonds between the collagen molecules to prevent breakdown by microorganisms and impart physical qualities of flexibility and suppleness. The ability of the leather to accept and retain the impressions of decorative tooling and stamping is also an important property.

After tanning, a lubricant is applied to the leather to maintain flexibility and prevent drying and cracking. Lubricants have usually been animal fats, but plant, mineral and synthetic oils have also been used. After tanning, dyes are applied to the leather by padding or spraying.

Parchment is made from the flesh side of split sheepskin, and vellum is made from the whole skin of calf, goat or lamb. Traditionally, parchment was used exclusively for writing and printing while vellum was used also as a covering material for books. Parchment and vellum (the terms are often used interchangeably) are prepared by soaking the skins in lime, stretching them tightly on a wooden frame and laboriously scraping and rubbing them with pumice, chalk and lime to produce an even and smooth surface. Vellum as a covering material can be distinguished from leather by its white or cream color and smooth, polished surface.

Deterioration of Leather

Despite its seeming superior properties of strength and flexibility, leather is an organic material that is highly susceptible to the effects of chemical and physical deterioration. Leather deterioration, sometimes called "leather rot" or "red rot," is caused by the degradation action of acids left in the leather from the tanning process or acids absorbed from polluted urban air. The process of acid deterioration is accelerated by high temperatures in libraries. Low relative humidity further desiccates leather and causes vellum and parchment to warp and distort. Stagnant, moist air during the summer months can promote mold growth. Dirt and dust will abrade the surface of the leather and provide nutrients for mold growth. Finally, the exposed spine of a leather bound book is subject to fading and desiccation from ultraviolet radiation in sunlight and fluorescent light. The overdry leather in the hinge area will subsequently crack and break when the book is opened and used.

Two examples of leather deterioration.

Preservation Issues

Leather bindings for new books are extremely uncommon and are usually executed only for some limited editions or one-of-a-kind fine bindings. Therefore, most of the leather deterioration problems experienced by libraries involve retrospective collections. Fortunately, many fine bindings or very valuable leather bound books have been carefully preserved in special collections or rare book departments. Utilitarian leather bindings from the late 17th century onward, however, are likely to be severely deteriorated.

Preservation treatments have been applied to leather bindings since the early 20th century, but there is no consensus among conservators as to the effectiveness of a particular treatment. In fact, the research that has been done seems to indicate that *no* treatment is of much benefit in combatting deterioration.[6]

One popular treatment, however, involves saturation of the leather with a 7% solution of potassium lactate followed by lubrication with a 60/40 mixture of neat's-foot oil and lanolin. Potassium lactate, a buffering salt, will *in theory* replace the protective salts washed out of leather during the tanning process and serve as a buffer against acid attack from polluted atmospheres. Leather dressing or lubrication with animal fats such as neat's-foot oil and lanolin supposedly restores suppleness and durability to leather that has become desiccated by exposure to light and heat or by oxidation of the natural oils over time. However, leather in an advanced state of deterioration accrues no benefits from treatment of any kind, and the unsightly powder is transferred during handling into the leaves and onto other books.

Leather dressings, in fact, provide no significant *preservative* benefits; they do not prevent deterioration and slow the rate only slightly. There is a danger of build-up on the leather from repeated dressings or seepage of overapplied oil into the text block. Dressing does, however, provide aesthetic benefits and some protection from mechanical wear and tear. More important, leather treatment provides an opportunity for cleaning and inspection by staff. Damaged bindings can be identified and protected and migration of acid from leather turn-ins arrested by interleaving.

Despite the dearth of recent research into the mechanisms of leather deterioration and the effects of various treatments, there is widespread agreement among conservators that leather deterioration can be retarded by controlling the storage environment. Eliminating agents of deterioration such as heat, light, dust, pollutants and extremes of relative humidity will retard chemical and physical deterioration. Additionally, the further protection of a custom-made protective box is highly recommended. A box provides a microenvironment that buffers the effect of minor fluctuations in temperature and humidity; shields the leather from dust, light and pollutants; and eliminates needless mechanical wear and tear.

BOOKBINDINGS

Structure, Materials and Manufacture

The written history of bookbinding is replete with detailed accounts of book decoration, while technical descriptions of the structure of specific bindings or the evolution of binding structures are rare. From a preservation point of view, decoration is of little interest, except that a preoccupation with "refinements" and superficial adornments tended to undermine the craft and produce bindings predisposed to deterioration and unreceptive to conservation treatments.[7]

The method of page attachment is the foundation of bookbinding and perhaps the aspect that is most representative of the development first of the craft, later of the trade and finally of the industry.

Early coptic books (gatherings of sections or groups of folded papers) were first held together by sewing each section through its fold to a common strip of leather. Later, sections were attached to each other without the leather strip by linking the sewing between the sections. The protective wooden boards at the front and back of the book were attached in the same manner as the sections.

This early structure would not adequately support large medieval manuscripts, and European bookbinders of the 8th century developed the technique of sewing sections onto bands or cords, which were subsequently laced securely into the wooden covers. Leather or vellum covered the backbone or spine of the book and extended onto the boards. The raised bands underneath the leather were clearly outlined on the spine. Metal clasps and corners held the book closed and protected the leather sides.

The evolution of bookbinding practices in the 15th, 16th and early 17th centuries did not involve dramatic changes in book structure. For the most part, books were produced one at a time by a single craftsman who matched materials and structure to the size and weight of the book and its intended use. Sewing methods were strong, with boards securely attached to the text. Endsheets and headbands were integral parts of the binding. Leather was used in its full thickness. There were many innovations, but they did not change the basic structure of the book or seriously undermine its durability.

During this period, pasteboard covers were introduced and eventually supplanted wooden boards. Heavy wooden boards and metal clasps had been necessary to counteract the tendency of the vellum to curl and cause the binding to "yawn," but they were not needed when paper replaced vellum as the common printing surface. The lighter pasteboard covers and smaller paper books led to the practice of shelving books upright instead of flat.

The covers extended beyond the leaves to protect the text. Shoulders were formed to accommodate the accumulated thickness of the sewing threads along the folds of the sections and the spine of the book became convex. This innovation kept the book from sagging forward when it was shelved upright. The procedure became known as "rounding and backing."

As the demand for books increased in the 18th century, the craft of bookbinding evolved into an organized trade, and specialization became common in the workshop. Abbreviated book structures were needed to keep up with the demands of production. Some changes were inventive and suited to the needs of the smaller, lighter books being produced. However, many changes made for the sake of economy and speed sacrificed the functional qualities of the binding while they emphasized false practices so that a book would *appear* to have the same type of binding as before.

For example, to speed up the process of sewing books into cords, cords were "sawn-in" or recessed into the folds of the sections so that sewing could pass behind the cords instead of wrapping around them (see Figure III.1). Fake cords were then glued underneath the leather on the spine to imitate real raised cords. Sections were also frequently sewn "two-on," or two at a time, instead of each section being securely fastened all along the fold. Decorative bands were glued to the head and tail of the spine or tacked loosely to the sections instead of sewn to the backs of the sections along with the other bands and laced securely into the covers. The sewing cords and covering leather (especially in the joints) were pared very thin to create a smooth surface for elaborate decoration. The result was early detachment of the cover boards. The odious technique of "tree calf" was invented; here the sides of a book were sprinkled or dripped with acid to create a pattern. The practice of substituting hollow backs instead of gluing leather directly to the backbone enhanced decorative possibilities but allowed the use of weaker leather because the spine

Figure III.1 Raised Cords (a) vs. Sawn-in Cords (b)

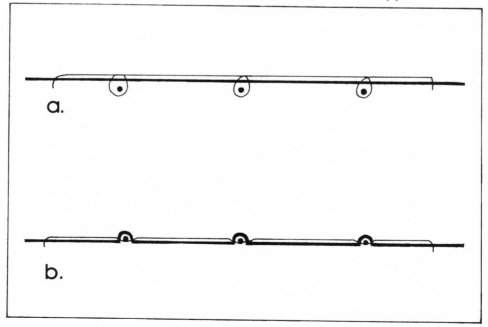

Tight back binding (a) compared to case binding (b).

would not have to flex as the book was opened. This practice resulted in a very weak joint or hinge area.

The Bookbinding Industry

Even with the shortcuts introduced in the binding trade in the 18th century, bookbinders were not able to keep up with the demand for books. The 19th century was a transition period where new inventions, mechanization and the application of business acumen revolutionized bookmaking.[8] Trade binderies were replaced by large edition or commercial binderies that mass produced books. The 19th century saw the universal acceptance of the cloth-covered cased book and the development of a machine to sew sections together.

Although paper cases were used for inexpensive books in the 18th century, the real impetus for case binding came when cloth was accepted as a covering material for books. Books were cased instead of "bound" because woven cloth could not be directly glued to the spine as it did not have the three-dimensional flexibility of leather. Cloth was first used in 1821 in England and was in widespread use in the United States by 1830.

Mechanization was proceeding at a rapid rate in the 19th century bindery, but sewing was still being done by hand. It was not until the development of mechanical sewing, in general, and the Smyth book sewing machine in 1878, in particular, that a satisfactory substitute for hand sewing emerged.

Full mechanization of the edition bindery was realized in the early 20th century. However, mechanization still involved many separate machines for the separate processes that were formerly done by hand. The forces that developed adhesive binding and paperbacks were inextricably connected with the search for a machine that would do it all—called straight-through or inline production. The fantasy was for paper to go into one end of a machine and the finished book to come out the other end.

Adhesive binding, which involves trimming the folded edges of sections and attaching the resultant single sheets together with an application of glue to the spine, was attempted long before full mechanization. In 1836 William Hancock used rubber for caoutchouc bindings, later called "perfect" bindings because Hancock boasted that they were "made to open perfectly flat." The adhesive binding was appreciated at once for its flexibility and durability—until the rubber dried out and the pages fell apart. Even after a disastrous beginning, the lure of eliminating the time-consuming step of sewing led to many more investigations and experiments.

Concurrently, paperbacks were gaining in popularity, and adhesive binding became associated with them. The real success and acceptance of adhesive binding did not come, however, until after World War II when synthetic resin (polyvinyl, acrylic and epoxy) adhesives were invented.

The modern commercial or edition bindery for manufacturing hardcover books is fully automated. In the production of a typical sewn and cased book, flat printed sheets are folded into sections, gathered in sequence and compressed, and sewn together through the folds. Protective endsheets are then attached to the book block, book edges are trimmed evenly, and the spine is given an application of glue. Rounding and backing creates the characteristic curved spine and shoulders for the cover boards to fit against. Decorative headbands, super (hinge cloth) and a paper lining are glued to the spine. At this point, the completed case that was separately constructed meets the book block and the two are glued together.

The adhesive-bound paperback production line, by contrast, is much more efficient and less time consuming. On one continuous inline machine, sections are folded, gathered and compressed; spines are trimmed and glued; and the preprinted cover is attached. Adhesive binding is also a widely used method of page attachment for hardcover books.

"Extra" Binderies

As bookbinding was transformed from a trade into an industry, special work and fine binding was still executed by "extra" binderies or individual craftsmen. These workshops catered to a clientele of bibliophiles and collectors and were not much affected by developments in the industry. Naturally, the quality of the work varied and some "craftsmen" caused permanent damage by binding inappropriately or insensitively. The most frequent abuses were trimming leaves, binding an early work in a contemporary style and obscuring or discarding historical or bibliographic evidence. Today, reputable hand bookbinders and book conservators provide an important service to libraries and use techniques and materials that are ethical, appropriate and conservationally sound.

Library Binderies

Binding establishments have also developed apart from the book manufacturing industry to serve the specialized needs of libraries. "Job" or library binderies bind and rebind paperbacks, books and accumulations of periodical issues. Production is done in quantity lots, but each lot is made up of assorted sizes and items with different binding requirements. Although machines are used at every step in production, the library bindery is labor intensive. With the exception of some binding of paperbacks, the library bindery does not use sophisticated inline production machinery like the edition bindery. Inline production is based on an exactly uniform product, whereas library binders must bind each book individually (although the line itself is organized along mass production principles).

The purpose of library binding is to provide a product that will survive use by multiple readers. The emphasis is on the *strength* of the binding and its ability to withstand abuse over time.

High quality library binding matches the production of the book block (page attachment, trimming and shaping the spine) to what is appropriate for an individual item. The type of sewing requested by a library or chosen by bindery personnel should be based on the quality of the paper, the width of the inner margins and the item's projected use.

Like the edition binder, the library binder constructs the case in a separate production line. Most cases are made with pyroxylin or acrylic-coated buckram (a thick canvas-like cloth). Synthetic cloths are also being used—especially for book and paperback binding. The book block and the finished case meet in a step called "casing-in." Unlike the edition binder, however, the library binder must contend with a production line where every case is a different color and size and every spine is titled differently.

The details of operating a large-scale library bindery are almost unfathomable. Because of the number of separate, distinct items that must be accounted for and the large number of personnel involved, record-keeping and personnel management occupy much of the bindery manager's energy. The application of computer technology to record-keeping is an important innovation in the industry.

Library binderies must be highly organized if they are to make a profit, yet as producers they must contend with a nonuniform production and as a service industry they must respond to the equally nonuniform demands of their customers.

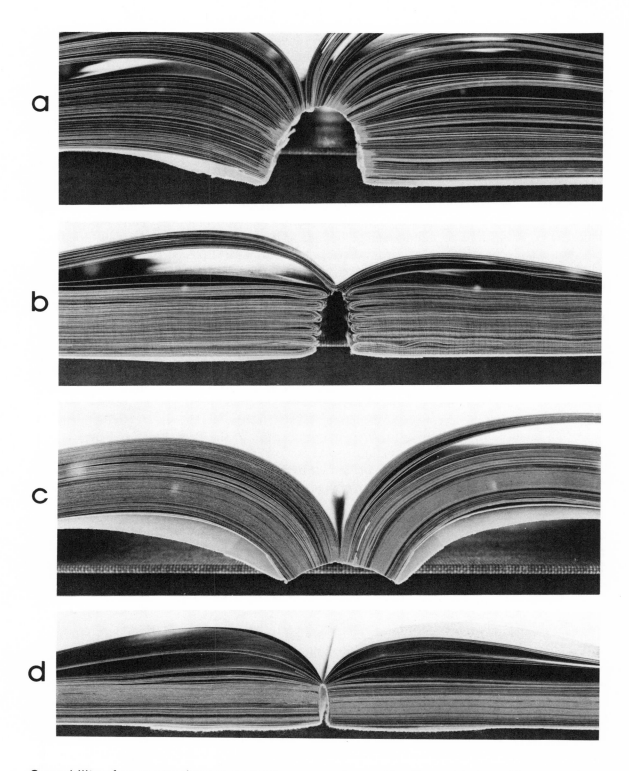

Openability of page attachment methods commonly used by library binders: (a) oversewing; (b) through-the-fold sewing; (c) cleat-sewing; (d) double-fan adhesive binding.

Deterioration of Bookbindings

A bookbinding is a structure composed of separate materials that must work together to protect the contents. Deterioration involves both the degradation of component materials and the breakdown of the structure. The *rate* of deterioration depends on the composition and quality of the materials used, the soundness of the structure and how the book is handled and stored.

Quality of Materials

Bindings are also greatly affected by the quality and kind of paper used in printing the book. As paper deteriorates, pages will be more likely to break away from the binding when the book is used. Bookbindings are composed of a wide variety of organic materials including linen, cotton or nylon thread; starch paste, animal glue or resin adhesive; paper or cloth backbone linings; decorated, printed or colored endsheets; bookboard or pasteboard covers; paper or bristol spine strips; linen, cotton or synthetic bookcloths and buckrams (starch-filled or coated); leather or vellum; decorated, marbled or laminated paper;

Detached text block with coated paper stock.

and dyes, colored stamping foils or gold leaf. The process of deterioration from physical and chemical agents, therefore, is extremely complex.

Heat will accelerate chemical changes in unstable materials causing desiccation and degradation. Acid will migrate from the endsheet or book cover to the title page and render it brittle and weak. Acid paste used to adhere book plates will stain endsheets. Acid leather or bookcloth turn-ins will damage the edges of the bookpaper. Heat will also speed up the natural aging of animal glues and cause them to become brittle and inflexible. Cover materials, especially the exposed spines of shelved books, are damaged by exposure to UV radiation from fluorescent lights or unfiltered natural light coming in through windows and skylights. Some bookcloth and leather dyes undergo dramatic fading as a signal of the problem, but all exposed fibers are subject to destruction by photochemical degradation.

Fluctuations in temperature and humidity will cause bindings, especially those that are improperly supported on both sides, to warp because the covering material, adhesive and endsheet that sandwich the cover boards will absorb moisture at different rates and to different capacities. Finally, the exposed binding is an obvious place for dust, dirt and atmospheric pollutants to accumulate. Not only is this unsightly but bindings are abraded by particulate matter and structurally weakened by the adsorption of gaseous pollutants.

Structural Soundness

Bookbindings also deteriorate as a direct result of faulty materials or methods or a structure that is unsuited to a book's size or the use it will receive. The premature deterioration of any of several component materials or structural elements can lead to breakdown of the whole binding.

Storage and Handling

A bookbinding can be thought of as a structure that is meant to protect a book when it is not being used and to readily expose the contents when it is being used. To accomplish this, the book block must be properly supported at all times. Support includes the internal support structure of the binding itself, as well as the external support provided by proper shelving. Internal support includes the method of page attachment; the shaping of the spine; the spine linings of glue, cloth and paper; and the method of attachment between book block and cover. External support means shelving books upright on their tails with even pressure exerted on both sides. The exception is very large books, which should be stored flat. Examples of inadequate external support are fore-edge shelving and leaning books. A sturdy binding can, of course, withstand more abuse than a weak or inappropriate binding. It is in every library's best interests, however, to minimize damage to bindings by providing the best storage conditions possible.

Since library books are meant to be used, a certain amount of wear and tear is inevitable. Some common abuses to be aware of are wrenching a book off the shelf or jamming it back on a crowded shelf, removing a book by hooking a finger over the headcap, throwing books, leaning heavily on a book while photocopying, bending covers back too far or breaking the spine by forcing a book open.

Preservation Issues

Publishers' Bindings

One of the most controversial issues in library preservation is the quality of publishers' bindings. A myriad of forces—social, economic and technological—have resulted in the production of bookbindings that are unsuitable for library use. Not all publishers' bindings are unsatisfactory. Many scholarly publishers and university presses continue to issue books with high-quality bindings. But many are unsuitable both for the public library, where books must tolerate frequent circulation for a relatively short period of time, and for the research library, where books receive infrequent use but must last in a "permanent" collection.

Publishers are not deliberately irritating libraries, they are running a business. The industry is under tremendous pressure to keep prices down in the face of ever-increasing production costs. Unfortunately, inadequately bound books purchased by libraries carry hidden costs that surface as rebinding, in-house repair and withdrawal. Libraries must also take into consideration the time and money spent to select, purchase, catalog and process an item, which soon becomes unusable because of its physical condition. Individuals and libraries alike bemoan expensive art and photography books that have hopelessly inadequate bindings for their size and weight.

Even more frustrating than books issued in less expensive formats (paperbacks instead of hardcover bindings) are bindings that are executed in a seemingly satisfactory style but with shortcuts. For example, rounding and backing becomes a useless (and temporary) affectation if the backbone of the book block is not also properly lined to maintain the shape.

These issues can perhaps be resolved by better communication among publishers, production managers, edition binders and librarians. The application of new products and technology that lower the costs of edition binding is desirable if the product can withstand the use it is expected to receive. On the other hand, libraries must make their needs and preferences known and be willing to pay the price for quality bindings.

Library-arranged Bindings

Another issue in the preservation of bookbindings is the bindings that libraries arrange for themselves. The library binding industry developed to meet the specific needs of libraries. Traditionally, the responsibility for choosing a suitable binding method for an individual book or periodical volume rested with the binder, whose expertise was rarely questioned.

Several developments have taken place during the last two decades, however, that have caused libraries to reexamine their role in the library binding process. First, economic forces have reduced the number of small binderies thus reducing personal contact between librarian and binder. Second, as the library binding industry has grown and become more mechanized, production capacities have increased and plants have become large and complex, making it more difficult to respond to preferences of individual libraries. Finally, as libraries have begun to see the effects of paper deterioration and have become more conscious of preservation concerns, they have become concerned with book *permanence,* while library binders have continued to emphasize the *strength* of a binding.

Discussions of book permanence have revolved around the issue of oversewing. An oversewn volume is extremely sturdy and will take much abuse; however, since the sections are joined by the piercing action of the multiple threaded needles, stiff or brittle paper will break off as the book is used. An oversewn volume will not open flat and tends to snap shut if it is not held open firmly. Additionally, oversewn volumes tend to have narrow inner margins because they are trimmed before oversewing and the sewing intrudes another one-quarter to three-eighths of an inch. The Library Binding Institute Standard for Library Binding (1981) only requires that "the sewing not infringe on the print." Some librarians have urged inner margins of at least three-quarters of an inch *before* trimming and oversewing, to ensure an inner margin of at least one-quarter inch after binding.

There are many other preservation issues surrounding library binding. The quality of the materials used is of concern to both binders and librarians. Some standards have been set but others are needed. There are constant problems with availability of materials, and the testing process to determine the quality and suitability of new materials is time-consuming.

Because library binding is a mass production process, individual treatment is difficult to obtain. Production lines are set up to maximize efficiency, and uniformity is stressed. If special treatment of a volume is warranted, it is the responsibility of the library to determine if library binding is appropriate. The library is in the best position to judge an item's physical condition, its value to the collection, how often and how it will be used, the likelihood of future rebinding and a myriad of other considerations. Library binding is complex, and librarians must have a clear understanding of products and processes if they are to make intelligent use of library binding services.

In-house Treatment

Librarians must also contend with the issue of in-house conservation treatment for damaged/deteriorated bindings. Even if one ignores the administrative realities of organization, staffing, costs and facilities, the issues surrounding in-house treatment for bookbindings are still complex. The need for conservation treatment can be greatly reduced by maintaining proper storage conditions and encouraging proper handling and use. Unfortunately, most libraries already accrued years of conservation problems before they launched preservation and conservation programs.

Damaged or deteriorated bindings are treated so that the contents or text can continue to be protected. Except for simple protective encasement (boxing), all conservation treatments for bookbindings (furbishing, repair, recasing, rebinding or restoration) alter the original physical item. Depending on the library, acceptable treatment may range from no treatment at all to making each item look brand new. What is appropriate for an item will depend on what is appropriate for a particular collection.

Libraries that are providing treatment for permanent collections emphasize soundness of structure and quality of materials. If possible, they will repair or restore the original cover rather than substitute a new cover. The original sewing will be retained or the book resewn after mending. Book blocks are never trimmed. Volume sets are treated uniformly, and decisions are often made in conjunction with a bibliographer or subject specialist. On the other hand, libraries that do not need to be concerned with maintaining collections for posterity can repair items much more expediently.

Sadly, the even larger preservation issue is the library that provides in-house treatment that is inappropriate and damaging—though usually well-meaning. Inappropriate repairs can cause more deterioration than if the binding merely experienced benign neglect. The use of impermanent materials will cause permanent damage, while repairs that violate the principles of book construction cause premature breakdown of the book's structure.

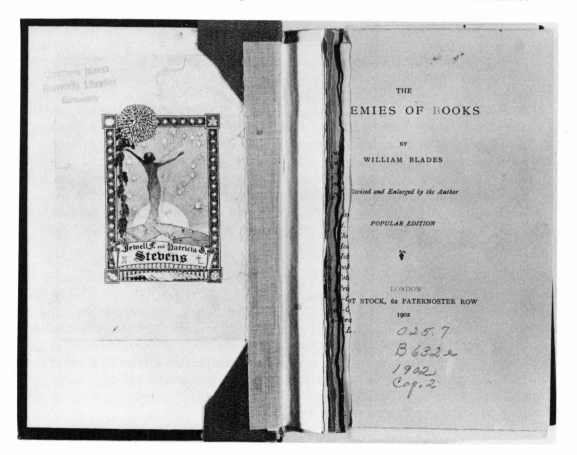

Damage caused by an inappropriate repair.

PHOTOGRAPHIC MATERIALS

Photographic materials, because of the complexity of their chemical composition and their physical vulnerability, present a constant preservation challenge. Although most libraries restrict the use of photographic materials that must be preserved in the original, most collections are comprised of materials that are meant to be used.

The composition of photographic materials and their preservation potential through proper manufacture, processing and storage should be of primary concern to libraries. Since libraries generally do not produce the photographic medium they mean to preserve for posterity (or even conserve for patron use for a reasonable time period), they are at the mercy of manufacturers and processors. The library world has little impact on the availability of raw materials and specific products, yet these materials form the basis for the preservation of the medium. Additionally, although the quality of proprietary products and their processing may vary considerably, libraries are usually unable to do expensive testing for permanence and are dependent on the claims or the reputation of manufacturers.

MICROFILM

Composition and Film Types

In the 1930s libraries in the United States began collecting microfilm copies of rare books and manuscripts held in foreign libraries. The use of microfilm soon expanded to include less esoteric items, but the impetus for collecting microfilm was still largely to supplement scholarly resources. Micropublishing has since grown to include original publishing. Libraries today acquire microforms as the *preferred* format for reasons of use, space or cost. Additionally, microforms are acquired to preserve the intellectual content of printed works whose paper has deteriorated to the point of being unusable.

Three film types are acquired by libraries—silver halide, diazo and vesicular. These are basic film types; there can be differences in composition of particular products that contribute to variable physical and chemical properties and result in different potentials for stability or deterioration.

Silver halide employs the same photographic process as conventional black-and-white photography. A gelatin emulsion containing fine grains of metallic silver is coated on one side of a transparent plastic film base—either cellulose acetate (ester) or polyester. The film is "exposed" in a camera by the effect of visible light on the silver. Because silver halide film is quickly exposed, it is almost universally used as the original recording medium, that is, for production of the master negative. Under precise conditions and in total darkness, the film is "developed" to bring out the image; the image is then "fixed" by immersion in a series of chemical baths. "Washing" removes residual chemicals, most importantly the sodium thiosulfate ("hypo") used as a fixing agent.

Diazo film is made by coating a resin containing diazonium salts and a coupling agent onto a cellulose acetate or polyester film base. The image is exposed by ultraviolet light and developed and fixed by ammonia vapor. Ultraviolet light exposes the image by decomposing the diazo component so that it cannot turn dark in the presence of ammonia. Because exposure is slow, diazo is not ordinarily used as camera film, but because it costs considerably less than silver halide, diazo is often used for service and distribution copies. Since there is only 4% loss in image definition for each generation (each time the image is photographed), a diazo "intermediate" is frequently made from a silver halide master negative and is used to make copies. The image quality of diazo film will depend on the legibility of the original document, the quality of the silver halide master negative and the proper duplication of the image onto diazo film. Duplication is accomplished by direct contact printing; ultraviolet light transmitted through the transparent image of a negative film exposes the diazo film in direct contact with the negative.

A vesicular film emulsion is composed of stable diazonium salts dispersed in a polymer layer. Like diazo film, vesicular film is exposed when UV light decomposes the diazonium component. The nitrogen gas given off is confined in the polymer layer. When the film is developed by heat, the gas expands in the softened polymer to form tiny bubbles or vesicles. Re-exposure with high intensity UV light fixes the image. Unlike silver halide and diazo films, vesicular film does not absorb light to create an image—the tiny bubbles diffract (scatter) the light. Vesicular film is used to make service and distribution copies. Since there is no wet processing or chemical processing involved, vesicular film is inexpensive to produce.

Deterioration of Microfilm

Microfilm deterioration is defined as a loss of image or of image quality. Image loss may result from abrasion of the emulsion layer, separation of the emulsion from the plastic film base or deterioration of the base. Loss of image quality refers to the degradation of photographic characteristics such as resolution (the sharpness of the image) or contrast (the difference between light and dark in the image area).

Storage Conditions

Proper film processing is vital to image preservation. Incomplete processing (including exposure, developing and fixing of the image) will cause degradation of the image regardless of film type. Unfortunately, libraries have little or no control over the quality of the processing when they purchase microfilm. Libraries do have the *potential,* however, to control microfilm storage conditions. Poor storage conditions will exacerbate the effects of improper processing, as well as cause additional deterioration.[9]

Different film types react differently to adverse storage conditions. Silver and vesicular films are resistant to light damage, but diazo images will fade when exposed to light. The most common danger is from a reader with film in it that is inadvertently left on. Vesicular and diazo films are resistant to high humidities, but silver film is highly susceptible. At 60% RH, mold thrives on the gelatin emulsion and the hairlike fungal growth will quickly obliterate the image. Short-term exposure to high temperature does not drastically affect silver or diazo films, but vesicular film will undergo complete image loss above 175°F

(80°C) from softening of the binder and collapse of the bubbles. Excessive heat can be generated when film is left in a reader to overheat or if film is near heat from a fire.

Although all plastic materials degrade with time, heat will accelerate the deterioration of plastic film bases. Cellulose acetate film subjected to hot, humid conditions will eventually become sticky and distort, and the image layer will separate. Polyester film, while more resistant to high humidity, will eventually degrade if subjected to high temperatures.

Adverse storage conditions also include exposure to gaseous air pollution and particulate matter. Dirt and dust settling on microfilm will abrade the emulsion layer and cause image loss. Atmospheric pollutants cause deterioration of the film base as well as chemical degradation of the photographic image. Silver halide microfilm is sensitive to a wide variety of pollutants including sulfur dioxide, paint fumes, peroxides, ozone and ammonia. "Redox" blemishes are caused by a reaction between silver halide film and contaminants given off by rubber bands, printing inks, acid cardboard boxes and other gaseous pollutants. The silver image becomes soluble and redeposits as red or yellow spots.[10]

The Kalvar film scandal of the early 1970s was a case of reverse deterioration. Metal storage cabinets rusted, and cardboard boxes embrittled from fumes of hydrogen chloride given off by a particular vesicular film. Although the problem has not been repeated, it is best to store diazo and vesicular film separately from silver halide.[11]

Handling

Careful handling and use and proper machine maintenance will reduce damage to the delicate emulsion layer of all types of microfilm. Since vesicular images are made by the diffraction of light off tiny bubbles, pressure from fingernails, malfunctioning equipment or pens and pencils will obliterate images. Fingerprints are a hazard to silver halide since salt from the hands will react with the silver. Clinching or winding roll films too tightly will cause damage from the abrasive action of dirt particles. Deterioration of microfilm images during handling and use can be reduced, but it can never be eliminated. For this reason, libraries usually make a distinction between storage and service (use) copies.

Preservation Issues

Libraries are naturally concerned with the permanence of their microfilm collections. Many libraries have had a policy of purchasing silver halide rather than diazo or vesicular film because experts insisted that only silver halide was "archival" or "permanent." In fact, silver halide only has the *potential* for being archival. For microfilm to be archival, it must also be processed and stored to meet archival standards. Since archival storage conditions allow only occasional, careful use and narrow parameters for temperature and humidity, *microfilm that is used by patrons cannot, by definition, be archival.*

When nonsilver microfilm technology emerged after World War II, the micrographics industry quickly switched from silver to diazo and vesicular films, which were cheaper to manufacture and process as well as more durable. Nonsilver microfilm now constitutes large portions of library collections. The issue of the permanence of silver halide versus the permanence of nonsilver films is fast becoming a nonissue as silver becomes literally unavailable. The issue now is whether master negatives (preservation masters) produced by micropublishers and large libraries meet archival standards. Many librarians have urged a central repository of preservation master negatives that would ensure archival storage conditions and continued availability.

Because the potential permanence of microfilm cannot be easily observed, standards have been developed to ensure a quality product. ANSI standards exist for silver halide film that specify film quality and properties before processing, chemical and photographic characteristics after processing, and storage conditions for processed film (see Table III.1). A National Micrographics Association standard describes production and inspection procedures that ensure the quality of first-generation silver halide microfilm.

Table III.1 Recommended Relative Humidity Range for Archival Storage

Sensitive Layer	Base Type	RH Range (Percent)
Microfilm		
Silver-gelatin	Cellulose ester	15-40
Silver-gelatin	Polyester	30-40
Heat processed silver	Polyester	15-50
General		
Silver-gelatin	Cellulose ester	15-50
Silver-gelatin	Polyester	30-50
Color	Cellulose ester	15-30
Color	Polyester	25-30
Diazo	Cellulose ester, polyester	15-30
Vesicular	Polyester	15-50
Electrophotographic	Polyester	15-50

Source: *Standard Practice for Storage of Processed Safety Photographic Film* (New York: American National Standards Institute, 1981), p. 10, ANSI PH1.43-1981. Copyright © 1981 by the American National Standards Institute. Reprinted with permission.

Although diazo film has not been standardized for archival keeping purposes, *American National Standard Specifications for Stability of Ammonia-Processed Diazo Photographic Film* (PH1.60-1979) sets a standard for the stability of physical properties and image quality of diazo film suitable for "long-term" records. Criteria are based on the dark aging stability of diazo images because diazo images are susceptible to ultraviolet radiation. Long-term is defined as a "minimum of one hundred years when stored under 'archival' conditions, providing the original images are of suitable quality." Archival storage conditions include archival storage enclosures, housing in a separate room or vault equipped with constant, accurate temperature (70 °F; 21 °C) and humidity (30% RH) controls and protection from fire hazards.

Although archival standards do not exist for vesicular films, these films might turn out to be as "permanent" as silver halide given the imperfect storage conditions in most libraries and the fact that most libraries contain microfilm collections that are used, not

Microfilm inspection station, New York Public Library.

merely stored. Predictions of permanence are based on accelerated aging tests, and the validity of these tests cannot be determined until enough time has passed to compare the effects of accelerated aging with aging under normal conditions.

Clearly, most libraries do not meet the requirements for archival storage—*whatever* the film type. The use of nonsilver film for service copies seems acceptable (and inevitable) providing there is some assurance that whoever is responsible for master negatives produces, processes and stores them for permanence.

PHOTOGRAPHS

Libraries are concerned with photographs—black-and-white and color prints, negatives and slides—as a medium that stores information. Aside from the possible value of a photograph as an original historical artifact or a work of art, photographs contain important information that either cannot be found in any other source or is dependent on the medium itself for transmittal. Photographs present complex preservation problems both because of the newness of the process and the great variety in processes and products.

A photograph is an image composed of processed chemicals trapped in an emulsion or coating and supported by a material such as metal, glass, paper or plastic film. A black-and-white image is formed by densities of metallic silver, while a color image is formed by dyes.

Deterioration of Photographs

Photographs are subject to chemical attack because of the inherent instability of emulsion or support materials, the action of residual processing chemicals, attack from atmospheric pollutants or improper temperature and humidity conditions. Chemical attack can cause image fading or discoloration, separation of the emulsion from the support or decomposition of the emulsion or the support.

Film Base

From approximately 1890 to 1930, cellulose nitrate was used as the film base for negative images. Although there are variations in nitrate film stability owing to variations in manufacture and subsequent storage, all nitrate-based films decompose. Cellulose nitrate is highly flammable, especially in the later stages of deterioration. During decomposition, the film base discolors and becomes brittle. Meanwhile, the image fades and the gelatin emulsion becomes soft and sticky. Finally, the base softens and emits nitric acid. Decomposition is accelerated by high temperature and humidity; lack of ventilation can result in spontaneous combustion. Besides the extreme fire hazard of nitrate film, the nitric acid fumes emitted during decomposition are very damaging to any organic material stored nearby.

In the mid-1930s, "safety-base" film, usually cellulose acetate, began to replace cellulose nitrate film. Although cellulose acetate was tested by the National Bureau of Standards and certified more stable than cellulose nitrate, early negatives have exhibited a deterioration process of shrinking and separation of the emulsion from the film base and, in the later stages of decomposition, staining of the image. Since there has been a variety of acetate films manufactured and high temperatures accelerate the deterioration process, the condition of early safety-base films cannot be predicted by date but must be determined by individual examination and testing. Improvements in cellulose acetate films have resulted in a greater assurance of permanence if proper processing and storage can be assumed. In 1965, polyester film bases became available that were equal in stability to cellulose acetate and had superior mechanical strength, dimensional stability and resistance to extremes of temperature.

Quality of Paper

The quality of the paper support of positive photographic prints will affect the rate of deterioration of the image. Fortunately, printing paper manufacturers quickly recognized the important relationship between paper quality and the permanence of the image, so deterioration of the paper support is usually associated with the external forces that cause paper deterioration rather than inherent impurities.

The resin-coated printing papers recently marketed are widely used in commercial applications. Libraries acquiring resin-coated papers need to pay particular attention to storage conditions—especially variations in relative humidity. Since processing chemicals tend to collect at the edges of the print and can contaminate other prints, it is recommended that the edges be trimmed slightly prior to storage or the prints interleaving with a barrier paper. Because resin-coated papers have not stood the test of time, there is confusion over their potential for permanence.[12,13]

Processing

Deterioration of photographic images is frequently the result of residual chemicals left over from processing. Damage usually appears as a brownish-yellow discoloration or fading of the image. Proper film processing is dependent on strict adherence to conditions recommended by the manufacturer, including proper strength of solutions and proper agitation and timing. After the image is fixed, negatives and prints are washed to remove fixing chemicals and silver compounds. The effectiveness of the washing step is dependent on the pureness of the water, the rate of water change, water temperature and proper separation of the items. Quality control is vital in the photographic lab and can be achieved by adherence to standards.

Storage and Handling

Atmospheric pollutants will fade and stain images, degrade paper bases and decompose the gelatin emulsions and film bases. Perhaps the most common source of contamination, however, is from materials used to store, mount, mat, frame or mark prints and negatives. Plywood, chipboard, cardboard, and cheap paper and matboard have disastrous effects on photographs from the migration of by-products or acid degradation. The result is staining and embrittlement. Storage materials such as glassine envelopes and cellulose acetate sleeves are suspect, as are plastic reels that may contain volatile plasticizers or solvents. Unstable adhesives such as rubber cement used for mounting, pressure-sensitive tapes and the adhesive used to make storage envelopes have caused incalculable damage to original photographs. So has the indiscriminate use of marking pens and ink pad stamps. Paper prints are more vulnerable to deterioration than film, not only because they are hygroscopic and absorb atmospheric pollutants, but also because they are mounted for exhibit and more frequently handled.

Modern color photographs are composed of dyes that will inevitably fade with time. Drastic image fading has been observed after as few as 10 years. Fading is caused by complex chemical reactions. The rate of fading is accelerated by high temperature and humid-

Damage caused by the rubber cement used for mounting can be seen in this photograph.

ity, atmospheric pollution and exposure to light, both visible and UV (see Table III.2). The specific color process used and date of manufacture also have significant effects on the stability of the image.

Color image fading is indicated by a loss of highlight detail, reduced density and contrast, staining and alterations in the color balance. The ANSI publication *Method for Comparing the Color Stabilities of Photographs* (PH1.42-1969) describes a method for objectively comparing the color stability of photographic products and assessing the effects of temperature, humidity and light on image stability.

Image permanence can be achieved by producing black-and-white separation negatives from each of the dye layers and then reproducing the color by dye imbibition (absorption) of tricolor exposure onto color photographic material.* The process is very expensive and requires skilled photographic work. Currently, the best recommendation for prolonging the stability of color photographs and slides is low-temperature storage.† When color is not necessary to the informational value of the photograph, duplicate black-and-white archival prints can be made from the original.

Table III.2 Effect of Temperature on Dye Fading Rate at 40% RH

Storage Temperature	Relative Fading Rate	Relative Storage Time
30°C (86°F)	2	1/2
24°C (75°F)	1	1
19°C (66°F)	1/2	2
12°C (54°F)	1/5	5
7°C (45°F)	1/10	10
−10°C (14°F)	1/100	100
−26°C (−15°F)	1/1000	1000

The table shows that photographs stored at 86°F will fade four times as fast as those stored at 66°F.
Source: *Preservation of Photographs* (Rochester, New York: Eastman Kodak Co., 1979), p. 39.

Color printing processes such as offset lithography, gravure and letterpress have excellent color image stability when stored in the dark but are subject to fading when exposed to light.

Not only are photographic materials subject to a wide variety of chemical attack, but photographs are a fragile medium easily damaged by physical agents of deterioration. Emulsions and coatings are easily damaged by abrasion during storage and use or from particulate matter. Even minor scratches will obliterate part of an image.

---

*Kodak's dye transfer process.

†The Library of Congress facility stores color images at 35° F (1.7° C) and 35% RH. The John F. Kennedy Presidential Library vault maintains 0° F (—18° C) and 30% RH.

Variations in temperature and humidity exert mechanical stresses on emulsions by causing paper and film to expand and contract. When the humidity is low, both the gelatin emulsion and the paper of a print will dry out and the print will curl. Older prints whose paper and gelatin have become brittle are subject to cracking and breaking. High temperatures promote brittleness and accelerate the deterioration of film and paper supports. Relative humidities above 60% combined with temperatures above 70 °F (21 °C) promote fungal growth and warping. All photographic materials are subject to fading from visible as well as UV light. Storage in a dark, cool environment with an RH humidity near 30% will significantly prolong permanence of all photographic images.

Preservation Issues

The complexity of both historic and contemporary photographic materials precludes any simple methods of preservation and conservation. Mass treatments for original photographs will never be possible because each individual photograph varies depending on the specific process or products, the idiosyncracies of the photographer or photographic lab, the date of production, and the intervening history of storage conditions, handling and abuse.

The inspection of collections of photographs for signs of image degradation or fading is not a valid preservation tool since there is no way to compare the progress of deterioration from the time of the last inspection. Additionally, the quality of a photographic image is a subjective decision, and different individuals will have different tolerances for fading or color imbalances.

Because of their fragility and sensitivity to light, *original* photographs should never be exhibited or even frequently used. Most large photographic collections rely on duplication of the original as their primary preservation method. High quality modern copy films in combination with archival processing and storage can ensure preservation of the image and its informational value. The artifactual value of an original must often be weighed against the uncertainty and expense of restoration.

Archival copies of deteriorating originals involve the same quality control checks as the production of archival master negative microfilm. Camera and film selection, preparation of the original, focus and exposure, darkroom and printing procedures, and storage conditions will all affect the quality and permanence of the copy.[14] Early photographic processes (such as daguerreotypes) and badly damaged prints present special copying problems.

The preservation of photographs can be significantly enhanced by storage at 65 °-70 °F and 30% RH. The optimum situation of low-temperature storage is the only viable alternative for fugitive color materials. However, retrieval of photographs sealed for storage at 35 °F can be rather complicated. Few institutions will be able to provide optimum storage, since the installation and maintenance of a special storage environment or a low-temperature storage vault is very expensive.

MOTION PICTURE FILM

Although preservation of motion pictures has mainly concerned repositories with major film collections, many smaller institutions have motion pictures that warrant preservation. Motion picture film is subject to the same deterioration problems associated with still photographs—physical damage to the emulsion, chemical attack from improper processing or storage, degradation of the film base and fading of color images. Retention of physical properties, such as strength and flexibility, is more critical for motion picture film than for still photographs, however, because of the stress put on film during projection.

Temporary dimensional changes in film caused by fluctuations in temperature and humidity, and permanent dimensional changes caused by the release of volatile solvents from the film base will affect the distance between film perforations and consequently the match between projector sprockets and perforation pitches. During projection, the potential for physical damage is great because of the number of images involved and the fact that the film is mechanically moved as it is used.

Color motion picture films produced after 1952 are extremely unstable chemically and subject to fading and color distortions in as few as five years. Many important films have already faded irretrievably. The original Technicolor process, used from 1928 to approximately 1952, was expensive and necessitated the use of bulky cameras; however, the color film from that era has not faded. In the early 1950s, Eastman Kodak Co. developed and marketed a cheaper color process. The film was quickly and universally adopted by the film industry despite the inherent instability of the color images.

A particular color film type exhibits specific qualities of speed, grain, sharpness, color reproduction and image stability. Film manufacturers maintain that since these characteristics are chemically interrelated, the improvement of one characteristic can only be achieved at the expense of another.

Preservation Issues

The conversion of cellulose nitrate base film to safety film is an urgent issue in the preservation of motion picture film. Although the necessity of conversion is well known, the sheer bulk of material worthy of conversion represents staggering costs. Conversion of commercially produced feature films has progressed because of the obvious investment value of preservation, but money for the conversion of important documentary and historic films in the public sector is woefully inadequate.

Color motion picture films can be preserved by separating the color information into its primary records for storage on separate reels. Color separations for a feature length film cost $15,000-30,000 so the process is only feasible for a fraction of the color films produced.

Low-temperature storage is currently recommended by film archivists and manufacturers as the most practical method of preservation. Both cellulose nitrate decomposition and the fading of color films are significantly retarded under cold-storage conditions.

Because organic materials are subject to continual deterioration, preservation of the original physical item involves, at best, retarding the *rate* at which deterioration progresses. Nowhere is this principle more graphically illustrated than with motion pictures. There is no way to stop the deterioration of cellulose nitrate film because the base is inherently unstable. Likewise, color films whose chemistry is combined in the film emulsion will inevitably fade. Storage at below freezing temperatures will apparently retard deterioration, but it makes access difficult. To protect the original, a system for preservation must be combined with provisions for accurate reproduction of reference copies. Tight budgets will often make it difficult to justify paying for both storage and replication.

If the current emphasis concerning preservation of unstable photographic materials is on the preservation of the *image* through accurate reproductions, then future emphasis may well be on storage of the image *information* through digital coding. In a reproduction or analog system of preservation, each copy generation experiences some loss in image quality, whereas in a digital system the image is converted to a recorded code that can be copied indefinitely. Should this promise of a "permanent" technological solution to image degradation ever materialize, archivists and librarians will be forced to reevaluate the importance of retaining the original physical artifact.

SOUND RECORDINGS

History and Composition

Sound recordings comprise an astonishing variety of formats, materials and machines. Further, recording technology continues to develop, and a new generation of laser and electronic recordings is emerging in the commercial market.

Although the first commercial sound recordings were available in the 1890s, the Library of Congress did not begin collecting sound recordings until the early 1900s. By that time, sound technology already included (to name a few) tinfoil cylinders, wax-coated cardboard cylinders, wax discs, vulcanized rubber discs and shellac discs. Playback equipment had also evolved and improved.

In the early 1900s, standardization became the major issue. In the 1920s, electrical sound recording vastly improved the quality of recorded sound. However, because of the ability to manipulate the frequency of the sound system (equalization), recording studios were also able to manipulate the *authenticity* of the recordings. It was not until 1953 that an equalization standard was adopted.

During the 1930s, noncommercial recording with electrical recording processes made possible sound documentation of important historic events and everyday life. The "elusiveness" of these recordings (recorded on materials such as cellulose nitrate and cellulose acetate), and the fact that they could only be played back a few times without significant deterioration, presented a significant preservation problem.

After World War II, improved plastic technology made possible long-playing vinyl chloride discs, and sound recordings became widely available. With the long-playing, better quality vinyl discs, stereophonic recording became a reality. Quadraphonic discs became available in the late 1960s.

Although magnetic sound recording on wire was first invented in 1899, it was not until 1936 in Germany that the first magnetic tape recordings were made. After World War II, tape recording was universally accepted by the recording industry. Magnetic tape recordings have been made on bases of paper, cellulose acetates and—most recently—polyester. Preservation problems have centered on the thickness and composition of the base. Multitrack recording became popular for professional recording and broadcasting, increasing the variables associated with the authenticity of the sound. The cassette tape format—using a thinner base and smaller, simpler playback equipment—is widely used in the consumer market and comprises significant portions of the sound collections of libraries and archives.

Digital sound recording, which is not yet standardized, offers the possibility of high quality, permanent recordings (see Chapter VIII).

Deterioration of Sound Recordings

Like other organic materials, sound recordings are subject to chemical, biological and physical deterioration. High temperature and humidity will encourage chemical degradation and fungal attack, resulting in pitting and distortion of the sound.

Fortunately, many sound recordings *are* stable chemically—providing the humidity is kept at 50% or below. Genuine shellac "cures" as it ages and becomes less subject to deformation. Vinyl discs properly stabilized during manufacture are permanent. However, there are many different materials, and some of these are subject to chemical degradation, embrittlement, cross-linking of polymers, condensation of shellac, loss of extenders, and so on. Recordings made on cellulose nitrate or acetate bases are definitely unstable and subject to complete decomposition through loss of plasticizers during exposure to heat, light and humidity.

Because of the manner in which sound recordings are made and used, dimensional stress caused by fluctuating temperature and humidity and improper positioning and storage is extremely detrimental. Disc recordings are easily warped. Besides proper support for the width of the record, discs must be kept *strictly* vertical at all times. Slanting causes warpage and warpage causes distortion of sound. Theoretically, shellac and vinyl are subject to very slow "flowing," and some sound archives have recommended rotating the edge placement every 5 to 10 years.

Magnetic tape recordings on polyester base are stable when stored properly. However, tape stored on reels is under tension, and this tension must be maintained correctly or distortion and loss of sonic content will occur. Tape should never be stored after being rewound because "rewind" and "fast forward" tension is too tight. Tape is extremely sen-

Disc warpage can be caused by exposure to heat or improper storage.

sitive to fluctuating temperature and humidity and cycling will cause distortion, "print-through" (transfer of magnetic particles on a tape layer to an adjacent tape layer) and loss of iron oxide coating. Cycling should be no more than ±5 °F and ±10% RH.

Although magnetic tape erasure because of proximity to magnetic fields is theoretically a preservation hazard, in practice there is little danger, providing tapes are not in close proximity to electric motors, high-voltage lines or transformers.

Cassette tape recordings are a convenient but unstable medium for long-term storage of sound recordings. The thin base material can be easily broken and will allow print-through. Sound information for permanent retention that was recorded on cassette tape must be rerecorded on reel-to-reel magnetic tape.

All sound recordings are extremely susceptible to damage from dirt and dust. Proper packaging (jackets, sleeves and boxes), filtration of air and cleanliness of playback equipment are essential preservation measures.

Preservation Issues

The preservation of sound recordings is immensely complex because of their diverse composition. This diversity is compounded by the necessity of preserving original playback equipment as well as original recordings. In cases where the original physical recording does not have artifactual value or when it is impossible to save because of advanced deterioration, rerecording is the most effective method of preserving the sound content.

Like microforms in libraries, sound recordings require the use of machines to transfer information to the user and are a reformatting of the original form of the information.

Unlike microforms, however, sound recordings seek to duplicate intangible and highly subjective information. Thus, not only are sound archives concerned with the physical object itself (wax cylinder, vinyl disc, magnetic tape) and the machine used to transmit the sound, but also with the integrity or authenticity of the recording. Because acoustics are so easily manipulated, both the original sound and the quality of the recording are of interest to the sound archivist and must be a paramount concern during rerecording onto a more permanent medium. The sound restoration of "noisy" recordings is possible with special technology. However, the authenticity of the sound is at stake; filtering to remove unwanted noise is a last-resort technique but particularly justifiable for nonmusical recordings when the semantic or verbal content is more important than the tonal content.

Providing an optimum storage environment is the most important preservation tool for all types of sound recordings. When storage conditions are optimum, many sound recordings are very stable. Stable temperature and humidity, security from disasters, eradication of particulate and gaseous pollutants, permanent and durable enclosures and proper physical support or the absence of dimensional stress constitute optimum storage conditions.[15]

Finally, the correct use of recordings on properly maintained equipment is vital to extending their useful life. Sound repositories may want to consider making only *copies* of the original recordings available for use, preserving the original as a master copy.

VIDEO TAPE AND COMPUTER TAPE

Magnetic video tape is inherently impermanent. Manufacturers have emphasized improved technology and ease of production without concern for the archival-keeping qualities of the medium. Nevertheless, the pervasive influence of television and the ease with which important productions, events and documentation can be reproduced on video tape make its preservation essential.

Video tape can be analyzed in terms of its physical performance by testing physical and chemical properties, such as expansion of the polymer base or tensile strength. The thickness of the base material has important implications for preservation because thinner tapes are more likely to exhibit print-through and dimensional changes.

Video tape can only be "played" a limited number of times before there is significant "drop-out" (complete loss of information caused by a loss of the recorded signal) and binder degradation. Each time a tape is run, it picks up dirt and dust, which are transferred via the tape head along the entire tape. Additionally, during playback, tape is in direct contact with the decoding head and minute amounts of the emulsion (image layer) are scraped off. Useful tape life can be extended, however, by proper environmental control, meticulous care of playback equipment and proper physical storage and handling. Just as with magnetic tape sound recordings, video tape should be stored "played," not rewound.

Magnetic computer tape is subject to deterioration not only from use (stretching, imbedding of dust), but also from deterioration of the plastic base. Even when stored in optimum conditions, tape has an estimated shelf life of only 10 to 20 years—depending on the particular manufacturer.

Absolute control of humidity is recommended to prevent cinching, layer adhesion and embossment. Storage in too low humidities will increase production of static electricity that attracts dust to the tape. Early tapes may be subject to shedding of the coating from fungicides used in their manufacture that gradually deteriorate. Fortunately, tapes manufactured in the 1980s are of much better quality than those made in the 1960s and early 1970s.

Because important, often vital information may be stored on computer tapes, tape vaults are common to ensure protection from fire and other disasters. Proper tape preservation includes temperature and humidity control to 70°F ± 5° and 50% RH ± 10%,[16] eradication of dust and dirt, protection from exposure to magnetic or electrical fields (including lightning protection on the building), upright storage of reels and strict policies for handling and use. Since deterioration is gradual, defects can be spotted during annual playbacks and copies made of the affected tapes. Periodic rewinding under constant or programmed tension will help redistribute tape stresses and avoid print-through.

FOOTNOTES

1. Verner W. Clapp, *The Story of Permanent/Durable Book Paper, 1115-1970* (Copenhagen: Restaurator Press, 1972.), p. 18.

2. R.W. Hagenmeyer, "The Impact of Increasing Paper Consumption and Resource Limitations on Alakaline Papermaking," in *Preservation of Paper and Textiles of Historic and Artistic Value II,* ed. J.C. Williams (Washington, DC: American Chemical Society, 1981), p. 248.

3. W. Church, ed., *The Manufacture and Testing of Durable Book Papers, Based on the Investigations of W.J. Barrow* (Richmond, VA: Virginia State Library, 1960).

4. Council on Library Resources, Committee On Production Guidelines for Book Longevity, *Interim Report on Book Paper* (Washington, DC: Council on Library Resources, April 1981).

5. William K. Wilson and E.J. Parks, "Comparison of Accelerated Aging of Book Papers in 1937 with 36 Years Natural Aging," *Restaurator* 4 (1) (1980): 47.

6. Ellen McCrady, "Research on the Dressing and Preservation of Leather," *The Abbey Newsletter* 5 (2) (April 1981): 23-25.

7. Gary Frost, "A Brief History of Western Bookbinding—Without One Mention of Decoration," *The Abbey Newsletter* 2 (4) (February 1979): 39-43.

8. Frank E. Comparato, *Books for the Millions: A History of the Men Whose Methods and Machines Packaged the Printed Word* (Harrisburg, PA: The Stackpole Co., 1971).

9. Pamela W. Darling, "Microforms in Libraries: Preservation and Storage," *Microform Review* 5 (1) (April 1976): 99.

10. C.S. McCamy and C.I. Pope, "Redox Blemishes—Their Cause and Prevention," *Journal of Micrographics* 3 (Summer 1970): 165-70.

11. American National Standards Institute, *American National Standard Practice for Storage of Processed Safety Photographic Film* (New York: American National Standards Institute, 1979), p. 8.

12. Eastman Kodak Co., *Preservation of Photographs* (Rochester, NY: Eastman Kodak Co., 1979), p. 5.

13.Henry Wilhelm, "Color Print Instability," *Modern Photography* 43 (2) (February 1979): 92.

14. James H. Conrad, "Copying Historical Photographs," *History News* 36 (8) (August 1981): 21-28.

15. Jerry McWilliams, *Preservation and Restoration of Sound Recordings* (Nashville, TN: American Association for State and Local History, 1979).

16. 3M Co., Magnetic Audio/Video Products Division, *The Handling and Storage of Magnetic Recording Tape* (St. Paul, MN: 3M Co., ca. 1978).

IV

Developing Preservation Programs in Libraries

A preservation program should be based on the needs of a specific library. Although preservation has many principles that apply to libraries in general, the emphasis and direction of a program will be determined by a particular library collection, building, organization and history.

THE LIBRARY SETTING

Collection

The collection itself and the use to which it is put will in part dictate preservation goals. Is the collection large or small? Does it contain a larger portion of retrospective or current materials? Is the collection weeded or does the library intend to keep materials indefinitely? Do materials circulate out of the building? Is the collection heavily or infrequently used? Does it serve recreational, informational, instructional or research needs? Who uses the library? In a large library with diverse collections, all of these possibilities can be expected.

The physical condition of the library collections must be documented so that preservation goals and priorities can be discussed. A systematic perusal of the collection will uncover particular problem areas and is a necessary step in planning future conservation activities. The services of an expert consultant in conservation can be useful in conjunction with the investigative efforts of the library staff. A consultant's recommendations and observations will be an invaluable addition to planning, and his or her written report can be used to substantiate requests for improved conditions, additional staff or funds for the preservation program. The consultant may give a lecture or presentation to the library staff to generate enthusiasm and ideas for the incipient program.

Building

The library building itself and its internal environment have a tremendous impact on the physical well-being of a collection and thus on the direction of preservation planning. A large research collection housed in an old building and located in an urban area will have preservation problems unheard of at a relatively new, air-conditioned state university library. A building's age, floor plans, shelving and storage, and systems such as heating and cooling, ventilation, and air-filtration will all have had effects on material's preservation. Therefore, before specific planning for preservation can take place, preservation needs must be determined through a thorough examination of the building, environmental conditions and overall physical condition of the collection.[1]

Organization

The organization of a library and its institutional affiliation, if any, will determine what preservation and conservation model is best suited to meeting the needs of a collection. To whom does the head librarian or library director report? How are budget monies allocated? What are the lines of authority and responsibility within the library? Is the collection centralized or are there branch or department libraries? Out of which department are binding and repair activities currently managed? Is there a stack maintenance unit?

History

Any previous and current arrangements for physical treatment and maintenance will affect the subsequent organization and emphasis of an expanded preservation program. What has been the legacy of binding and physical treatment? Has the library had a history of dubious mending practices or benign neglect? Was there always a vigorous library binding program? Did the library purchase microfilm copies of serials rather than bind? Were paperbacks prebound? What has been the policy concerning seriously deteriorated items? Were rare and unique items in need of conservation treatment sent to a qualified outside conservator?

POLICY, STAFF AND ORGANIZATION

Once the needs of a collection have been determined and inadequacies in the building and its environment documented, a library is ready to begin establishing the framework for a preservation program. The plan for the program should take into account the present situation and should set realistic goals for improvement.

A policy statement on preservation can be instrumental in defining preservation principles, listing preservation and conservation activities and designating responsibilities.[2] In order for the policy to be effective, the library's governing group, department heads and staff should all be involved in the policy-making process. To be truly effective, the preservation effort must involve the whole library staff. When people are involved in making policy and understand why a particular policy is important, they will be more likely to be supportive.

A designation of priorities is an important part of the policy statement. Priorities are established based on a particular library, its purpose and the condition of its building and collections. They are needed because the task of preserving library resources is mammoth and never ending. Meaningful priorities for a preservation program can be established by balancing those activities designed to have the most significant and immediate impact on the condition of the collections with those designed to provide the library with a logical, unified and well-organized long-range program.

Organizing a preservation program is often a process of rethinking those library functions that may fall within the purview of both long-term preservation efforts and immediate conservation activities. "Preservation" is usually associated with planning or action that will retard the deterioration of library materials. Such activities as the monitoring of environmental control, the installation of screens to filter ultraviolet light from exhibit cases, the development of a disaster preparedness plan and the production of a staff training film are characteristic preservation efforts. "Conservation" usually implies those activities directly concerned with protective or remedial treatment of the physical item. Conservation includes activities such as protection through binding and enclosure, preventive maintenance through a systematic program of repair or sophisticated treatments such as deacidification. "Information preservation," or preserving the intellectual content of seriously deteriorated library materials, involves reformatting a physical item that cannot or need not be retained in its original physical format or medium.

Depending on the library, preservation activities may be organized into a single unified program, that is, an umbrella for all preservation and conservation activities, or a network of policies and procedures that are carried out by several departments or units within guidelines specified by the preservation policy. The possibilities for an *effective* organization for preservation are probably as diverse as the number of libraries developing such programs.

Whatever the organization, the most *efficient* way to organize a cohesive preservation program is to assign overall authority and responsibility to one person. This is usually impossible in all but the very largest or very smallest libraries because preservation affects so many different aspects of library affairs. Consequently, the authority to impose or enforce preservation policies usually comes from the library administration. One workable arrangement for libraries may be to authorize *preservation* policy (which often crosses departmental lines) through the library administration and assign *conservation* responsibility to an individual qualified to organize and direct conservation activities. This individual could also serve a staff function and advise on matters of preservation policy. The success of preservation (not unlike the success of bibliographic control or reference service) is dependent upon the recognition and support of the library administration. Without commitment, direction and enthusiasm from the top, very little can be accomplished.

The development of a preservation program inevitably involves some reorganization of library functions. Unfortunately, some staff may view change as either threatening or insulting. The library administration should encourage acceptance and cooperation by nurturing a broad base of support for preservation *before* imposing changes.

COST OF A PRESERVATION PROGRAM

A preservation program does not need to cost very much. A modest yet effective effort against the deterioration of library materials can simply be instituting policies consistent with preservation principles.[3]

Actually, most libraries already spend funds on preservation, such as to bind unbound materials, to prepare new materials for the shelves and to "mend" damaged materials. The reorganization of these activities within a single unit often improves efficiency, and provides a base for future development of expanded preservation and conservation activities. A preservation committee with a specific charge to examine conditions and make recommendations can significantly enhance the preservation of the collection if the library administration acts on its recommendations.[4]

Most libraries, however, will aim for a comprehensive program that includes the administrative considerations of preservation or preventive maintenance, as well as a program for actual conservation treatment. The major additional cost that libraries assume when they embark upon such a preservation program is for the staff position necessary to organize and direct conservation activities.

Some libraries assign a vacated position line to conservation. Other libraries redefine the job description of an interested staff member and assume responsibility for retraining. This new position can soon "earn its keep" by improving decision making for contract binding, by increasing the efficiency of materials preparation procedures and by upgrading repair activities.

Other clearly identifiable costs of preservation and conservation may include items such as contract binding, salaries and wages of staff assigned to a conservation department or unit, the cost of purchasing reprints or microfilm copies of brittle books, conservation supplies that are directly used in conservation treatments and new equipment purchased to monitor the environment. Many costs, however, are hidden in other budget lines. For example, the cost of changing bibliographic records to reflect the photocopying and withdrawal of a seriously deteriorated work would be subsumed in the cataloging budget.

Inevitably, the cost of preservation does cross departmental and budget lines; thus unless the entire library staff is convinced of the need for preservation, it may resent the additional time and trouble necessary to shelve books properly, or tell a patron that he or she cannot borrow a damaged item until it is repaired, or catalog a microfilm copy of a deteriorated item. A successful program cannot be imposed by the library administration but must become the goal of the entire staff.

Some of the cost of preserving a library collection may not even be part of a library's budget. Building maintenance, environmental control, fire detection and extermination services are often assumed by a parent institution. If inadequate building systems jeopardize the preservation of the collection, the library may have to alert many people outside the library and convince them about the importance of preservation before conditions are improved. For even though conservation scientists have established that library materials will last significantly longer at lower temperatures, it still may be difficult to convince a centralized physical plant to cool the library building to 70°F during the hot summer months.

Perhaps the most significant aspect of the cost of preservation is the very real cost of *neglecting* the physical collection. For example, an improperly shelved book will require repair or rebinding sooner than a properly shelved one. Libraries that use book drops for book return will be forced to repair or replace a much higher proportion of their circulated items than those that only use the circulation desk for returns. These are practical examples of the cost effectiveness of preventive maintenance. In addition, the neglect of preservation concerns results in incalculable costs of irreparable damage to materials of permanent research value or historic interest. A library collection is an enormous investment for the future, and it deserves to be protected.

Libraries planning to increase greatly the range and complexity of conservation treatments performed in-house or contracted for by a cooperative treatment center or private conservation enterprise will need to increase allocations to conservation. Some libraries seek grant funds to provide for new equipment or to enable the restoration of a valuable special collection. Some libraries transfer funds from other budget lines to make room for conservation activities. The most desirable monies, however, are those received because the library is successful in justifying the need for an increased preservation effort.

Costs for specific treatment options are discussed later in this chapter.

PRESERVATION PROGRAM STANDARDS

Environmental Control

A library is responsible for the preservation of those materials that it acquires, describes and stores for the library community it serves. A library should provide intellectual and physical control to those materials, as well as an optimum storage environment that enhances preservation of the collection. The single most important aspect of preservation is environmental control.[5]

Providing a proper storage environment includes protection against those specific agents, discussed in Chapter II, that cause library materials to deteriorate.

Recommended standards for the storage of library materials specify 68°–70°F and a relative humidity of 50% (see Chapter II). A temperature of 68°–70°F is a compromise between what is comfortable for people and desirable for library materials. Actually, as far as most library materials are concerned, the lower the temperature, the better. There is a point, however (approximately 50°F), when unless special procedures are followed, condensation will form on materials brought out of a cold storage area. The best situation is a building that separates stack and public service areas. Then cooler temperatures that retard deterioration are possible, and people can be made comfortable by regulating the temperature and humidity.

The library climate should be kept as close to constant as possible. Systems controlling humidity are as important as those controlling temperature. It is also important that changes in temperature and relative humidity be held to less than ±5°F and ±6% RH.

A hygrothermograph (center) being using to record the temperature and humidity.

While air conditioning is the norm in newer libraries, most air conditioning (cooling) systems do not specifically control humidity. Some control of high humidity does occur during the summer months when incoming air is cooled. But without a humdification system, humidity levels in the winter months will drop drastically—resulting in desiccation of paper, bindings and plastic films. Additionally, if thermostat systems are not working properly or are not capable of responding to rapid changes in the weather, damaging fluctuations in temperature and humidity will occur. Heating and cooling systems tied to a central physical plant are often particularly slow to respond to changes in the weather. Many libraries connected with a large institution experience rapid and drastic fluctuations in temperature and humidity—especially in the spring and fall.

A system of environmental control for a library building should not only maintain specified levels for air temperature and relative humidity but should also filter gaseous pollutants and particulate matter and circulate the "clean" and "climatized" air. Proper air circulation will prevent pockets of stagnant air or small areas where temperature and humidity levels do not meet standards.

Particulate matter is removed by filtration of incoming air. Common commercial filtration systems employ dry filters, oil bath filters or electrostatic precipitators. Though many libraries operate with electrostatic precipitators, they are not acceptable since they produce ozone, which promotes embrittlement of paper. Oil bath filters may not be advisable because they produce aerosols of their own. Dry filters provide excellent filtering efficiency if the system is properly maintained.

Gaseous pollutants are removed by passage of incoming air through treatment beds in the ventilation system where chemicals can absorb specific pollutants. Before such a system is designed, however, the percentage of specific pollutants must be determined.

Damage caused to library materials by exposure to ultraviolet (UV) light rays in sunlight and fluorescent light can be minimized by providing filters to screen UV rays, lowering light levels and keeping lights off when possible. Windows should have curtains to prevent direct or reflected light from falling on library materials, or a UV filtering screen should be applied to the inside of the glass. In stack areas, fluorescent light levels should be kept as low as possible or incandescent lighting should be used. In a closed-stack library, the stack area can be wired to permit lights to be turned off when they are not being used. When stack and public service areas occupy the same space, fluorescent tubes that contain UV filters can be used. Since these are more expensive than ordinary tubes, an alternative is UV filtering sleeves that fit over standard fluorescent tubes. The sleeves, however, must be tested periodically and replaced when necessary.

If environmental control systems are to function properly, they must be maintained on a rigidly specified schedule. Poor maintenance of air conditioning and humidification systems will eventually lead to water-damaged library materials. The effectiveness of an air-cleaning system is dependent on the timely changing of filters and recharging of the system. Systems should be designed and installed with maintenance in mind. Often a library attached to a parent institution will not directly supervise maintenance crews, and communication and control can be difficult.

Environmental control systems must also be monitored to determine if they are meeting the standards set. Periodic adjustment will always be necessary, and there may be occasions when immediate adjustment is needed. Systems purchased from distant companies can be a problem if there is no one available to maintain them or to solve on-the-spot problems. Each system should be equipped with built-in monitors so that non-maintenance library personnel can check the effectiveness of the system. Independent monitors can be used to periodically check the accuracy of system monitors so that recalibration can be performed when necessary.

Physical Control

The preservation of library materials includes provisions for proper storage, shelving, handling and circulation or use. Different kinds of library materials may require different storage conditions depending upon their physical and chemical make-up, their structure or format and their value or intended use.

Some aspects of the physical storage, handling and use of library materials present areas where the preservation of the collection can be enhanced and damage and deterioration averted. Systematic cleaning and stack maintenance activities can prevent deterioration by removing dirt and grime, and can help detect signs of insect infestation and mold growth, or items needing conservation treatment. Likewise, routine reshelving aids preservation because of the opportunity to shelve leaning volumes or volumes placed on their fore-edges correctly and to designate items for binding or repair. Custom protective enclosures can be provided for individual items during the systematic examination and refurbishing of a special collection.

Shelving and Storage

The purpose of library shelving is to provide ready access to the collection. Libraries with stacks that are closed to the public view shelving as a means of storing the collection when it is not being used, while libraries that encourage browsing see stacks as a continuation of public service areas. Regardless of the viewpoint, shelves function as physical support for books; their structure and arrangement should ensure the preservation and effective use of the collection. The shelving arrangement must be flexible enough to allow for expansion of the collection. Tightly packed shelves lead to damage from wrenching books off the shelf and forcing them back on.

When stacks are meant for browsing, there should be enough room to allow easy access to every shelf. If a patron is cramped, he or she will be unable to handle volumes carefully. A table or empty shelf should be available at regular distances so patrons will not be forced to prop books open against other books or to hold several books while looking for others and consequently drop all of them. Footstools should be readily available so users will not have to perch precariously on tiptoe to jostle a book off a high shelf.

The shelves themselves should be easy to clean and wide enough to provide ample support for the books. The painted surface should be smooth without being slick. There should not be any sharp edges or corners, and every shelf should be equipped with a bookend to keep books upright. Leaning books or shelving casebound books on their fore-edges destroys the shape of the spine, causes the book block to pull away from its cover and breaks or tears the thin cloth and paper in the hinge area. Bookends should provide their greatest support at the base of the shelf. Their sides should be thick enough to prevent "knifing" book pages against the bookends when they are reshelved.

Optimum storage for flat paper materials (prints, maps, broadsides and manuscripts) and oversize materials is flat storage. Thus a library storage environment must include adequate flat storage for both oversize and letter-size materials. Convenient and nondamaging access to the materials, as well as suitable tables for their use, must also be available.

Microforms have many applications in a library—as original documents, as preservation copies of deteriorated or space-taking paper originals, as use copies of fragile materials and as copies of documents owned by other libraries. In all instances, microforms that are used will deteriorate and at some point become unusable. If permanent retention of a microform is intended, use copies must be generated as they are needed from a duplicating master negative. A master should be kept in a rigorously controlled environment, preferably a separate storage room at 60°F and 45% RH.

Rare, unique or special collections are customarily stored and used in a separate area that is subject to more stringent security measures than the rest of the library. Because of the value of these materials, measures for physical and environmental security also frequently exceed those for the general collection. A fireproof vault may be included in a rare book room, or halongenated fire extinguishing systems may be used instead of the less expensive sprinkler systems. However, in research libraries, much of a collection may represent material of permanent research value, and "rare" materials will be found throughout the collection. It is most important to keep in mind that this generation's assignation of "valuable" may not be the same as the next generation's.

Handling

Although a certain amount of wear and tear is inevitable when library materials are used, damage caused by improper handling and use can be reduced in a library where preservation is a priority. Minimizing the inadvertent damage caused by ignorance or carelessness and the deliberate abuse caused by selfishness or maliciousness requires sensible policies backed up by constant and unswerving enforcement.

The attitudes of the library administration are reflected throughout the library. Library staff will respond positively to preservation when they realize that the administration is committed, and library patrons will be impressed by a preservation "atmosphere" in a library.

The process of educating the library staff about preservation may require retraining or raising the consciousness of the existing staff conducting formal orientation and training sessions for new staff, and reminding the entire staff on an informal but continuous basis of the importance of preservation and conservation.

Educating the staff can involve such activities as a lecture by a conservation expert, a video tape that illustrates preservation concerns, or small-group orientation within the library. Staff assigned to a repair unit may attend a conservation workshop with the financial support of the library. A combination of these techniques is probably most effective.

Even the library that systematically exposes its staff to preservation concerns will have problem staff members who continue to treat materials roughly or are obstructive to preservation policy. Carelessness is inherent in some people, and not everyone working in a library behaves in a responsible and professional manner. Some people will need constant supervision and reminding and will inevitably cause damage to library materials. Others will need an occasional reminder from their supervisor.

The problem of educating library patrons on the proper care of library materials is much more challenging than that of educating staff. Patrons do not receive their paychecks from the library, and they cannot be required to view a video tape on preservation. A few may feel a general dislike for the "system"—a feeling that manifests itself as animosity toward the library. Frustration with library services may elicit "revenge" against library materials. Studies of academic library patrons have shown that they do not consider even direct mutilation of library materials a very serious offense.

If a library sets a good preservation example, the work of educating library patrons to preservation concerns is half done. Patrons have an almost universal ignorance of the actual costs of obtaining, cataloging and storing library materials. A preservation public relations campaign will alert patrons to their impact on the physical well-being of a collection and the cost of carelessness or deliberate mutilation.

To be most effective, preservation concerns should be advertised in an appealing manner that gets the idea across without harping. Some patrons will respond to pleas to save library materials for the good of mankind, but pointing out how they are hurting themselves will probably get more of a response. Simple instructions on how to handle and use library materials properly can help prevent damage caused by simple ignorance.

Educating library users is a necessary part of a preservation program and it can help prevent needless abuse. However, the problem of mutilation (like theft) is really not one of preservation but rather a matter for criminal prosecution. Studies have shown that the best deterrent to those who would steal or mutilate library materials is the very real possibility of prosecution. How a library handles mutilation and theft will depend upon the state laws, local laws, the institution and the philosophy of the library administration.

Circulation

Although it is obviously desirable for library materials to be used, most of the direct physical damage that accrues is through circulation and use. The best defense against damage is a collection that is properly maintained. Materials that are not appropriately protected by a binding or enclosure are especially vulnerable to damage. Materials that are already damaged or in a state of disrepair are subject to more serious damage.

The patron using library materials is concerned first of all with extracting information. The potential for damage to materials during use is practically limitless. For example, the emulsion layer of microfilm is very easily damaged and the image obscured by rapid movement through a reader, bindings are easily broken by placing them open and face down to mark the place, and large maps are easily torn when they are dragged out from under other maps. The photocopy machine is a notoriously damaging experience for bound materials, as patrons lean heavily on items to get a good copy.

Circulation of library materials out of the library building by direct patron borrowing or interlibrary loan exposes them to a myriad of hazards. Materials that circulate are often bounced along in a bicycle basket, left on an automobile dashboard in the sun, examined over dinner, read in the bathtub and mauled by eager toddlers or hungry pets. A library

"Save a Book" poster published by the Illinois Cooperative Conservation Program with Library Services and Construction Act funds. Simple, graphic instructions educate patrons on how to prevent damage to books.

that allows, and even encourages, circulation must accept that a certain amount of damage is inevitable. One purpose of special collections is to protect materials that are too valuable to risk the hazards of circulation.

Libraries concerned with preservation may want to consider restrictions on the use and circulation of certain categories of materials. For example, patrons wanting to borrow an item in disrepair may be asked to return for it the next day so that it can receive rush treatment. Circulation, especially of fragile or brittle materials, out of the building may be denied and their photocopying restricted.

Automatic Book Return Systems

Automatic book return systems are not recommended since books are easily damaged by mechanical systems that jostle them about, allow them to bump against one another, permit abrasion of the binding or drop them any distance—however slight. The best method of book return is for items to be returned to the desk where they were charged out. Though it is true that humans can be injurious to books, they can be taught to be careful. On the other hand, poorly designed mechanical or automatic systems, once installed, cannot be reasoned with.

In the case of a public library that emphasizes public service, book "drops" outside the building may be justified—the trade-off for the service is fewer circulations per volume and frequent replacement of volumes as a result of damage from rain, overflowing boxes and vandalism. Inside the library, a slot that opens to a gradual slide leading to a table is acceptable providing the table is emptied *as soon* as it is full.

Some libraries, however, insist on an automatic or mechanical system for the return of circulating materials. When automatic systems are used, the library should (1) ensure that a minimum of abrasion and bumping occurs; (2) determine the maximum capacity of the system and chart it against the maximum possible volume of book return within the max-

Book "drops" often result in damage to volumes from rain, overflowing boxes and vandalism.

imum time the system would be unattended; and (3) visit another library where the system is used to see it in operation.

DISASTER PREPAREDNESS

The purpose of disaster preparedness is to maximize preventive measures that can be taken to protect an existing library building and collection from devastation resulting from fire, flood, tornado, earthquake, a building system's failure, etc. Preventive measures include a written plan of action outlining salvage procedures to minimize damage to a collection in the event of a disaster.

Fire

The protection of library collections from fire is complicated by the nature of the materials themselves and the way they are stored and used. Library materials are in many cases irreplaceable and in most cases uninsured. Libraries contain highly combustible, compact fuel that will feed any fire that manages to get started. Detection is a problem because there are many remote areas; in a large library the staff is unable to supervise the entire stack area. To make matters worse, water from high pressure hoses used in fire-fighting causes additional serious damage—bindings warp, colors bleed and pages stick together. Salvage operations are complicated when damaged buildings cannot be entered immediately, since wet paper is subject to mold growth almost immediately.

Two major considerations for the protection of a library building and its contents from fire include (1) construction features, and (2) arrangement of the functional areas and utilities within the building. (Of course, site location is also an important factor to consider.) These factors are important regardless of the method of fire detection or the building's extinguishing system. If a building was constructed with the fire hazard in mind, then a possible fire may be prevented or, if a fire is started, it may not spread uncontrollably.[6]

Building Construction

A building constructed of "fire-resistant" materials is not necessarily "fire proof." It may be that the contents of the building will burn completely, but the building itself will remain standing. In any case, all materials, even fire-resistant materials, will burn and/or disintegrate if the fire is hot enough.

In order to fight a fire effectively, the building must allow for access by the fire department. A complete plan of the building indicating stack areas, aisles and entrances, windows and knock-out panels, utilities and priority collections, catalogs and records must be available. The fire hazard exists around the clock, not just during library hours; a fire-fighting force without a plan for access wastes valuable time in forceable entry.

The physical security of collections should not hamper either fire fighting or safety for staff and patrons. Requirements for exits are outlined in local building codes, but many libraries channel all traffic from the stacks through a single circulation desk and a single exit. Neither collection security nor people security need be jeopardized if the fire alarm system is integrated with exit systems.

Arrangement of Areas

The principle of compartmentalization is perhaps the single most important aspect of fire-prevention planning. In the past, construction of tier upon tier of self-supporting metal stacks created a chimney effect, encouraging the spread of fire. This type of construction has been rejected, except in cases where aesthetic considerations unwisely outweigh fire safety. In fact, any vertical opening that allows passage of flames between floors is inadvisable. Compartmentalization will confine fires to the areas in which they start. Stacks separated by fire-resistant floor construction and further compartmentalized by fire doors, resist the spread of fire. Stairways, elevators and pipe shafts should be enclosed. Service areas should be compartmentalized and/or separated from stack areas because they are high-risk areas for fires. Stacks separated from public service areas and used only for storage can receive maximum fire protection.

Heating, electrical and air-conditioning systems should be installed and maintained so that they will not increase the fire hazard. Boilers and furnaces can be cut off from the rest of the building by a fire resistive enclosure and/or installed in a separate structure. Heating and air-conditioning ducts and pipe shafts should prevent the passage of flames between floors. Inadequate maintenance of utility systems within library buildings has been the cause of numerous fires. Preventive maintenance performed periodically and according to systems specifications can lessen fire risks.

Automatic Extinguishing Systems

Even if a library building is constructed of fire-resistant materials and has fire doors, compartmentalization and the services of a good fire department, it still should be furnished with automatic systems for fire detection and extinguishment. Automatic detection systems operate by sensors which, depending upon the system, respond to a temperature change, the light flash of a fire or the presence of smoke or invisible products of combustion. To be effective, every detection system should be able to notify the local fire department, trigger an alarm in the building, indicate the location of the fire, shut down the ventilation system and recall elevators.[7]

An automatic extinguishing system will contain a fire or put it out. Extinguishing systems for libraries use either water or gas. Although water can cause extensive damage to library materials, it has been repeatedly proven that modern automatic sprinkling systems can effectively suppress fires with minimum water damage to collections. When sprinkler heads operate independently, water is discharged only from those sprinklers activated by the detection system. Recent developments in the salvage of water-damaged library materials are a further incentive to installation of sprinkler systems.

Gas systems for the suppression of fire use either carbon dioxide or halon (a halogenated hydrocarbon). Carbon dioxide will extinguish a fire by smothering flames, but it is not recommended for libraries because of the great and immediate danger to people.

Halon is a liquefied, compressed gas that extinguishes a fire by interfering with the combustion cycle. It is harmless to people in exposures up to five minutes. Halon is very effective and particularly advantageous for libraries because it does no damage to books and manuscripts. However, it is an expensive system relative to automatic sprinklers; a false discharge may cost as much as $30,000. The use of a dual detection system—where two separate sensor systems must be triggered to activate the extinguishing system—will prevent expensive false alarms. Automatic detection systems, like all other building systems, should be periodically checked to be sure that they are operating properly.

Water Damage

Almost all disasters involving libraries result in water-damaged materials. Storms, floods, tornadoes and high winds bring water; water is used by fire fighters to extinguish fires; and earthquakes cause broken water pipes. Man-made calamities usually involve water from overflowing cooling or humidification systems and leaky plumbing or bursting pipes. Damage caused by the water from natural disasters is increased by the accompanying dirt and debris.

Special precautions should be taken by libraries located in areas where frequent storms or flooding occur. Libraries with recurring water problems should not store library materials in the basement, or at least not place materials on the bottom shelves. Water detection devices can be installed, and the water sensing unit can be connected to a central alarm system. However, large-scale damage can happen almost instantly if water pipes above shelving break. Likewise, dripping from an overflowing humidification system can go undetected for long periods and ruin important materials before the problem is even noticed.

A well-maintained building will prevent many conditions that can lead to a disaster, but only good luck can protect a library for all time from all potential calamities. It is imperative that every library be prepared to act quickly to salvage irreplaceable library materials in the event of a major or minor disaster.

Preparedness for Salvage Operations

Disaster preparedness includes an assessment of the existing library building to determine potential hazards. The building and its detection and alarm systems, fire extinguishing systems and climate control systems should be examined and problem areas noted. Areas such as the roof, physical plant, duct-work, food service or lounge, shipping and receiving and conservation treatment facility can present special hazards. A schedule for periodic inspection and monitoring should be instituted.

Development of a written disaster preparedness plan will enable a library to act expediently and react appropriately to a disaster.[8] The disaster plan should include the designation of key staff members who would authorize and supervise salvage operations; the identification of priority collections for immediate protection and salvage; lists of necessary services, equipment and supplies; and a step-by-step procedure for salvage operations.

The designation of a disaster "team" to organize and supervise salvage operations should include someone, usually an administrator, who can authorize expenditures, cut through red tape and elicit cooperation from all those involved. If a library is part of a larger institution, there may already be a procedure for responding to a disaster and a designated safety or security officer. However, the library will also need to designate specific staff members and delineate responsibilities. If no specific person has been assigned preservation responsibility, a small disaster preparedness committee can be charged with developing a written plan. A large library may have a building manager who is knowledgeable about the building and its systems and can direct efforts to stabilize the environment, ensure the safety of workers and reduce the danger of rampant mold and mildew growth. Such a person can also act as a liaison with central janitorial services, electricians and plumbers, and assemble necessary equipment and supplies. Local sources of equipment and supplies should be listed in the disaster plan so that salvage efforts can proceed with a minimum of confusion and delay.

A specific person, most logically a librarian with preservation responsibilities, can become expert in the salvage and restoration of water-damaged library materials. The development of staff expertise in this area is vital if *additional* damage to affected materials as a result of improper handling or treatment is to be averted. This person would be responsible for obtaining current information on the treatment of water-damaged library materials, devising a salvage procedure and establishing contact with services for freezing, vacuum-drying, fumigation, photographic processing and smoke and soot removal. If additional technical information is needed, this person can contact conservators and others who have had experience in the salvage and restoration of water and/or smoke-damaged materials.

Subject librarians, department heads, bibliographers and curators should be responsible for assigning priority ranking to collections. In the event of a disaster, these priority collections would be salvaged first. The list of priority collections should be keyed to *exact* locations and become a permanent part of the disaster preparedness plan. Actual floor plans that include shelving and storage arrangements can be appended to the plan and updated as necessary.

A major disaster will necessitate the involvement of volunteers or temporary paid help. Because wet materials can be easily damaged, it may be best to identify library staff members who would volunteer to help in salvage operations. To minimize confusion and coordinate efforts, volunteers at the disaster site can be organized into "work teams" with a group leader or be supervised by a member of the library's disaster team. Salvage can be exhausting and depressing work, and supervisors should arrange for refreshments, rest periods and regular relief by fresh workers.

Responding to a Water Disaster

A typical procedure for responding to a disaster involving large-scale water damage follows.

1. Establish the safety of the affected area.

2. Stabilize the environment. The temperature and humidity should be kept as low as possible. The season, weather and condition of the building systems will affect how quickly temperature and relative humidity can be controlled. Mold will flourish at 70ºF and 70% RH even on "dry" materials. The usual rule is that wet materials are subject to mold growth after 48 hours.

3. Assemble necessary equipment and supplies.

4. Assemble the work teams.

5. Remove water-damaged materials that will be frozen from the affected area.
   a. Remove wet materials by a human "chain."
   b. Pack materials for freezing as close to the disaster site as possible.
   c. Pack the wettest materials first.
   d. Materials that will be frozen will be packed in plastic milk crates and coded as to location.
   e. Transport materials to a freezer facility.
   f. Transport frozen materials to a facility for vacuum drying and, if necessary, fumigation.

6. Wet photographic materials should be kept wet and cold and moved immediately via a refrigerated truck to a photographic facility for reprocessing.

7. Remove water damaged materials that will be air-dried from the affected area. (Coated paper cannot be air-dried or the pages will "block"—stick together in one mass.)
   a. Set up the area for air drying well away from the affected area if control of temperature and humidity will be a problem.
   b. Cover large tables with unprinted newspaper. Use fans and dehumidifiers to circulate the air and keep temperature and humidity down.
   c. Remove damp materials via book trucks to the drying site.
   d. Place damp books upright and open the covers slightly. Do not fan the pages open. Support the book block with small squares of book board so that the contents will not sag forward and pull out from the cover and the spine will retain its shape.
   e. Just before drying is complete, lay books flat with the spine hanging over the edge of the table and weight them with paper-covered bricks.
   f. Fumigate the materials after they are completely dry.

8. Clean and sterilize the affected area.

9. After air drying and fumigating damp materials, arrange for necessary repair, rebinding and restoration.

10. After vacuum drying frozen materials, acclimate dried materials for a period of six months to restore moisture equilibrium. Arrange for necessary repair, rebinding and restoration.

CONSERVATION TREATMENT OPTIONS

Environmental control, physical control and disaster preparedness are activities central to a comprehensive preservation program. Their implementation will significantly enhance the overall condition of a collection and will help prevent large-scale damage from occurring. There are, however, deteriorative processes over which libraries have no control, such as the deteriorative processes that weaken bindings during routine use and embrittle paper during aging. These require the intervention of conservation treatments (see Figure IV.1).

The decision making that accompanies the selection of a conservation treatment is part of collection development. By allowing materials to deteriorate beyond the point of usability, libraries limit access to information and frustrate users. By altering the physical item through the intervention of treatment, libraries may alter the bibliographic item.

For the purpose of developing a rationale for treatment decision making, conservation efforts can be divided into (1) maintenance activities (for new materials being added to the collection or those materials still in reasonably good condition) and (2) the disposition of deteriorated items that have been designated for long-term retention. Eventually, many items being maintained will also have to enter the decision-making routine for long-term retention. The reevaluation process for long-term retention is necessary if collections are to be *dynamic* rather than static and are to serve patrons by being responsive to their needs. Few libraries will be able to afford the luxury of preserving, in their original state, everything they have ever accessioned or cataloged.

Preventive Maintenance

Preventive maintenance is as important a concept in library preservation as it is in automobile maintenance or health care. The protection afforded by environmental control, proper shelving and handling practices, and the more active maintenance procedures of selective binding, mass deacidification, proper storage containers and timely repairs can significantly reduce the need for later restoration or replacement. Thus, in the entire scheme of library operations, maintenance of the physical collection is cost effective. Central to a maintenance program is the deliberate protection of items *prior* to their being made available for use, through conservation treatments such as mass deacidification, library binding, and the use of protective jackets, folders and boxes.

Mass Deacidification

Chemical stabilization of acid book paper by mass deacidification (see Chapter VIII) will prevent subsequent weakening and embrittlement of the paper from acid deterioration. *Paper that has already become brittle, however, will not be restored to former strength and flexibility through deacidification.* In an ideal maintenance program, each paper item being added to the library's permanent collection would be tested and those items with an acid pH would be deacidified. Arranging for treatment would involve (1) contracting for the service; (2) screening and testing incoming materials and designating them for treatment; (3) transporting materials to the treatment facility; and (4) keeping accurate records

Figure IV.1 Conservation Treatment

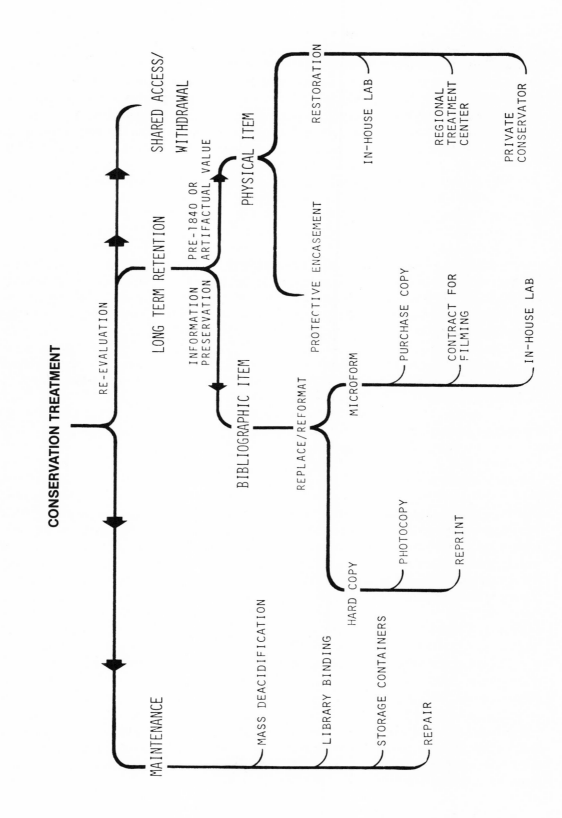

on items sent and returned. Realistically, the addition of a deacidification step to the already cumbersome routines of acquisitions, cataloging, binding and marking would even further delay the process of making information available to patrons. Further, the expense of deacidification would have to be added to today's frozen or even shrinking budgets for new materials. On the other hand, if the technology is available to ensure that acid paper will be made permanent if deacidified, then libraries should take advantage of the treatment for their permanent collections. If materials destined to deteriorate are knowingly added to "permanent" collections, then libraries must hope that in the future it will be technologically, financially and practically feasible to convert deteriorated materials to other media that can conveniently and satisfactorily transmit information to users.

Library Binding

Library binding is the most common, and often the only, conservation activity routinely practiced by libraries. It is the responsibility of the library to communicate product specifications to the library binder (see Chapter III). In order to make appropriate decisions on the suitability of library binding for certain types of materials, staff must be familiar with every aspect of bindery production. This usually means periodic trips to the binder's premises.

A contract for library binding should do more than specify prices; it should clearly state acceptable binding methods and materials and delineate responsibilities. For example, a library should always reserve the right to choose the method of binding. Some issues to consider are: the initial and projected condition of the book paper; method of sewing (including oversewing, machine through-the-fold sewing, hand sewing, and adhesive binding); margins; trimming; rounding and backing of spines; and types of covering material.

Storage Containers

Proper storage containers for unbound paper materials, maps, manuscripts, microforms, photographs, phonograph records, magnetic tapes and discs and for items with unusual formats are important for preventive maintenance. To meet conservation standards, a container must provide protection against mechanical damage caused by movement; physical damage caused by particulate matter, abrasion or pressure; and chemical damage caused by the migration of impurities from adjacent materials or the container itself. Depending on the structure, containers can also serve as buffers against fluctuations in temperature and humidity and protection from ultraviolet light rays and some atmospheric pollutants. Examples of common containers are map folders, manuscript storage boxes, microfiche envelopes and motion picture film cans.

Repair

An active and well-organized book repair program is a vital maintenance activity. Since 1840, libraries have not only seen a sharp decline in the quality of paper, but in the quality of book manufacture as well. The inadequacy of publishers' bindings has meant that libraries are forced to repair volumes, or have them rebound by a library bindery, almost as soon as they are used. Since a library binding for every new acquisition is out of the question, the maintenance of a collection depends on the development of a series of simple in-house repairs.[9-11] An ideal program would include periodic, systematic perusal of the shelves for materials in need of repair. The need for repair can, of course, be greatly diminished by proper storage, shelving, handling and use.

Long-Term Retention

Since libraries will not want to retain unusable materials, items that are seriously deteriorated must enter a decision-making process for long-term retention—to determine if they should be withdrawn, restored or reformatted (see Chapter V for discussion of this treatment). The following questions will need to be asked about every item: Should this item be kept in the collection? Is the paper brittle? Can it be commercially rebound or repaired in-house? Would a protective box be appropriate? How is it used? How often is it used? Does it have value as an artifact? Does it need to be in hard copy format? Is a commercial reprint available? For how much? Is a commercial microfilm copy available? Has another library filmed it? Are they planning to? Is it too long to photocopy and bind? Should the original be discarded after replacement? How much would it cost to have it restored?

The answers to these questions are not always simple. There may be disagreements about issues such as what should be kept, how many copies should be kept, what constitutes brittle, the advisability of binding or repair, the quality of a reprint and the choice between film stocks and formats. There is also the consideration that when money is spent on replacement, it cannot be spent on new books. Finally, library staffs may not want to make these decisions, or simply may not have the time to make them.

TREATMENT: THE DECISION-MAKING PROCESS

Even with all the issues and controversies, libraries are still left with the primary consideration—can this item be used? If it cannot and it is kept without restoring or reformatting, then the library must restrict or deny its use. This results in what many libraries euphemistically refer to as "restricted access" or "storage." Not restoring or reformatting is a type of decision making since, left alone, a deteriorating item will eventually turn to dust. Are libraries wise to expend huge sums for online bibliographic control of their resources if significant portions of the collections are physically disintegrating? Can libraries justify the retention of materials that cannot be used? Clearly, this is where an overall collection development policy that includes preservation must enter in.

Preserving Intellectual Content

Fortunately, not all library materials need to be kept in their original state, or even format. If appropriate to the individual item and its projected use, the information contained in the item can be preserved by replacement in microformat. This is not a panacea, however, or even a simple option.[12] Some types of information would be lost by reformatting; information is sometimes dependent upon the original format; microfilm is not the preferred format for some items; microfilm is only "archival" if it is the right film, filmed correctly, processed correctly and stored and used properly. After all, there is no point in substituting one impermanent medium for another. Additionally, not every deteriorated title is available commerically, and in-house labs and contracts for outside filming are both complicated undertakings. Even with all the problems, microfilming is still the foremost preservation tool for deteriorated paper stock. In fact, the vast number of items that have *already* deteriorated make microfilming the *only* option in many cases. Coupled with cooperative filming programs among libraries, microfilming is an impressive treatment option for preserving and sharing information. (Microfilming is discussed in more detail in Chapter V.)

Preserving the Physical Item

What if a library is compelled to retain a seriously deteriorated book physically—because it has artifactual value or the content is dependent on its original format? For example, half-tones, color reproductions, etchings and other illustrations are not very satisfactorily microfilmed or photocopied. If the paper is brittle, each page can be laboriously deacidified and strengthened by lamination and the book rebound. Such a process is expensive, and skilled services are difficult to obtain. A protective box would buy some time, which is the rationale behind the Library of Congress's Phase Box Program. Damaged items are boxed and their characteristics and condition noted so that they can be retrieved and grouped for treatment in the future.[13] For example, the treatment for an ordinary 18th-century volume with a damaged binding, but strong paper and the sewing still intact, would usually be leather treatment and boxing. If the paper quality permits and the expense is warranted, the book could be rebound and the new binding executed to be compatible with the period of the book's production. This is an especially appropriate treatment option for important books that are not in their original bindings.

Choosing the Treatment

Who in the library will make the difficult decisions about treatment options?[14] Subject specialists and bibliographers are in the best position to know an item's informational value, instrinsic value, value to the collection as a whole and expected use. Reference librarians who act in a collection development capacity are also concerned about the disposition and treatment of deteriorated items. Treatment options, in general, are based on what is technologically, financially and practically feasible. The option for a particular item is based on what is appropriate in terms of its condition, value to the collection and present and projected uses. Not all items in the same condition warrant the same treatment. Even the determination of "condition" may be a matter for some deliberation.

In a library with a comprehensive preservation program, decision making is best accomplished through liaison between the subject specialist and the preservation librarian or conservator whose job it is to be knowledgeable about treatment options. The selection of a conservation treatment is a collection development decision. There are reasonable short-cuts to this process. A philosophy and framework for decision making in individual libraries can be developed to expedite routine decision making while ensuring that impor-

Custom-made protective
enclosures for rare/fragile
materials.

tant decisions are made by the appropriate people. See Chapter VII for a discussion of decision making as it relates to rare books and special collections. The determination of categories of items for treatment can simplify decision making by setting parameters for treatment options. For example, new paperbacks that are sewn in signatures rather than adhesive bound might constitute one category of materials. In this case the library might make the unilateral decision always to retain the signature format by providing a hard cover casing rather than choosing the less-expensive option of an oversewn binding. A group of items that constitutes a discrete collection is another case when decisions can be made en masse. This kind of decision making does *not* ignore the fact that each individual item may be a separate and unique problem. However, it is safe, for example, to make the decision to provide acid-neutral envelopes for all the thin pamphlet material in a discrete collection without going through the process of making individual decisions. If libraries are to expect results, then it is imperative that they recognize and apply practical solutions.

The intelligent use of conservation treatment options requires coordination throughout the library of all the processes that affect the physical item and all the people who are involved in making treatment decisions—including decisions concerning withdrawal or reformatting. Trained and experienced paraprofessionals and conservation technicians can do an excellent job making decisions for maintenance, library binding, routine repair and protective encasement—providing that a framework for decision making has been developed and professional librarians are available for advising on bibliographic matters, and collection development and budgeting.

Costs

How much will treatment options cost libraries? Maintenance activities, although they initially cost money, will save money in the long run. If, for example, it costs $7 (including transportation, treatment, in-house processing and record-keeping) to have a book deacidified before being used, then it may be wise to spend the money on treatment now rather than wait for the book to deteriorate and be forced to spend $20 to $30 to replace it or reformat it and change the bibliographic record. Likewise, a simple remedial repair executed in time may eliminate the need for a costly repair later.

Unfortunately, many libraries have a history of inappropriate maintenance activities, such as leather volumes that were "treated" with shellac, books that were "mended" with surgical tape and photographs that were "protected" by being mounted on acid mat board with rubber cement. The costs of unsuitable practices and inappropriate treatments are difficult to calculate. At the very least, the useful life of materials is considerably shortened. And it is a sad fact that the bulk of most conservators' work is repairing damage that could have been avoided—time that could have been spent treating items worn out through normal handling and use or providing protection for vulnerable items.

Replacement of a badly deteriorated item takes time and costs money. An initial search must be made to check holdings, to locate missing volumes or other copies or editions, and to determine replacement options and costs. It takes time to make a final decision and acting on that decision takes more time. Reprints are not cheap, and a single title wanted in microform may be buried in an expensive microfilm series. An in-house lab represents a major expense, yet a librarian may spend months working with a commerical filmer before a quality product is produced on a regular basis. If the library intends to retain the *physical* item, a protective box made in-house may cost anywhere from $4 to $25, or more. Custom commercial boxes start at $20. A simple cased rebinding for an ordinary book would take even an experienced technician approximately eight hours to execute. A typical restoration job by a conservator may cost $150 to $300.

Within the limitations of a library's particular preservation options, it is desirable to determine the estimated cost of each particular option. Such cost figures are an integral part of decision making. For example, if a library determines that the average unit cost of repairing a book in-house is cheaper than sending it for a new library binding, it may decide to increase its capabilities and do more book repair. Likewise, certain rules can be established for decision making based on a library's experience with costs. For example, it may be cheaper to search for and purchase a microform copy than to arrange for the filming of the library's own deteriorated item.

Routine book repair station, Morris Library, Southern Illinois University at Carbondale.

Librarians must consider responsible custody of their collections as part of their professional responsibilities. By taking an active role in conservation treatment decision making, librarians will ensure that they continue to be directly involved in the composition of their collections.

MODELS FOR ORGANIZING PRESERVATION PROGRAMS

The following (see Figure IV.2) are models for organizing preservation programs in a range of library sizes and types. Every library collection is unique and most libraries will not *exactly* fit one of the five levels of preservation organization suggested by the models; however the models can be used as a guide for organizing preservation and conservation activities. See Appendix 1 for sample job descriptions for preservation and conservation personnel. (Footnotes for Chapter IV follow Figure IV.2.)

Figure IV.2   Preservation Program Models

PRESERVATION ACTIVITIES Level*	1	2	3	4	5
development of a preservation policy statement		x	x	x	x
development of a disaster preparedness plan	x	x	x	x	x
standards for environmental control	x	x	x	x	x
monitoring the environment		x	x	x	x
information preservation program including withdrawal or replacement of brittle books	x		x	x	x
cooperative filming projects				x	x
microfilming contract with a commercial firm					x
cooperation with reprint and microform publishers				x	x
library binding specifications and contract	x		x		x
mass deacidification specifications and contract				x	x
preservation responsibility for certain subject areas in agreement with other libraries					x
microfilming of rare/fragile materials to reduce handling of originals		x			x
standards for handling and use, loans and exhibits	x	x	x	x	x
education programs for staff and patrons	x	x	x	x	x

CONSERVATION ACTIVITIES Level	1	2	3	4	5
fumigation		x		x	x
storage containers	x	x	x	x	x
exhibit support design and installation		x		x	x
marking	x		x		x
preparation of materials for library binding	x		x		x
pamphlet binding	x		x		x
simple book repair for general collections	x		x		x
extensive book repair for general collections			x		x
leather treatment	x	x	x	x	x
simple protective folders		x	x	x	x
protective encasement		x		x	x
arranging for treatment of artifacts not within the conservator's area of expertise		x			
stabilization of book structures		x		x	x
selective in-house binding of new acquisitions				x	
deacidification		x		x	x
restoration of original bindings				x	
conservation rebinding				x	x
treatment documentation and fragment files		x		x	x
arranging for sophisticated scientific support/analytical services				x	x
arranging for custom protective encasement and occasional sophisticated conservation treatment	x		x		
simple flat paper repair and encapsulation	x		x		
flat paper repair, encapsulation, matting and mounting		x		x	x
conservation/duplication of photographic images		x		x	x
conservation/conversion of plastic base materials		x		x	x

*Level refers to type of library and collection, explained further below.

Figure IV.2   Preservation Program Models (Cont.)

STAFF (FTE)	Level	1	2	3	4	5
professional librarian		.2		1.0	1.0	1.0
professional conservator			1.0		4.0	1.0
paraprofessional, library		1.0		2.0	1.0	3.0
clerical		1.0		2.0	2.0	4.0
conservation technician			2.0	1.0	6.0	2.0
part-time assistants		1.5		4.0		8.0
volunteer			1.5		2.0	
	Total	3.7	4.5	10.0	16.0	21.0

SPACE (square feet)	Level	1	2	3	4	5
office/s			120	120	300	500
processing		500		750		1500
workshop/laboratory		225	625	625	1500	1200
	Total	725	745	1495	1800	3200

Level 1:

Small college library or large public library with a heavily used core collection of standard works and current resources and a small retrospective collection. Includes a small collection of rare books, manuscripts and unique local history materials.

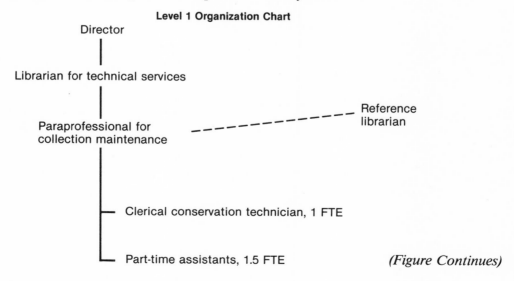

Level 1 Organization Chart

(Figure Continues)

Figure IV.2   Preservation Program Models (Cont.)

Level 2:

Historical society library or discrete historical collection pertaining to a particular geographic region or specific subject, person, topic or time period. Includes original documentary resources and artifacts, as well as secondary research materials and reference works in support of the collections. Collection includes a wide variety of artifacts not limited to books and flat paper materials. Active exhibition and education programs.

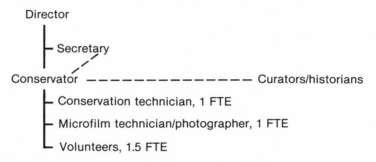

Level 2 Organization Chart

Level 3:

University or large college library with a heavily used core collection of standard works and current resources and a moderately used retrospective collection. Includes several small branch or department libraries and a small separate collection of rare books and manuscripts.

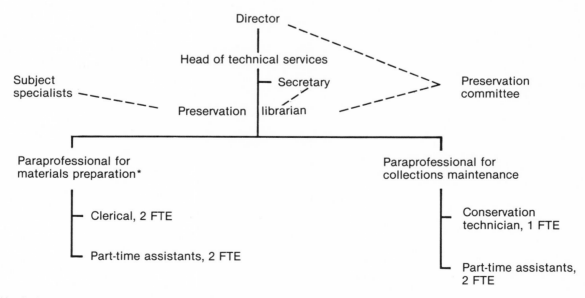

Level 3 Organization Chart

*Includes binding preparation and marking.

Figure IV.2   Preservation Program Models (Cont.)

Level 4:

Specialized research library or separate special collections library associated with a large research library. Includes collections of rare books, manuscripts, photographs, ephemera and other unique materials pertaining to one or several particular fields. Includes secondary research materials and reference works in support of the collections. Active exhibition program and popular collections that are heavily used.

Level 4 Organization Chart

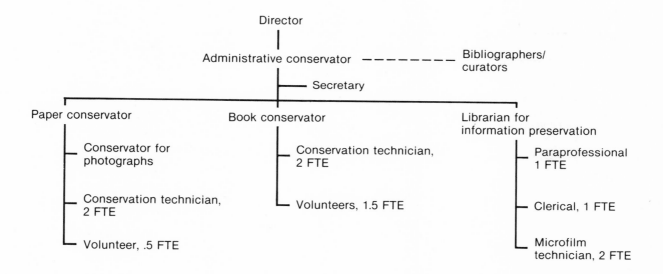

(Figure Continues)

Figure IV.2   Preservation Program Models (Cont.)

Level 5:

Large research library with diversified collections organized into one central or main library receiving moderate use and numerous branch or departmental libraries receiving heavy use. Includes a large separate collection of rare books, manuscripts and photographs.

Level 5 Organization Chart

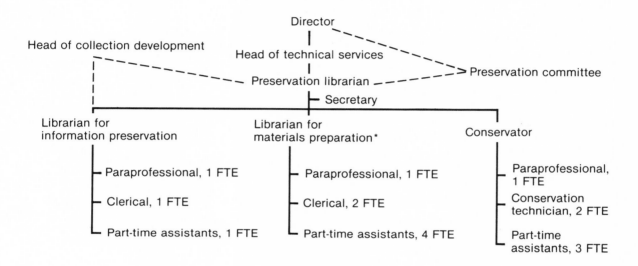

*Includes binding preparation, marking and preparation for mass deacidification.

FOOTNOTES

1. George M. Cunha, *What an Institution Can Do To Survey Its Conservation Needs* (New York: New York Library Association, Resources and Technical Services Section, 1979).

2. Carolyn Clark Morrow, "A conservation policy statement for research libraries," University of Illinois, Graduate School of Library Science *Occasional Papers Series,* no. 139 (July 1979).

3. Pamela W. Darling, " 'Doing' preservation, with or without money: a lecture on carrying on a preservation program," *Oklahoma Librarian* 30 (4) (October 1980): 20-26

4. Robert H. Patterson, "Organizing for conservation: A model charge to a conservation committee," *Library Journal* 104 (10) (May 15, 1979): 1116-19.

5. Paul N. Banks, "Preservation of library materials," in *Encyclopedia of Library and Information Science, Volume 23,* eds. A. Kent, H. Lancour and J.E. Daily (New York: Marcel Dekker, 1978), pp. 180-222.

6. National Fire Protection Association, *Recommended Practice for Protection of Libraries and Library Collections* (Boston, MA: National Fire Protection Association, 1980).

7. Timothy Walch, *Archives and Manuscripts: Security* (Chicago, IL: Society of American Archivists, 1977).

8. Hilda Bohem, *Disaster Prevention and Disaster Preparedness* (Berkeley, CA: University of California, April 1978).

9. Jane Greenfield, *Wraparounds,* 1980. *Tip-ins and Pockets,* 1981. *Paper Treatment,* 1981. *Pamphlet Binding,* 1981. *The Small Bindery,* 1981 (New Haven, CT: Yale University Library).

10. Carolyn Horton, *Cleaning and Preserving Bindings and Related Materials* (Chicago, IL: American Library Association, 1969).

11. Carolyn Clark Morrow, *Conservation Treatment Procedures: A Manual of Step-by-Step Procedures for the Maintenance and Repair of Library Materials* (Littleton, CO: Libraries Unlimited, Inc., 1982).

12. Pamela W. Darling, "Microforms in libraries: preservation and storage," *Microform Review* 5 (1) (April 1976): 93-100.

13. Margaret Brown, Donald Etherington and Linda McWilliams, *Boxes for the Protection of Rare Books:Their Design and Construction* (Washington, DC: Library of Congress, 1982).

14. Robert DeCandido, "Preserving our library material: preservation treatments available to librarians," *Library Scene* 8 (1) (March 1979): 4-6.

V

Preserving the Intellectual Content of Deteriorated Library Materials

by Gay Walker

Any volume can be repaired and restored—given an unlimited budget. The cost of repairing bindings on nonrare books to obtain a structurally sound binding with no cosmetic restoration may be fairly reasonable. The cost of repairing a book's brittle paper, however, can be thousands of dollars and the paper will be no stronger than before. Clearly, such time-consuming and expensive work must be reserved for those items that are unique, rare or important to the collection or the history of that title.

Libraries are faced with decisions concerning the preservation of huge numbers of research items in academic, historical and research library collections that are primarily important for their intellectual content. Libraries, especially academic libraries, will have to realize that they do not have to save *every* title in the original format.

RETAINING ORIGINAL FORMAT

This chapter deals with the preservation of the intellectual content of library materials. It is important, however, to be familiar with items that *should* be considered for their artifactual value and be retained in their original formats. These materials fall into several categories discussed below.

Unique Materials

Unique materials include rare books and special collections, as well as manuscripts and books with important marginalia, decorations or valuable ownership marks. The paper used for manuscript notes by a famous figure, or an original specimen of his handwriting, may be of importance to researchers; decorations such as a fore-edge painting are important for their historical and artistic merit; ownership marks such as bookplates or autograph signatures make a book worth maintaining in the original format.

Items with Historical Value

It is important to retain certain original copies for their research value. For example, the first edition of a famous author's work, such as James Joyce's *Ulysses,* is of considerable research value.

Items with Aesthetic Value

Many volumes are important for the aesthetic value of their printing or binding. Special illustrations, including color illustrations, engravings, etchings, lithographs, other prints and artists' books, are materials that may be retained in their original formats.

The above categories identify many types of library materials that should be considered for retention in their original formats. However, the majority of library titles fall outside these categories. Clearly, if a deteriorated work is important *primarily* for its intellectual content—its information value—then it should be preserved by reproduction in a stable format.

IDENTIFYING ITEMS FOR PRESERVATION

There is usually no difficulty in identifying items in poor physical condition. Shelvers and shelf readers see them constantly, circulation personnel see them as they are charged and discharged, readers bring them to the attention of staff, bibliographers and curators identify them in reviews of specific subject areas, and inventories turn up many. A systematic perusal of the stacks to identify items in poor condition can be made, and records on items requiring attention can be kept. Depending on the size of the collection, circulation policies, whether the library has open or closed stacks, the capacity of the preservation and conservation staff and relationships with other library units, it may be sufficient to train circulation personnel to identify books in poor physical condition and to set them aside for routing to preservation staff. In this manner, those items that are being used are the first to receive attention.

No matter how preservation candidates are identified, some check should be made at the point of circulation to control the activity of books in poor condition. Fragile books should not be allowed to circulate but should be consulted only in the library, either in the preservation unit or under the control of the circulation unit.

When deteriorated books arrive in the preservation unit, they should be examined briefly. Those items that can be commercially rebound or simply repaired can be processed immediately, and volumes with only minor cosmetic damage can be returned to the shelves. This screening may take place immediately if circulation personnel know the selection criteria well. The condition of the paper medium in these volumes is critical. If the paper is strong, the volume can be maintained in its original format. If the paper is brittle, then replacement or reproduction is recommended. Once the remaining items are charged to the preservation unit or otherwise recorded so they may be consulted by readers, they are ready for the decision-making processs.

RESPONSIBILITY FOR DECISION MAKING

The decision of what to do with each deteriorated volume may be made in several ways; each should include a check of the card catalog and the shelves to identify other editions that may be relevant to the title, a check for the availability of a commercial reprint or microform and a review by a subject specialist or bibliographer to ensure that each title will be handled in accordance with library policies.

An important requirement for a decision-making program is a staff member who coordinates the searching steps needed for each title, oversees the control of volumes requiring attention, translates the information gathered on each title and provides prices and recommendations to the subject specialist. In a small collection, the head librarian can authorize a preservation officer to make many of the decisions. This could be done most easily if the contents of all items unique to the collection are to be maintained in *some* format. In larger collections, a bibliographer who may also be the preservation officer should review volumes for their subject value, rarity and importance to the collection. Subject specialists are responsible for shaping the present and future collection, and they should choose replacements for deteriorated items on a competitive basis with new acquisitions.

The preservation officer should be responsible for setting up routines, developing decision options and seeing that these options are carried out. It is desirable to establish as many options as possible so that the most suitable alternative for each item may be chosen.

THE SEARCH

A search is carried out to gather information on the relation of each deteriorated book to the rest of the collection, to ascertain the availability of that title on the commercial market and to establish the condition of other editions or relevant volumes in the collection. Those deteriorated items that have poor bindings but good paper and can be repaired may or may not be included in the search. If an item with good paper is not suitable for commercial rebinding, then a protective box may be an alternative, or the search may be conducted to ascertain if the expense of hand rebinding is warranted. A seriously deteriorated item that is primarily important for its intellectual content would normally not be restored if there are cheaper alternatives of replacing or reformatting. If the item may be rare and transferred to a special collection, it may be searched to establish its relation to other holdings. In this case, the step to locate commercial replacements may be skipped.

A policy incorporated in some search procedures is to examine every accessible edition, copy or volume of each title during the search procedure and to review all deteriorated items during the decision-making period so that the title will be handled only once. This thorough approach helps avoid duplicate searches for the same title. In addition, although decisions are made on an item-by-item basis, the information required for each decision is gathered on a title-by-title basis, and decisions made without this specific information can do irreversible damage to the collection. It is easy to assume, often incorrectly, that there are many copies of an important or popular work when discarding a worn copy. The copy, however, may be a first edition or otherwise significant to the collection. Money spent repairing items with brittle paper can stretch much further in buying reprints located in trade bibliographies, and duplicate searches are expensive and time-consuming.

The three-part search of holdings, commercial replacements and other editions or copies helps the bibliographer identify the work and provides information for decision making. Figure V.1 shows a sample layout for a search form; 5″×8″ ruled index cards also work well. After the deteriorated volumes are received and screened for easy-to-repair books, they are charged out so that they may be located by readers. The basic information about the book—the call number, author, title and imprint (place of publication, publisher and date of publication)—is added on the search form at this time. Relevant comments are also noted including lacunae, if the item is a pamphlet, or if it is rare or recommended for transfer. The search card is kept in the book until it is pulled for the search.

The information developed during the search includes the following:

1. Verification of the book's basic information and addition of any missing data;
2. Whether the item in question is the only copy in the library;
3. The call numbers and dates of publications of all other copies and editions of the title;
4. Whether this book is the only work in the collection written by that author;
5. Whether there are collected works by the same author, which include the title in question;
6. The dates of the author's life;
7. The number of volumes in the set and the number of copies of that edition;
8. For translations, the existence of original language editions;
9. The condition of all other accessible editions, volumes in the set and copies;
10. The availability and cost of commercial reprint and microform copies.

A searcher normally batches the search cards in groups of 20 to 40, or perhaps those from a shelf of books. The first part of the search is a check of the card catalog. The search cards are alphabetized by the authors' last names (or other main entry), the card catalog or data base is checked, and the information listed in items 1 through 6 above is noted on each card. Editions of titles by prolific authors (i.e., Shakespeare) may be searched separately where other copies by the same editor are listed. Search cards with incomplete or incorrect entries may be verified in the shelflist, and monographic series titles or series offprints may need to be checked under two entries. Other editions are noted on the search card in sequential order by date of publication so that the edition history and holdings may be seen at a glance.

Figure V.1   Sample Search Form

Call Number	Author:	Dates:
	Title:	
	Imprint:	
	Other editions or copies:	
Pam? ☐		
Repair? ☐		
Collected works:		
BIP:	NRMM:	
GtR:	BBIP:	
BOD/SIM:	NIM or foreign:	
GtM:		Searcher: _____
Decision:		
		Bibliographer: _____
		Date done: _____

   The second part of the search consists of checking a standard list of trade bibliographies for reprints and microforms to identify those titles available on the commercial market. The trade bibliographies include the current updates of those bibliographic tools listed in the first group below. Titles not found in the first group would be checked in the second group. A non-English title would be checked in the trade bibliography for its language if the library purchases from foreign sources.

First Group

   • *Books in Print* (New York: R.R. Bowker Co., annual update). A listing by authors (two volumes), titles (two volumes) and subjects (three volumes) of books currently available in the United States from American publishers or through American distributors. Publishers report their sales lists on a voluntary basis so this tool, like the other trade catalogs listed here, is not totally comprehensive. Entries are listed as they are reported, so there may be several spelling variations in names and various combinations of initials or one or more forenames. Thus, entries for the same author or title may be separated from one another. A search by title may be easiest. The information listed is fairly complete and usually includes the ISBN, the Library of Congress card number, the publisher's series title, type of binding, whether illustrated and the price.

• *Guide to Reprints* (Kent, CT: Guide to Reprints, Inc., annual update). A two-volume listing of reprinted titles by main entry; reported as available by reprint houses. Some foreign reprinters are listed. Often the date of the original edition is given along with the republication date, but one or the other may be missing. Reprints are defined as "materials that have gone out-of-print and are now back in print by virtue of a photo offset process . . . or any other process which involves reproduction of the original text as opposed to resetting text."

• *Books on Demand* (Ann Arbor, MI: University Microfilms International, annual update). A listing by author, title and subject (one volume each) of those titles that were out-of-print but are now available from University Microfilms International (UMI) (UMI prints the copies from its microfilms). All titles in the catalogs are available in hard copy at the listed price, and most are available on 35mm or 16mm microfilm or microfiche at half the listed price ($12 minimum). Illustrations, particularly half-tones, do not come out well in these editions; silver prints of illustrations are sold separately ($1.50 each with a $6 minimum). The original books filmed are not always clean copies, but the paper used is low in acid or acid-free. Paper masters are made and reproduced for those titles with AG3-200 or AG3-2000 in the UMI number and can be expected to have more satisfactory illustrations. The ISBN and UMI numbers are given along with the price of each volume.

• *Serials in Microform* (Ann Arbor, MI: University Microfilms International, annual update). A listing in one volume of serial titles available from UMI on archival record film (35mm, 16mm or microfiche), which meets the ANSI Standard PH1.4. Nonsilver film is available at 15% less than the listed price. Most current titles are available only if a hard copy subscription is purchased by the library. Some backfiles are listed with an "inquire" note and are not available until enough inquiries are received or the filming process is finished. The number of titles listed makes this an important catalog for locating serial titles. The ISSN and UMI numbers and the contents and cost of individual reels are given.

Second Group

• *Guide to Microforms in Print* (Westport, CT: Microform Review, annual update). A listing of titles by main entry available in microform (film, fiche, ultrafiche and micro-opaques) in one volume. These titles are sold by commercial micropublishers in the United States and Canada and many foreign sources. The more recent updates incorporate *International Microforms in Print*. The ISBN or ISSN is given but the rest of the entry is brief with no details on reel contents or individual reel prices.

• *National Register of Microform Masters* (*NRMM*) (Washington, DC: Library of Congress, annual updates [not current]). This title consists of 12 volumes as of this writing; six represent the 1965-1975 cumulation with annual volumes since then through 1980 (1978 was published in two volumes). All annual volumes must be checked along with the 10-year cumulation. A listing of titles by main entry is available from commercial and noncommercial sources that have reported titles to the National Register Office. Prices are not given. The LC card number and portions of the title available from each supplier are listed, as is an indication of format and whether the negative film is maintained under archival conditions. There is approximately a two-year lagtime until newly filmed titles are listed. The *NRMM* plans to go online with the *National Union Catalog* (*NUC*) some time in the future. Entries have been reviewed by the Library of Congress (LC) staff before inclusion and therefore follow LC cataloging practice for entry format.

• *Newspapers in Microform: United States 1948-1972, 1973-1977* and *Newspapers in Microform: Foreign Countries 1948-1972, 1973-1977* (Washington, DC: Library of Congress). A listing by main entry of titles reported to the NUC Division at LC by libraries and institutions in the United States and Canada. Prices are not given, but most are available from the library or commercial publisher in microfilm.

• *British Books in Print* (London: J. Whitaker & Sons Ltd., annual update). A listing of books by author, title and subject (two volumes) in one alphabet, which is published and sold in the United Kingdom.

• *Canadian Books in Print* (Toronto: University of Toronto Press, issued quarterly with three complete fiche editions and one hardcover edition). A listing by author, title and subject (two volumes) of books published in Canada based on information supplied by the publishers.

• *Verzeichnis Lieferbarer Bücher: German Books in Print* (Frankfurt am Main: Buchhandler-Vereinigung GmbH, annual update). A listing by author and title in one alphabet (four volumes) of German-language books printed in the Federal Republic of Germany, Austria and Switzerland, and other books distributed in the trade.

• *Les Livres Disponibles: French Books in Print* (Paris: Cercle de la Librairie, annual update). A listing, in French, of books by authors, titles and subjects (three volumes) published in France and elsewhere.

• *Libros en venta en Hispanoamérica y España* (New York: R.R. Bowker, updated irregularly). A listing by author and title of Spanish-language books printed in Spain, Latin and South America, and elsewhere.

• *Catalogo dei libri in commercio* (Milan: Editrice Bibliografico, Associazione Italeana Editori, annual update). A listing by authors, titles and subjects (three volumes) of Italian-language books printed in Italy and elsewhere.

• *Guide to Russian Reprints and Microforms* (New York: Pilvax Corp., 1973). A listing by main entry (one volume) in one alphabet of books in reprint and microform published in many countries. Many are still available, but there are no updated editions.

There are a number of other catalogs and bibliographies that are generally less useful than those listed above but may be helpful for specific groups of books. The Philadelphia Bibliographical Center and Union Library Catalog's *Union List of Microfilms* (1942-1949 cumulative and 1949-1959 cumulative in two volumes) precedes the *NRMM* and lists over 77,000 titles, by main entry, that are available on microfilm. Most of these titles are rare books and pamphlets. The *Catalog of Reprints in Series* (Metuchen, NJ: Scarecrow Press) lists volumes available in publishers' series and is not very relevant to the search described here. LC produces cataloging slips in sheet form from its Cataloging in Publication (CIP) program. Slips for reprints include full cataloging information and prices sometimes; they are important for corroboration of publication and price and may provide information unavailable elsewhere.

Other important sources of republication information are the cataloging data bases. Networks such as the Research Libraries Information Network (RLIN), the Online Computer Library Center (OCLC) and the Washington Library Network (WLN) list reprints and microform copies held and cataloged by member libraries and by LC on its MARC tapes. Verification in this medium is important if it is suspected that an advertised title was never published. Some reprint dealers list titles that never appear because they are waiting for a certain number of orders. A few reprinters are unethical and should be avoided.*

Dividing the standard bibliographies into the two groups listed above shortens the search although it presumes a preference for hard copy reprints. All titles are searched in the first group of bibliographies. Those found are removed; those not found are searched in all other appropriate bibliographies. All catalogs in the first group are checked for each title since different prices and suppliers may be listed. Items that appear in *Guide to Reprints* do not automatically appear in *Books in Print*. Also, some titles that are listed in *Books in Print* as reprints are not reprints; rather, they are original editions that have been in storage. The paper quality in this case is likely to be the same as that of the deteriorated volume. This is the reason the out-of-print market is unsatisfactory for obtaining replacements except for recently published volumes that are missing or badly mutilated. Serial titles should automatically be checked in the first two catalogs listed in the second group since a microform replacement is often more sensible for long serial runs. Noting the commercial availability of the title on the search card marks the end of the second part of the search. Search cards for books that are the only copies in the collection or for which no relevant, accessible editions exist are placed back in the deteriorated volume to await a decision.

The third part of the search is the examination of relevant volumes in the stacks so that the condition of other copies, volumes in the set or editions may be noted. Relevant

---

*A list of some reprinters found to be unsatisfactory was printed in *American Libraries,* November 1977, p. 541. The list concentrates on those firms believed to be operated by Frank or Michael Gille, who often take payment and never deliver.

volumes are examined by removing them from the shelves and flipping through to check paper quality and hinge strength and to locate obvious mutilations. Any deteriorated volumes of the title being searched become part of the decision-making session along with the original volume. A relevant volume in good condition may be shown to the bibliographer as a good example of what remains on the shelf. This step completes the search.

The search of a batched group of 20 to 40 titles may take one and one-half days, or an average of 20 minutes per title. After relevant volumes are charged, the search card is placed back in the original volume, and all editions are gathered together for the decision-making period with the appropriate subject specialist.

THE DECISION PROCESS

Some collections may have clear-cut guidelines covering certain subject areas such as out-of-scope topics or pleasure reading. The preservation officer may make decisions in these areas, but most items should be reviewed by a subject specialist. The decision-making period works well if the preservation officer or other preservation staff member reviews each title with the bibliographer. This is quickly done (25 to 50 decisions can be made in an hour) since the bibliographer has the expertise of the preservation staff available for recommendations, translation of the searching information and estimated costs of the various alternatives, and the volumes remain under the control of the preservation staff. The books to be reviewed may be placed on a book truck that is either taken to the bibliographer's desk or reviewed in the preservation area. This routine avoids the loss of books that are sent to bibliographers without preservation personnel involvement.

OPTIONS

The more options available to the bibliographer, the greater the likelihood that the best decision, based upon the present and projected use of the item and the value of the item, can be made for each title. With the supervision and advice of the preservation officer, decisions can be made consistently and with some assurance that valuable objects or unique information are not lost to the collection. General decision guidelines are an important tool in this process.* They articulate preservation policy and will aid new bibliographers in learning about options.

After a decision has been made on each title, those to be withdrawn, reshelved as is, boxed or transferred should be processed immediately. The rest should be retained in the preservation area under restricted access until the option has been carried out. Six categories of possible options follow.

Commercially Available Reprints

One satisfactory option is the replacement of a deteriorated title with a hard copy reprint. (Many reprinters use acid-free paper.) In this way, an exact replacement of the text

---

*Two examples of brief decision guidelines are available from Stanford and Yale libraries.

is obtained in the same physical format. The deteriorated volume should be retained in the preservation area until the replacement is cataloged to avoid loss of text and so that the original may be compared to the reprint. If the contents are not duplicated exactly in the reprint, it may be necessary to reproduce the original title instead. It is helpful to test the paper quality of the reprints or new editions and to maintain a list of publishers and test results for future selection among publishers. A number of pH pens and pencils* and other simple methods† are available for testing the acidity of paper.

Commercially Available Microform

Microform replacements for deteriorated or incomplete holdings have both advantages and disadvantages,** but they provide adequate replacements for many library materials in poor condition. The advantages include space savings over the hard copy originals (up to 90%), much lower cost than hard copy reprints (unless microform is produced in-house) and the reduction of awkward folios, newspapers and multivolume sets to fewer physical units in a standard format. Disadvantages include the necessity of maintaining special storage and reading areas for microforms, the purchase and maintenance of special equipment to enlarge, read and print copies of microfilm, the prejudice many readers and library staff still harbor against this format because of its less-accessible information, and the ease with which some microforms may be torn, scratched and the text obliterated by dirt and fingerprints.

Microfiche may be suitable for the reproduction of monographs, pamphlets or reports that are updated regularly. It is easier to find your place on a fiche than on film, but more units are required to contain as much information as a microfilm reel and fiche are more likely to be misplaced or misfiled. Microfiche requires special fiche readers, as do ultra-microfiche and micro-opaques. Ultramicrofiche has the highest reduction ratio (above 92 ×) of all the microforms, and the smallest defect or dust speck can obliterate quantities of text. Some micropublishers produce only ultramicrofiche, and you should make sure that your library owns the equipment necessary to read ultramicrofiche before any is purchased.

Standard microformats are 35mm safety base (a triacetate, cellulose ester is common) microfilm, 16mm safety base microfilm for technical reports, patents and the like (an adapter is available that fits on the 35mm reel uptake arm for easy manipulation), and 4″×6″ microfiche. Micro-opaques are less popular formats, but there are readers available

---

*Available from TALAS, 130 Fifth Ave., New York, NY 10011; Conservation Resources International, 1111 N. Royal St., Alexandria, VA 22314; and other supply houses that sell archival materials.

†A paper-testing kit developed by the W.J. Barrow Laboratory is available from Applied Science Laboratories, Inc., 2216 Hull St., Richmond, VA.

**Further discussion of microforms, their acquisition, handling, storage and bibliographic control, and the control of micropublication from library volumes is available in many books and articles, one being the "Guidelines for the Handling of Microforms in the Yale University Library," *Microform Review* 9(1) (Winter 1980): 11-20, 9(2) (Spring 1980): 72-85. An excellent compilation of papers on microforms is contained in *Microforms in Libraries: A Review* edited by Albert James Diaz (Weston, CT: Microform Review Inc., 1975).

that can enlarge both microfiche and micro-opaque cards. Microcards, such as those sold by Microcard Corp., are photostatically produced micro-opaques that are photographically fixed. Micro-opaque cards such as those sold by Readex Microprint Co. are produced by miniaturized printing with no photographic chemicals.

There is often a choice of microformats and film bases available, and each library must set its own standards of acceptability. The only film base for which standards have been set is safety base film made of cellulose ester or polyester. Specifications do exist for diazo film (ANSI PH1.60-1979), but silver halide (or silver-gelatin type) is the only type of film production for which archival processing standards exist. Archival storage standards exist for all types of film (ANSI PH1.43).

The debate continues over the acceptability and longevity of the other two major film types, diazo and vesicular (see Chapter III for details), but all three have both advantages and disadvantages. However, given the proper storage conditions, silver halide still appears to have the longest life expectancy. Other types may be preferable for service copies.

If the library decides that 35mm silver halide film should be the microformat whenever possible, it should be prepared to pay a premium for it, in some cases up to 50% more than for diazo film. The library that insists upon silver halide might send out notices with each order stating that 35mm silver halide safety base film is the acceptable format and that any other format must receive approval before purchase. Spot tests should be made on microforms purchased commercially to ensure their quality.

Withdrawal

A bibliographer may decide to withdraw a deteriorated item for many reasons: it is out of scope, there is an exact duplicate or the contents are elsewhere in the collection; it has been superseded and is not needed for historical value; it is no longer important for the collection. If an item is to be withdrawn, it should be marked so that it will not come back to the library as a returned book. Usually, the call number label and the bookplate are marked out, date due slips or pockets are removed, and the title page and/or endpapers are stamped "withdrawn" or "discard." Disposal of these items may be a problem in many state-supported libraries where all withdrawn volumes must be physically destroyed. In other cases, however, discarded books may be sold at library booksales.

Transfer

In some cases a deteriorated item may be retained for its artifactual value and transferred to a noncirculating or special collection. It may be placed in a protective wrapper or box or repaired in some way before transfer. A copy can be made or a commercial replacement ordered if a copy is required for the circulating collection.

In-house Photocopying

When titles are unavailable on the commercial market and must be retained in hard copy, an in-house program of photocopying may be established. Photocopying retains the hard copy format for items receiving heavy use, it solves the immediate need for information in the library at a reasonable cost, and the copy on acid-free paper will stand up to use longer, in most cases, than did the original. Photocopying onto acid-free paper* generally costs less than the production of a negative film, and the cost of binding is roughly equivalent to the cost of generating a positive film copy for use as a service copy.

There is some question as to the permanence of the print in the electrostatic and other photographic methods of copying. Longevity of the copy also depends on the proper functioning of the machine and the paper used. The print produced by some machines, especially in the quick-copying techniques, tends to be short-lived (a matter of years but not necessarily decades). Many copiers, however, such as the Xerox 4000 and 4500 and the Kodak 9500 produce copies that manufacturers claim should last well over 100 years. Those that produce a thermoplastic image by heat and pressure fusing through electrostatic charges are most highly recommended since this method produces the most permanent copy.†

Some testing has been done, including the National Bureau of Standards' *Evaluation of Archival Stability of Copies from Representative Office Copying Machines* [NBSIR 74-498(R)] and the related American Society for Testing and Materials D 3458 standard *Specification for Copies from Office Copying Machines for Permanent Records* (contained in Part 20 of the *Annual Book of ASTM Standards: Paper, Packaging; Business Copy Products)*. Further *independent* testing needs to be done to identify those machines that can produce permanent copies and to promote the acceptance of this method as a preservation option.

Photocopies may be bound in three formats, depending on the size of the original text, so that recataloging for size changes is avoided. The two-page opening in small books with a text area less than 9″ from one side to the other may be photocopied on one side in a standard location. After collation, the finished copy may be bound across the top and trimmed at the sides. This trimming will reduce the book to regular octavo size.

The second and recommended format is the double-sided copy. One side of a book page is copied on one side of the paper and the other side of the page is registered and

---

*One acid-free paper, Xerox XXV Archival Bond, is available through Xerox. Permalife, the permanent/ durable paper developed by W.J. Barrow and the Standard Paper Manufacturing Co. of Virginia now produced by Howard Paper Co., is available from most paper distributors. Other acid-free text papers from mills such as S.D. Warren, P.H. Glatfelter Company, Olin Corp., Finch Pruyn and Co., Allied Paper Mills, Curtis Paper Co. and Mohawk Paper Mills are also available through paper distributors.

†A manager in the Fusing Technology Area at Xerox states: "From our knowledge of the fixing process, we do not expect Xerographic toner images, which are well fused initially, to sustain any significant degradation in fusing over a 100-year period. If adequate toner to paper adhesion is developed, no loss in adhesion should be expected even when the copies experience changing environmental conditions. The toner itself is composed of a carbon black filled hard thermoplastic polymer. Both the carbon black and the polymer are stable materials and, therefore, the toner should not suffer any loss in mechanical strength either due to prolonged sunlight (i.e., ultraviolet) or to extreme humidity exposure. In fact, the Xerographic toner image should be more permanent and resistant to environmental exposure than the paper itself."

copied on the other side of the paper. The Xerox 4000, 4500, 9400 and 9500 and the IBM Copier 3 can produce double-sided copies with an internal mechanism for turning the paper over. The bottom edge is trimmed and the inner edge bound in a double-fan adhesive binding or by oversewing. Since the inner margin can be as wide as desired, the copy can be photocopied easily by readers.

The third format is to fold the single-sided opening and bind along the free edges, but folding is a time-consuming job and makes a more difficult format to bind.

Fold-out plates and outsize maps may be copied on several pages and then glued or taped together using an acceptable pressure-sensitive tape.* These folded sheets must extend beyond the copy's edge to alert the binder to the special handling requirements. Pockets can be made for plates that need to be retained. Each loose plate retained in a pocket should be marked and placed in a noncirculating collection for further protection.

Part-time students, employees or volunteers may be used as photocopy operators. Since mistakes such as omissions, duplications and incorrect positioning are easy to make the copy must be checked again by a responsible staff member before binding. The collated copy must be perfect and in binding order since it will usually be bound as is. Incomplete books should be completed before binding. Copies of the title may be located in *NUC* and the *Union List of Serials* or *New Serials Titles* and borrowed through interlibrary loans for photocopying.

The photocopy operator should be shown how to disbind books in the fastest and easiest way with an Exacto knife or scalpel and a cardboard work surface. Photocopying is best done from flat sheets that are either in a gathering or in individual leaves. Some volumes will need to be reproduced without disbinding and should be copied on a photocopier with the glass plate next to the machine edge so that the volume need not be opened beyond a 90-100° angle.

Hard copies may be produced through microfilming and Copyflo (printing from the film directly onto roll paper) for approximately three times the cost of photocopying. A negative microfilm copy is generated by this method, but few libraries have in-house capabilities to produce Copyflo copies. Binding Copyflo copies can be difficult as well, especially if the cutting is done inaccurately so that the image does not fall consistently in the same location on each sheet.

In-house Microfilming or Microfiching

When deteriorated titles are not commercially available, an in-house microform program may be the answer. There are many advantages in microfilming a deteriorated volume, especially to the library community as a whole. Microfilming preserves the information indefinitely, and the master copy serves as insurance if disaster befalls the service copy. Once a title is filmed, it need not be done by any other library. As long as the

*Ademco or Filmoplast P tapes, available from TALAS, are recommended.

microfilm master is retained only for producing copies and is listed in *NRMM*, other libraries may purchase service copies. It is a very cost-effective approach to salvaging texts of those items likely to be deteriorated in many libraries at the same time.

If the library has a photographic services department, an agreement should be worked out for technical standards and handling routines. Unless the photographic department is organizationally related to the preservation unit, preservation staff will also need to establish their involvement in the preparation of volumes for filming. It there is no in-house photographic unit, a satisfactory agreement can usually be negotiated with commercial service agencies (see below). Microfilming is often chosen for the reproduction of serial or newspaper runs, collections of materials in a single subject area, and multivolume sets or monographs that receive low-to-moderate use.

Important aspects of microfilming are proper processing and maintaining correct technical standards to assure the longevity of the product. The storage and handling of the film are also of the utmost importance to its lifetime, but they mean nothing if the film has been incorrectly produced. Specifications for the actual filming of library materials are in three pamphlets published by the Photoduplication Services, Library of Congress.* They detail the technical and bibliographic targets recommended for standardized filming, define many of the terms used and clearly describe and illustrate the filming process. Other standards applicable to the technical processing of microfilm include several promulgated by the American National Standards Institute (ANSI), and the National Microfilm Association (NMA).† Both ANSI and NMA revise and update standards on a regular basis.

COPYRIGHT

Every effort must be made to observe the copyright law when reproducing titles in-house, either in hard copy or microform. If the item cannot be located in the standard list of trade bibliographies and catalogs given earlier, then one copy may be reproduced to replace the deteriorated original according to Section 108, subsection (e) of Public Law 94-553, which went into effect January 1, 1978. Also, if only new editions of items no longer in copyright are available with different scholarly apparatus (i.e., notes or introduction), then the original item may be duplicated. The great majority of the deteriorated items that need reproduction will have been published between 1850 and 1940, and most of these titles are out of copyright (U.S. titles printed through 1906 are definitely out of copyright). Titles from many foreign countries published through the 1950s, many of which were printed on highly acidic paper, may also be under copyright. These would need to be searched for commercial availability before making a single copy as a replacement.

Specifications for the Microfilming of Books and Pamphlets in the Library of Congress (Washington, DC, 1973); *Specifications for the Microfilming of Newspapers in the Library of Congress* (Washington, DC, 1972); *Specifications for Microfilming Manuscripts* (Washington, DC, 1980).

†ANSI PH1.28-1976 (*Specifications for Photographic Film for Archival Records, Silver-Gelatin Type, on Cellulose Ester Base*); ANSI PH1.41-1976 (*Specifications for Photographic Film for Archival Records, Silver-Gelatin Type, on Polyester Base*); ANSI PH1.43-1979 (*Practice for Storage of Processed Safety Photographic Film*); ANSI PH1.25-1976 (*Specifications for Safety Photographic Film*). NMA has also produced guidelines which should be observed whenever possible, particularly their publication MS104-1972, *Inspection and Quality Control of First Generation Silver Halide Microfilm.*

FILMING PROCEDURES

The balance of this chapter is devoted to a discussion of microform programs, including in-house filming procedures and quality control.

Preparation for Filming

Titles to be filmed must be prepared, usually by preservation personnel. The first step in preparing materials for filming is a check for completeness. A reasonable effort should be made to film the complete title so that it need be filmed only once, is in sequential order and can replace deteriorated copies in other collections. As previously noted, if the title is incomplete, other locations can be identified in *NUC,* the *Union List of Serials* or *New Serial Titles*. Missing titles may be borrowed through interlibrary loan. A copyright notice should be attached if appropriate.

After examining each item for completeness and correct order, the item and the information necessary for the bibliographic target—the name of the author, the title truncated to a reasonable length, the place and date of publication and the number of volumes (optional)—should be sent to the person who makes the targets. Often a copy of the catalog card is filmed immediately preceding the text of the book. Targets may be made by placing individual letters on a menu board or by one of several machines available for this purpose. The words on these targets will be eye-legible on the film so that a microfilm reader need not be used to identify the contents. Unusual instructions such as rush notices, no cutting, an order for more than a single positive copy, for no positive copy or for Copyflo hard copy should also be sent to the photographic division.

Serial volumes can be sent for filming to fill up each reel in order. Monographs and pamphlets may also be batched for filming by sending enough at one time to fill a complete reel, or several complete reels. This saves film storage space, and the positive service copy may cost the same for a partial reel as for a full one. It should be ascertained if there are special cataloging requirements for monographs on microfilm. Some libraries find it easier to place only volumes in the same general subject area on the same reel so that one person may catalog a reel containing many titles. In other libraries, one staff member may catalog all the monographic microfilms so this need not be a concern.

Photographic services personnel should check the volumes for special instructions and proceed to make up the necessary targets according to LC specifications. Extra space is left between volumes when filming so they are easy to locate on the reel, and each volume should be preceded by a bibliographic target with the appropriate volume number indicated.

If the item is not disbound, filming should be done using a book cradle to avoid damaging the binding. The cradle (two boards with a spring system that holds each half of the open book independently) supports the book so that the surface of the open pages is on a fairly even plane in relation to the camera lens. A glass plate may be used to keep the text on one plane if the book opens easily, but the book should not be forced open.

Microfiche may also be made in-house if proper facilities are available. However, most microfiching is done in commercial establishments. It is more likely that the library's photographic department has equipment to produce microfilm, which may then be stripped, placed in fiche pockets and reproduced in the fiche format. Microfiche is especially suitable for pamphlets and monographs up to 98 pages, so that each fiche represents one title, or for ephemera or documents and manuscripts. Producing copies from a fiche master is simple and inexpensive with a fiche duplicator. The ANSI standard on *Specifications for Microfiche* (PH5.9-1970) should be followed for work with fiche.

Quality Control

Quality control is necessary to ensure that the microform meets the specifications for proper filming and processing and that it is as complete and accurate as possible and will last a long time given proper storage conditions. Many checks should be made during filming to obtain proper resolution, contrast and density; processed film should also be checked routinely. Every reel, or a sampling from each processed batch, should be checked under a microscope or $10 \times$ enlarger for resolution, with a densitometer for density, and on a reader or at a rewinding station for contrast changes or other bibliographic or physical faults. Every reel *should* be checked frame by frame for completeness, correct sequence, accuracy of bibliographic and other target information, correct spacing between units, correct contrast and positioning and faults missed during filming.*

Chemical testing, either in-house or by a commercial lab, may be done on a sample of processed films. There are two residual thiosulfate tests that may be performed in-house as described in the ANSI standard PH4.8-1971 on *Methylene Blue Method for Measuring Thiosulfate and Silver Densitometric Method for Measuring Residual Chemicals in Films, Plates and Papers.* It may be desirable to send samples out for methylene blue testing.

A sample of negative films, in particular, should be examined regularly (every five years or so) to ensure their continued good condition. Although the photographic unit is responsible for the quality of its product, the ordering unit must be assured of that quality. The best way to do this is to spot check the processed reels, carefully examining a few reels frame by frame.

It is the responsibility of the photographic unit to produce a perfect copy that is as complete as the original. Although many units do not have the personnel to check films frame by frame, this activity is highly desirable, especially if film copies may be sold through *NRMM* or institutional advertising. If a few frames must be spliced in to correct or complete a film, it may be necessary to refilm several frames on either side of the retakes so that there will be enough film for splicing. The use of an end-to-end butt weld splicing machine, which uses heat, is the best method for splicing film. Given the proper temperature, this splice is smooth and permanent for all types of safety base film. The

---

*Allen Veaner's work, cited earlier, will aid in evaluating the processed film as will the NMA's standard on *Inspection and Quallity Control of First Generatioln Silver Halide Microfilm* (MS103-1972).

machine, however, is expensive (around $2000 or more). There is a special film cement that can be used, but it must dry overnight and it leaves exposed edges, as does the film splicing tape available at most stationery stores. The tape, a transparent archival quality product, is faster and easier, and is acceptable for service copies.

Commercial Microform Service Companies

Most large cities have commercial microfilming companies, some of which are service agencies that work on a contractual basis. Both microfilm and microfiche capabilities are usually available, and most requirements for quality standards, filming sequence and special targets can be negotiated and should be carried out to the ordering unit's satisfaction.

Terms of insurance coverage, transportation, turn-around time and actual requirements and standards for filming should be reviewed carefully and agreed upon in writing. Some microfilm companies may want the rights to publish the titles being filmed or to retain a negative film copy. The rights to the film should be made clear before filming begins. Such a relationship can be very satisfactory both for the library and the agency as long as both parties can communicate freely with each other and any problems are dealt with immediately.

MICROFORM STORAGE AND ENVIRONMENT

Much has been written about proper storage for microforms in libraries (see Chapter III), but few libraries are able to meet the recommended levels of 40-55% relative humidity (RH) and 50-75°F for service copies and 30% RH and 65°F or lower for negative masters. It is very expensive to maintain the environment at a constant RH and temperature, but it is imperative that all libraries with a negative microform collection make every attempt to attain these levels. A library is, in a sense, maintaining these titles in trust for the rest of the nation so that other libraries may obtain copies and avoid the expense of duplicate filming.

Films should be stored on plastic reels in acid-free boxes and in metal cabinets to eliminate dust and provide some control over radical fluctuations in environmental conditions. Acid-free button-string ties work well if the film needs to be held in place on the reel. Fiche should also be stored in cabinets (or a revolving tub type of storage unit) in individual acid-free envelopes that prevent the fiche from sticking during hot, humid weather, protect the separate fiche from extra handling and provide easier control for retrieval and storage. Acid-free board stock can be cut into 4"×6" sizes to use as dividers and deterrents to the curling of fiche.

LOCAL BIBLIOGRAPHIC CONTROL OF MICROFORMS

All internally produced microfilms should receive full cataloging as soon as they are processed under the same priority system applied to books. Most books filmed in preservation programs are from the library's collection and will be replaced by the film, so it may be possible to use the original book's catalog card with a new call number and film note. Master films, usually negatives, should be stored in an environmentally-controlled area separate from service copy films; the catalog information for these masters may also be maintained separately. Masters should be used only for the reproduction of positive copies or duplicate reproduction negatives, and access to first-generation masters should be restricted to those who process orders for reproductions or print the copies. A separate shelflist for masters may be set up, and these titles may be represented in the card catalog only by a note stating: "Master Available for Reproduction." This alerts readers and inter-library loan personnel to the easy availability of a film copy. If the catalog is automated, then the restrictions applicable to master films can be included with the shelf number for each record.

A most important step in cataloging films produced internally is to send a copy of the catalog card to *NRMM,* which is soon to become part of *NUC.* Both are to be automated, which means that film entries will become accessible sooner.

The call number, often an accession number preceded by a code indicating polarity, format or subject, should be marked on the item. It is recommended that a pressure-sensitive label be applied to the header area of microfiche (the top one-half inch) or that the number be marked on the fiche itself with a permanent marker since the fiche envelopes, which are often labeled instead, are easily misplaced or damaged. The microfilm box should also be labeled, and though the film leader could be labeled, boxes are less prone to loss or damage than fiche envelopes. Both the boxes and the envelopes should be made of acid-free stock.

Master microforms can be bibliographically controlled on a local level as long as the catalogers are willing to handle and process them. Their work is made easier if the records for the original hard copies can be used to produce the film records. It is helpful if one person in the cataloging department coordinates microfilm cataloging; if he or she does not actually do all the cataloging, at least that person is able to answer questions and direct the workflow.

NATIONAL BIBLIOGRAPHIC CONTROL OF MICROFORMS

The major difficulty in the bibliographic control of microforms is the lack of cataloging for large sets sold by micropublishers. These sets may contain hundreds of titles. Cooperative cataloging projects and exchanges of cataloging information are becoming common since no one library can catalog every title without massive rearrangements of priorities and funding. The titles in these sets need individual cataloging to allow full access to the contents. When such sets are represented by a single set of cards under the overall title, acquisitions and interlibrary loan personnel may order titles that duplicate those in unanalyzed filmed sets and readers cannot locate needed titles. Joint cataloging efforts are essential, and more libraries are cooperating in this area.

The Association of Research Libraries (ARL) is actively involved with preservation and microfilms. Jeffrey Heynen is the manager of the ARL project to coordinate the bibliographic control of microforms. The focus of the project is on the cataloging of large micropublishers' sets of microforms, and announcements of those being cataloged by various libraries will be made in the *RTSD Newsletter* and elsewhere. Most micropublishers produce bibliographies, indexes or listings of titles in each set. A few have attempted to produce cards and card sets that are available for purchase along with the film, but these are not always done according to Anglo-American Cataloguing Rules (AACR) and may be impossible to interfile in the card catalog. The ARL project may encourage publishers to catalog these sets at the source.

The Reproduction of Library Materials Section of the Resources and Technical Services Division of the American Library Association (ALA) has sponsored a Subcommittee on the Bibliographic Control of Microforms that has been a forum for spirited discussion and the exploration of cooperative cataloging projects. Several cataloging changes caused by AACR 2 directly affect microform cataloging. Specific formats are being developed within the Research Libraries Group (RLG) for negative microform records, and the New York Public Library is now working on transferring records for their very large negative microfilm collection (110,000+ reels) into the RLIN data base. Several hundred serial titles filmed by the New York Public Library during the 1970s do not appear in *NRMM,* so this project will aid considerably in distributing new filming information. RLG libraries plan to input all negative film records held by the membership and maintain an up-to-date online record of films along with titles earmarked for filming or in the process of being filmed.

NRMM is a major tool in the bibliographic control of microfilms. The lagtime for publication is about two years, with approximately 280,000 records in the pipeline as of this writing. Going online with *NUC* will be helpful. This invaluable tool is the only listing of most negative microfilm titles generated in libraries. Another helpful, if old, tool is Felix Reichmann and Josephine M. Tharpe's *Bibliographic Control of Microforms,* which was sponsored by ARL under contract with the Office of Education. It contains a good compilation of bibliographies and lists of filmed titles in sets with some cataloging information and a study of the problem.

MAJOR FILMING PROGRAMS*

Many commercial micropublishers film large collections of library materials in specific subject areas on an ongoing basis. In addition, major filming programs are underway in academic institutions and cooperative groups, which tend to cover areas of less interest, or marketability, to the commercial publisher. Taken together, these groups are converting huge numbers of titles to microforms, but there is still much to be done. Seminars on the Acquisition of Latin American Materials (SALAM) has issued an index to approximately 1100 titles filmed under its sponsorship over the last 20 years, which includes all formats of Latin American and Caribbean publications. The index cumulates the titles listed in SALAM's *Microfilming Projects Newsletter.*

The Cooperative Africana Microform Project (CAMP) within the Center for Research Libraries continues to sponsor the filming of African materials. Although the film entries

---

*I am indebted to John Baker (Chief, Conservation Division, New York Public Library) for much of the information in this section.

in its 1977 cumulative catalog are included in *NRMM,* it has issued a supplement of about 1500 titles filmed btween 1976 and 1979 that has not yet reached *NRMM.*

Some 12,000 Southeast Asian titles on film have been listed and published by the Singapore University Press in its *Masterlist of Southeast Asian Microforms.* The titles are drawn from the holdings of 43 institutions.

The Canadian Institute for Historical Micro-Reproduction has so far filmed 6000 of an estimated 50,000 targeted titles in the National Library of Canada's retrospective bibliography, *Canadiana, 1867-1900.*

Harvard University is microfilming titles from the Widener Collection on a large scale under Title II-C grants and with major funding from the Littauer Foundation (for Judaica materials). The Harvard Law School has also initiated a microfilming project covering retrospective serial titles in several law-related fields. The American Theological Library Association hopes to film theological titles published from 1850 to 1929 in addition to their present serial filming program. See Chapter VIII for a description of its survey project.

The Library of Congress has a large ongoing preservation microfilming program that concentrates on deteriorated titles identified by the various collection curators. They are also working through the American history section systematically marking titles for filming or repairing.

Research Publications, Inc. (RPI), a commercial micropublisher, is involved with a number of large-scale filming projects, including the American Fiction Collection, 1906-1910, the post-1850 portion of the Goldsmith-Kress Collection of Economic Literature, and City Directories of the United States, a joint project with the Library of Congress. RPI has also announced plans to film all titles in the *Eighteenth Century Short Title Catalog* (500,000-600,000 titles), which may take 15 to 20 years.

The French plan to film some 670,000 volumes in the Bibliothèque Nationale's Department of Printed Books over the next five to ten years. The Bodleian Library at Oxford University has initiated a project to film pre-1900 titles.

Cooperative microfilming programs have been carried out on a small scale in the past, and this activity is likely to become a trend in the future. The Research Libraries Group has undertaken cooperative filming in the late 1970s and is considering a new program now. The Library of Congress has long had a cooperative filming agreement with the New York Public Library, and other programs are currently underway. Cooperative programs not only share the cost and responsibilities, but they take advantage of complementary holdings so that more complete items are filmed while avoiding duplication. Such co-operative efforts will undoubtedly strengthen and broaden local preservation microfilming and encourage the establishment of more filming programs. Such cooperation also empha-sizes the necessity of standards to be followed by all filming units. The Library of Con-gress specifications mentioned earlier are the most important and provide a critical founda-tion of any preservation microfilming program.

CONCLUSION

Options for the treatment of brittle books provide some solutions for the preservation of the intellectual content of library materials. They are in use in several preservation programs, but like all other handling and repair techniques, they must be carried out with a good deal of common sense. Libraries must choose those formats and options that are appropriate to their collection and work out the procedures and routines to fit their unique set of circumstances.

VI

Case Studies of Preservation Programs

The following case studies of seven preservation programs illustrate solutions to the preservation problem in seven distinctly different libraries. Although each program was developed to meet the particular needs of a specific library, there are definite similarities in approach and organization. An analysis of these similarities suggests a model for developing a successful preservation program.*

SIMILARITIES IN PRESERVATION PROGRAM DEVELOPMENT

Perhaps the most obvious similarity is that each library emphasizes different aspects of preservation and conservation based on its specific organization and collection. Thus, the Folger Shakespeare and the Indiana Historical Society libraries emphasize full-scale conservation treatment of unique or rare materials, while the libraries of Rutgers University and Southern Illinois University (SIU) emphasize the routine maintenance of general collections supporting curriculums. Because of the emphasis on exhibition at the Folger and Indiana Historical libraries, conservators at these institutions are heavily involved in exhibit installation and monitoring. The preservation program at Rutgers is decentralized because its libraries are decentralized, while conservation activities at SIU are centralized to reflect a library under one roof and with one fiscal administration.

Another obvious similarity is the timing of the programs. In every case, expansion of the preservation program, or planning for it, took place in the early 1970s. The similarity in timing was no accident but reflected the state-of-the-art of library preservation. Whereas previously libraries had considered "mending," "binding" and "restoring" low-level manual activities, libraries in the 1970s began to view preservation and conservation on a broader scale and as part of collection development. The commitment of the library ad-

---

*The Selected Bibliography at the end of this book lists published articles describing other exemplary programs.

ministration to preservation and the integration of preservation with the rest of the library's functions was vital to the initial and continuing success of the programs.

In each case, development of a broad approach to preservation involved a redefinition of those activities that constitute preservation accompanied by administrative reorganization to facilitate the coordination of preservation efforts. In each case, employment of a professional to develop and organize the program was recognized as essential. Programs that emphasized physical treatment tended to employ conservators in the top position, while those with less-specialized collections hired librarians to oversee activities. Regardless of the job title, direction and planning from a professional whose sole responsibility is preservation and conservation has been a key element in successful program development (see Appendix: Sample Job Descriptions for Preservation and Conservation Personnel).

In all seven libraries, a knowledgeable library staff is considered paramount to the success of the program. Staff involvement among the seven programs ranges from viewing training presentations on handling and use, to responsibility for recognizing and designating damaged items, to performing minor repairs, to decision making in consultation with preservation staff. Conservation librarians in the public service units of the New York Public Library (NYPL) have a variety of preservation responsibilities; curators at the Folger are directly involved in treatment decision making; subject specialists at SIU and Johns Hopkins make retention decisions for brittle books; special interest groups at Rutgers determine preservation policies. No matter what the mechanism, formal liaison between preservation staff and the rest of the library is an important element in a broad preservation program.

All seven libraries serve as resource centers for preservation information. Dartmouth served as a pilot library in the Association of Research Libraries Preservation Project to develop a self-study process for libraries. The planning process involved a detailed assessment of preservation needs followed by the development of a phased plan to improve preservation conditions. Rutgers, Indiana Historical, SIU and Johns Hopkins periodically offer workshops to assist other libraries. SIU is involved in the development of the Illinois Cooperative Conservation Program, and the Folger and Johns Hopkins libraries have instituted formal apprenticeship and internship programs.

Perhaps most significantly, these seven programs (along with other established programs) provide a testing ground for developing solutions. For example, NYPL, as a member of the Research Libraries Group, Inc. (RLG), has input NYPL master negative records to form the basis for an automated data base for preservation microfilming records. Libraries with established preservation programs cooperate with other libraries that are struggling to solve preservation problems. In a field as new and uncharted as library preservation, the development and dissemination of standards, specifications and procedures are considered important outreach activities. The obvious similarity in approach in these seven programs suggests that libraries are learning to cope with preservation in a systematic manner. Every program, for example, includes stipulations for environmental control and monitoring and disaster preparedness.

Another similarity among the seven programs is the existence of in-house treatment facilities. The workshops, like the programs in general, are tailored to the needs of the individual libraries. In every case, however, efficiency, workflow and economies of scale are emphasized. Some libraries develop unit cost figures for treatment to assist them in planning and budgeting. Those with more sophisticated workshops have organized workspace, supplies and equipment in order to enhance productivity. Conservation treatment, like other library activities, can benefit from scrutiny of procedures to determine what is appropriate, as well as what is efficient.

What impetus was there for these and other libraries to start preservation programs? In many cases informed and far-thinking library administrators or other concerned individuals have sparked a concern for preservation throughout the library. In some cases grant funds have been catalysts for preservation programs or have allowed the purchase of sophisticated equipment or the conservation of an important collection. A consultant's report or library planning study has often provided direction for initial program development. In every case, however, the establishment of a formal program has marked the acceptance by the library of its responsibility for the preservation of its collections.

The following case studies were written by a preservation staff member at each library. In examining them, it will be useful to consider overall organization of the program; lines of authority and responsibility; functions and activities in the program; number, experience and training of the staff; capabilities of the workshop; and statistics, such as number of treatments performed, costs and percent of the budget allocated to the program.

DARTMOUTH COLLEGE LIBRARY

Philip N. Cronenwett, Curator of Manuscripts

The Dartmouth College Library is a system of eight libraries, the oldest of which was constructed in 1928. Serving a graduate and undergraduate population of 4300, the library maintains a collection of 1.3 million volumes, 1 million maps, 1 million microforms and about 5 million manuscripts. The preservation problems in the library are typical of those of a library founded in the 18th century.

For many years, there was no directed or concerted effort to preserve or protect the library's holdings. There were sporadic oiling and cleaning projects, but these were never organized into a program. The lack of a preservation program was documented in a 1976 survey prepared for the library by the New England (now Northeast) Document Conservation Center. The report indicated several avenues of approach, including the development of an organized program, and recommended the creation of a position for an officer with preservation training.

Staff and Facilities

In 1979, a librarian with preservation training was appointed to the staff. While the position carried responsibilities aside from that of preservation officer, there was time to create a rudimentary preservation program, and space was allocated for a small workshop. Funding was obtained from the Landauer Bequest, an endowment for new and innovative programs within the library, to equip and supply the workshop.

The workshop serves the special collections of the library. Because of size and staff limitations (a full-time work-study student and a supervising officer) it is not possible to perform work for other divisions of the library. Flat paper cleaning, deacidification and repairs are the major tasks of the shop. In addition, books are cleaned and treated and minimal repairs are made to bindings. Extensive binding repairs or restorations are done by an external fine binder. When it is necessary to use volatile materials in the treatment of paper, the manuscript must be taken to one of several laboratories on campus available for the library's use. Approximately 5000 volumes and 15,000 manuscripts are treated and repaired annually.

The greatest difficulty with this system is the need to find and train students each term. Much of the 10-week term is spent in training the student to a minimal level so that materials can be treated. As part of the long-term planning for the library, it is deemed vital that a full-time staff member be appointed as a conservation technician.

OMS Preservation Planning Program

In 1980, Dartmouth was selected as one of the three pilot libraries to test the Preservation Planning Program developed by the Office of Management Studies (OMS) of the Association of Research Libraries (ARL). The program allows a library to study its preservation program, or lack thereof; to develop recommendations to improve environmental conditions and disaster preparedness; and to enhance preservation awareness and programs. The Preservation Planning Program took six months and 2200 hours of staff time, but the results already have proved its worth. The library's preservation program, hitherto scattered and fragmented, was thoroughly examined, and 18 recommendations, to be carried out over the next 10 years, were presented to the librarian. These include a complete reorganization of preservation within the library, installation of climate control systems where they are lacking, hiring of additional staff and educating staff and patrons. Included with the program was a manual of practices to inform staff of basic preservation issues.

The primary recommendation of the Preservation Planning Program study team was the establishment of a standing committee on preservation. This committee is charged with preservation development and oversight throughout the library system. It has studied the 18 recommendations developed during the Preservation Planning Program and has begun implementing them. A complete reorganization of existing preservation programs is contemplated, and work will begin on enlarging the program. This will be difficult in the next several years as a result of fiscal constraints, but the committee believes it is imperative to increase funding for preservation and to appoint a qualified, full-time preservation officer.

An important outgrowth of the ARL/OMS Preservation Planning Program was the involvement of staff on all levels. A sharp rise in the growth of staff awareness of preservation and conservation was apparent during the six months of the test. The preservation committee will use films, lectures and slide presentations to enable the staff to acquire more knowledge of preservation. A program for patron awareness is also envisioned.

A third key feature of the new preservation program is stack maintenance. All materials new to the library system, except publisher's shipments, are fumigated in a vacuum fumigation chamber before they are processed and placed in the stacks. This is particularly important with materials that will be housed in special collections. Several members of the bindery preparation staff are also involved in stack maintenance. Approximately 20 hours per week are spent cleaning, treating and inspecting volumes in the stacks. Materials that are found to have damaged or fragile bindings or paper are flagged so that the appropriate selection officer can review the materials and make a decision to repair, replace or rebind. Approximately 45,000 volumes are cleaned and inspected annually. One of the goals in the coming year is to increase the hours spent on this project.

A fourth feature of the new program was the establishment of a disaster team to develop a manual and procedures to deal with emergency situations. Only months after the team was organized, a humidification unit malfunctioned and damaged some 500 volumes. It was clear from the work of the disaster team that preparedness is an essential part of any preservation program.

While the organized preservation program is a new part of the Dartmouth College Library system, it is of major importance. The budget remains modest at $12,500 per year for staff and supplies, but with a well-organized program the impact is great. Grant applications now have a preservation component as an integral part. Collection development policies contain sections on preservation, and prospective staff members are questioned about their preservation knowledge and awareness during interviews. The result is a preservation effort that will have continued impact on the library and its holdings.

RUTGERS UNIVERSITY LIBRARIES

Susan Garretson Swartzburg, Preservation Librarian

In order to understand the preservation problems faced at Rutgers and the approach taken to resolve them, it is necessary to understand the University's history. Originally chartered in 1766 as Queen's College, it was the eighth institution of higher education to be established in North America. Its purpose was (and is today) "the education of youth in the learned languages, liberal and useful arts and sciences."

In 1816 Queen's College suspended its undergraduate curriculum and became a theological seminary. By 1825 the undergraduate college was revived and renamed for the head of its Board of Trustees, Henry Rutgers. Thus, it is reasonably safe to assume that the original collection of books that supported the needs of the Queen's College undergraduates is now a part of the collection in the seminary library and that the Rutgers collections date back to 1825.

In 1864 Rutgers became the land-grant institution for New Jersey. This designation led to the multicampus public university that Rutgers is today. While Rutgers is one state university, the schools and colleges that comprise it are physically separated and retain a great deal of independence.

The collections at Rutgers University Libraries are curriculum-related. Preservation activity within the system is directed toward providing an environment that will preserve general collections as long as possible.

Staff and Facilities

Rutgers began its preservation activity in 1972. By 1974 the position of preservation librarian was created and authorized to survey the situation at Rutgers and determine what was to be done. During the next five years, however, there was little money available to implement programs, the preservation librarian was assigned additional tasks, and the library experienced serious administrative problems. While the situation was frustrating, useful time was spent identifying problems in the unit libraries (located in three separate areas of New Jersey) and increasing the awareness of the university administration; this was essential before any substantial programs could be undertaken. Additionally, the preservation librarian identified individual items and special collections that required the attention of a conservator as funds became available. In 1979 serious preservation activity began.

Responsibilities

The first priority was to clean out the Alexander Library's sub-basement, which was poorly ventilated and very dirty, where all materials out of the ordinary had been stored since the library was constructed in 1956. Several important collections that enhanced the library's research capabilities, including valuable collections of 19th and early 20th century books, were identified and grouped together. Collections that range beyond the research focus of Rutgers are in the process of being deaccessioned—deposited in collections at other institutions or sold at auction. The majority of the material, however, will be housed in a compact storage facility, now under construction on the Rutgers-Piscataway campus. The storage annex will provide an appropriate environment for these and other lesser-used but valuable materials, and the books will be cataloged and made available to the scholarly community.

Rutgers would have preferred to restore or to prepare phase boxes for volumes in poor condition *before* their transfer to the annex. However, funds for such a project have not been available. Condition reports are prepared on the materials in these collections in the hope that fragile material can be filmed or repaired upon user request. A program of phase boxing will be implemented at the annex as soon as the books are moved there. Rutgers is working closely with the Research Libraries Group (RLG), through its preservation committee, to seek solutions for the preservation problems that all libraries face. Developments in mass-deacidification and laser disc technology are awaited as Rutgers considers the long-term preservation of the material that will be housed in the annex.

Workshops

The Rutgers collections do not merit the attention of a full-time conservator, but a small workshop may be established in the annex. In the meantime, workshops on caring for and repairing books have been given for the library staff. In 1980 workshops based upon the slide-tape presentation, ''Preserving Harvard's Books,''* were given for the circulation staffs and others in the unit libraries. The situations illustrated, which are typical of those encountered at Rutgers, raised awareness of many problems in the unit libraries and increased the ability of staff members to work toward solutions. The program will be repeated periodically.

Each unit library has assigned the task of making simple repairs to a qualified staff member. Several staff members attended workshops on basic repair techniques given by the Northeast Document Conservation Center, and further training in basic repairs as well as the centralized purchase of supplies will be arranged for as needed. The goal is for simple repairs to be done accurately in-house.

In 1980 the position of collection management librarian was created. In addition to other duties, the collection management librarian is responsible for stack maintenance. Written shelving instructions are being prepared, and there are plans to develop a training program for the shelvers within a year.

Also in 1980 the university librarian introduced the concept of Special Interest Groups (SIGs) to address basic library problems using a task force approach. In a system such as Rutgers, with its emphasis on group decision making and management, this is a satisfactory method for developing a variety of preservation programs and for preparing preservation policies and procedures. The preservation librarian, who has an excellent reference collection covering all aspects of conservation and extensive vertical files, serves as the information center for the library system and the region.

In 1980-1981, the serials SIG surveyed current library binding practices and expenditures throughout the system. Specifications for library binding that are appropriate for each unit library are now in preparation; the goal is to have them in effect by the 1982-1983 academic year.

In 1981 the preservation librarian gave a workshop for the map SIG, and the group is preparing guidelines for the care of maps. In spring 1982, the microform SIG gave a workshop on the care of microform collections, for which they will develop guidelines. In addition, the microform SIG will examine current procedures and develop specifications for microfilming archival material in-house if it is decided that the library will continue this operation. While the preservation program at Rutgers moves forward slowly, it moves forward steadily, with the ''grass roots'' support that makes a preservation program work.

---

*A slide-tape presentation emphasizing proper storage, handling and use. Developed by Doris Freitag, conservator at Harvard, and available for rent. Similar aids have been developed by (to name a few) the University of Wisconsin-Madison Library, Yale University Library, the Newberry Library and the Nebraska Historical Society.

INDIANA HISTORICAL SOCIETY

Pamela M. Najar, Conservator

In June 1977 the privately endowed statewide Indiana Historical Society moved into the 1976 addition to the Indiana State Library and Historical Building. Included in the addition was a restoration laboratory, designed by state archivist John Newmann, to be shared by the State Library and the Historical Society. The restoration laboratory, together with a generous endowment from the estate of the late Eli Lilly, enabled the Historical Society Library, under the leadership of head librarian Thomas Rumer, to commit substantial resources to the development of an active, in-house conservation program.

The Indiana Historical Society Library was opened to the public in 1934 to provide a repository for "the collection of all materials calculated to shed light on the natural, civil and political history of Indiana." The present collection has a wide range of materials relating to 18th and 19th century Indiana and the Old Northwest; it includes 2000-3000 rare books, 25,000 pamphlets, more than 1000 pre-1900 maps, 500,000 manuscripts, more than 15,000 early photographs and prints, and a collection of broadsides and other ephemera. In addition, special collections of 20th century material are being developed, especially in the areas of black and ethnic history, social service agencies, labor history, Indiana architecture and railroad history. These 20th century collections include over 700,000 manuscripts, 100,000 photographs, 5000 architectural plans and 8000 volumes of related secondary and research material.

Staff and Facilities

The conservation section, which reports to the director of the library, includes two full-time professional conservators and part-time student assistants. Facilities include the 800-square-foot restoration laboratory, which is supplied and administered primarily by the Historical Society, and a 12′x14′ work area within the main Society library stacks. The laboratory is used for all work involving water, chemicals and specialized equipment; the stack work area is reserved for examination, documentation and simple cleaning and mending. Large-scale cleaning operations, sorting for fumigation and similar tasks are done in the library's processing area, adjacent to the laboratory.

Great effort has been made to bring and keep these facilities up to date. Laboratory equipment includes several large work tables, two fume hoods, a compressor and spraying apparatus, a vacuum fumigator, a 3′x5′ sink, utility sinks and trays, presses, a hand sheet former, an analytical microscope, a pH meter and other essential small tools and equipment. The stack work area has a large work table, large storage drawers and shelves, a utility sink, a stereo microscope, environmental monitoring equipment and the conservation reference library. The basic equipment was purchased during the building expansion. The Society attempts to add equipment as the need develops and the budget permits.

Responsibilities and Services

The primary responsibility of the conservation section is collection maintenance and restoration within the Historical Society Library. More than half of the staff's time is devoted to duties such as environmental monitoring, consultations with curatorial staff on storage policies and cleaning and repairing collections. Long-term projects include reboxing manuscript collections in acid-free boxes and folders, making acid-free wrappers for bound manuscript volumes, treating and building phase boxes for the rare book collection, developing methods to deal with the photograph collection, which includes large numbers of odd-format and nitrate materials, and developing a disaster preparedness plan. In addition, the staff maintains environmental monitoring equipment, supervises the sending of secondary source material to a library bindery, targeting at least one manuscript collection per year for complete cleaning and repair. The conservation staff also prepares the Society's exhibition program, which includes restoring individual items for display and designing and preparing safe and attractive mountings and exhibit equipment.

Perhaps one-fourth of the conservation staff's time is devoted to the needs of other cultural and historical institutions in Indiana. Restoration services and workshops are provided at a reasonable cost when time is available; and consultation, lecture and disaster assistance services are given free of charge in most cases. In addition, a library of books, pamphlets and periodicals, as well as information leaflets written by the staff to answer commonly asked questions, are available for reference.

The conservation program at the Historical Society has been well supported financially from the very beginning. It currently absorbs about 17% of the Society Library's $360,000 budget, about the same as is devoted to acquisitions. A rough breakdown of the 1981-1982 conservation section budget includes:

$41,200	salaries and benefits
$12,000	storage and display supplies
$ 7,000	laboratory supplies and equipment
$ 1,000	conservation library/reference materials

Some aspects of the budget should begin to decline as remedial projects, such as reboxing manuscript collections and box making for rare books, and laboratory equipment purchases are completed. Personnel costs, however, are likely to increase; to maintain standards, purchases of quality storage materials will continue as the collections grow.

It should be noted that the budget is designed primarily to meet the needs of the Historical Society's collections and to develop the restoration laboratory as a resource center. The costs of providing consultation, disaster assistance and lecture services to other institutions and individuals are subsidized by the charges made for outside restoration work. Thus, aside from the obvious overhead costs of space and equipment, these extension services pay for themselves.

In the future, the Historical Society hopes to encourage the wider development of conservation resources and to extend more help to other institutions in Indiana. For the present, as Robert K. O'Neill, current director of the Society Library, has said, "The Indiana Historical Society Library is privileged to have an active, nationally known and highly respected conservation program. We feel that this is a valuable asset to the Indiana Historical Society, the State of Indiana, and the historical and cultural community as a whole; and we hope to be able to continue to maintain and develop it to its fullest potential."

THE FOLGER SHAKESPEARE LIBRARY

Karen Garlick, Assistant Conservator

The Folger Shakespeare Library is an independent, privately endowed educational institution. Its Shakespeare collection is unsurpassed, and its holding of English Renaissance works are the finest outside Great Britain. The resources of the library range from late medieval to modern times and cover British, Continental and American materials.

The Folger has had a department dedicated to the care of its books since shortly after its opening in 1932. Robert Lunow, a German-trained bookbinder, was the in-house binder for a long time, during which the bindery functioned as a technical adjunct to the curatorial and administrative divisions of the library, attending exclusively to book repair and rebinding with an emphasis on skillful execution of craft techniques. Though the Folger was a pioneer in providing care for the collection at a time when most libraries ignored the condition of their collections, the broader aspects of conservation concern that characterize the efforts of conservators today were not considered. The library viewed the bindery as a low-level service unit, reflected by the nonprofessional status accorded the position of binder. As supervisor, the curator selected books for treatment and assigned the type of work to be done.

In the early 1970s, the library entered a new phase of development and expanded activity in response to the conservation needs that had begun to be defined in the professional literature. After the retirement of Mr. Lunow, Johannes Hyltoft was appointed conservator and began the conversion of the bindery into a conservation department. The department was elevated to professional status within Central Library, one of three library divisions, and the position of conservator was made directly responsible to the associate director. The workshop was reorganized to permit the execution of work governed by conservation principles, as well as traditional binding practices. Specialized equipment was purchased for use in conjunction with permanent and durable materials. The expanded treatment capabilities allowed the application of conservation methods and techniques to works of art on paper and manuscripts, as well as books.

For the first time, measures geared to retarding deterioration or preventing damage to the collection were taken. The department instituted a program to monitor the temperature and relative humidity. Charts that resulted from this program documented the inability of the physical plant systems to maintain optimum environmental conditions and became an important factor in demonstrating the urgent need for the library's renovation. During the two-year renovation in 1979-1981, about half of the $8 million spent was allocated to the total reworking of the physical plant systems. Both the old and new areas of the library now maintain close to ideal temperature and relative humidity readings. At the same time, a conservation committee was formed to evaluate general library procedures, review specific questions (such as requests for library loans) and recommend courses of action to the administration. A stack maintenance program began that included leather treatment, cleaning of the stack areas and dusting of books.

Staff and Facilities

From 1977 to the present, the conservation department has been staffed by Frank Mowery, head conservator, and Karen Garlick, assistant conservator. During this time, the workshop facilities have been significantly improved. With a $15,000 grant from HEW, Title IIC in 1978, the department made several purchases to upgrade old equipment and to acquire new and more sophisticated equipment, such as a fume hood, stereo microscope, a deionizing and recalcifying water system and a photographic documentation set-up. The library's engineer built a leaf caster from plans drawn up by Mr. Mowery that incorporated features from other machines. The leaf caster has made possible the treatment of the 4000 "Tamworth Castle Papers," an important manuscript collection for Renaissance social and political history, that were so weakened and deteriorated by extensive mold and rodent activity that they could not be satisfactorily mended and strengthened by traditional repair techniques.

The library renovation program roughly doubled the size of the workshop to 1000 square feet and provided separate areas for benchwork, chemical work and finishing. Each conservator now has a working surface of about 6′ with a built-in light table, individual press and conveniently located storage space for pressing boards, blotter paper and the like.

Items in need of treatment are identified in several ways: when accessioned, cataloged, used by staff and patrons and during yearly shelf reading. Any staff member may place items that require minor repairs on a special conservation shelf on the secured stack area level. Once or twice a month the shelf is emptied and the items treated en masse to make efficient use of conservation time and to ensure that materials are back in place as soon as possible. The curator maintains a list of materials that need boxes (phase or clam-shell) to protect valuable bindings, to prevent further damage to items that await treatment but do not have priority, and to protect unbound books, pamphlets and manuscripts. Priorities for boxing are called to the attention of the conservation department; otherwise, the list is consulted periodically and a group of materials attended to at the same time.

Priorities among items requiring extensive treatment are determined through a review by the curatorial and conservation staff. Curatorial decisions are based on an item's artifactual value, collective or individual importance with regard to the collection, and prior and anticipated use. Because of the nature of the collection, options such as reformatting and purchasing other editions or alternative titles are not considered. Conservation priorities are based on an evaluation of the current condition and an assessment of the condition in relation to the life expectancy of the item if no treatment is given. Because of the relatively small size of the collection, the value of individual items and the general good condition of the items, the conservation department is not pressured by an overwhelming number of deteriorated or damaged items. The department can usually justify the recommendation of full restoration in cases where other libraries, facing a different set of realities, might have to compromise. The selection and execution of a particular treatment is governed by the principles of reversibility, respect for an item's integrity and an awareness that any treatment should be as limited as possible.

Responsibilities

Work on a daily basis covers a wide range of techniques and is concentrated on rare materials, unless an individual circumstance dictates otherwise. Serial binding and standard rebinding of modern books is done by a library bindery. Paintings, tapestries and objects (furniture, sculpture, ceramics, etc.) in the collection are sent to area conservators for maintenance and treatment. For bound items, in-house treatment ranges from boxing and minor repairs, to rebinding, rehinging and rebacking, to full restoration. Paper treatments include simple tests and analyses (pH, lignin, alum, rosin), dry and wet cleaning, deacidification, traditional Japanese and Western paper mends and leaf casting, cold lining, and polyester film encapsulation.

Currently, the treatment documentation system is undergoing revision. With the new photographic documentation set-up, all items receiving extensive treatment are photographed. The short documentation form previously used is being expanded to a checklist to allow the comprehensive recording of all pertinent information in a standardized and easy manner. The practice of tipping into a book a summary sheet containing a collation and brief description of treatment will continue. All fumigated items will not only be listed on a master sheet, but will have the date of fumigation noted—at the back of books and on the inside cover of a box for unbound items.

The conservation department is also responsible for overseeing the library's semi-annual exhibits, including installation and dismantling, construction of cradles and monitoring of light levels. From 1979 to 1982 the department was involved with a unique traveling exhibit, "Shakespeare, the Globe, and the World," that contained the library's finest rare books, manuscripts, documents, paintings, works of art on paper, playbills and artifacts. Dr. Nathan Stolow, conservation consultant to the exhibit, worked with the department on designing the special packing crates and exhibit cases that, among other features, contained silica gel panels for humidity control. At each site, the Folger conservation staff supervised the registration of every item, compared the condition of the items against the photographic and written records, installed and dismantled the exhibit, checked footcandle levels (limited to five) and ultraviolet light readings and distributed five hygrothermographs throughout the exhibit for continuous monitoring of the temperature and relative humidity.

In 1980 the staff orientation program was expanded to include an introduction to conservation. It includes a slide-lecture on the proper handling and storage of library materials, followed by a tour of the workshop. The department hopes to include the slide-lecture as part of the orientation for new readers to illustrate the reasons behind the rules for use of rare materials.

In the past, the library has received several grants with a conservation component. In 1976 a National Endowment for the Humanities grant to make accessible the extensive collection of theater promptbooks included the microfilming and basic conservation of all the materials. The employment of two conservation technicians under this grant marked the beginning of the library's commitment to a professional training program. These informal apprenticeships were expanded into a formal intern program. An award of a $350,000 conservation endowment (to be matched by Folger) from the Andrew W. Mellon Foundation will be used, in part, to continue the intern program and pay a modest stipend.

Current projects of the conservation department call for the completion, administrative approval and implementation of a disaster plan drafted by conservation staff; the addition of a conservation technician to the workshop to do minor paper and binding repairs so conservators will be freed for intern training and more technically demanding treatment; the compilation of a conservation source book containing formulas and techniques for staff and intern consultation; expansion of the conservation library; and the purchase of an ultrasonic welder for polyester film encapsulation.

Over the course of 12 years, the Folger Library has evolved from an institution with limited in-house binding activities to an institution with a full-scale conservation department. The library includes conservation as an integral element in both its departmental organization and its apparatus for formulating policy, demonstrating its commitment to the preservation of its unique and valuable collection.

MORRIS LIBRARY, SOUTHERN ILLINOIS UNIVERSITY

Debra Willett, Collections Maintenance Supervisor

Southern Illinois University at Carbondale is the main campus of a state supported university system. Morris Library, with holdings of 1.8 million volumes, is one of the largest open-shelf, subject division, academic libraries contained in one building. It serves the curricular and research needs of Carbondale's 24,000 students and 1500 faculty and is one of the four Research and Reference Centers in the Illinois Library and Information Network (ILLINET). The library is organized into five major divisional libraries: humanities, social studies, education/psychology, science, and the undergraduate collection. Special collections (university archives, rare books and manuscripts) and learning resources (media and instructional support services) are also housed in Morris Library but are fiscally separate. The law and medical libraries are completely separate.

There are distinct advantages to conservation in being a centralized library. Materials to be treated are conveniently located, which enables collections maintenance activities to be better coordinated. Because all the divisional libraries and technical services belong to one fiscal unit, conservation service charges and associated record-keeping are eliminated. Bureaucratic red tape is reduced by dealing with one library administration.

Although the bulk of the collection is general research materials, there is a blend of the contemporary and the antiquarian (for example, the Diderot encyclopedia [1751] is located in the general stacks). The focus of conservation activities is on the materials most heavily used—those returned to circulation and those selected by divisional staff. These books are charged to conservation and delivered weekly for treatment. Damaged items for which there is a patron request are handled on a rush basis.

A conservation policy statement was approved by the library affairs administrative council in 1980. It gives authority to conservation programs, outlines areas of responsibility such as disaster preparedness and environmental controls, and describes proper stack maintenance and conservation treatment practices. The conservation staff has authority to make treatment decisions while the divisional staff has the final retention decision.

The conservation and binding section is a unit within the serials department. Historically, binding preparation was linked to the serials department because of the large number of serials titles being bound. The section includes the conservation lab and local bindery, library binding preparation and marking. Each of the three areas is staffed by a supervisor who reports to the conservation librarian.

Staff and Facilities

The conservation program began in 1975 with sound conservation techniques for book repair (i.e., eliminating use of tape). The program received its first real impetus, however, in 1978 with the hiring of a conservation librarian in conjunction with a $60,000 grant funded by NEH, the John Dewey Foundation, and Corliss Lamont, philosopher/philanthropist. The purpose of the grant was twofold: to restore the John Dewey papers and to begin a comprehensive conservation program. Grant funds provided equipment and supplies for the Dewey restoration project, as well as custom-made storage areas and work stations that facilitate smooth workflow and better use of space. In 1981, the library received commitments from the university to continue the program past the grant period.

The conservation and binding section is allocated 5.4% of the library budget, including salaries and wages. Expenditures for fiscal year 1980-1981 were broken down as follows:

$ 64,047	salaries (excluding fringe benefits)
	professionals: 1 FTE
	paraprofessionals: 4.5 FTE
$ 44,144	wages
	student assistants: 6.3 FTE
$ 94,000	contract binding
$ 5,671	conservation supplies
$ 750	brittle book replacement costs
$208,612	

Because conservation work is labor intensive, it is critical that the library administration provide strong support for the student work force. For example, in the total cost for operation of the local bindery, student labor accounts for 36% of the conservation budget:

$ 23,140   salaries   [unit cost for routine treatment = $3.08]
$ 16,977   student wages
$ 6,421   supplies/replacements
—————
$ 46,538

Student wages for the conservation and binding section amount to 11% of the library's student work budget. This does *not* include stack maintenance activities such as reshelving, binding pick-up or shifting, which are handled by divisional personnel.

Conservation occupies 2500 square feet, half of which is used for materials and binding preparation. The local bindery/conservation lab is located in a 25′x50′ room. Generally, the local bindery operates as a production workshop, where routine repairs are batched for maximum efficiency. Workers maintain a standard rate for the seven major categories of book repair and protective encasement. A detailed manual including philosophy and step-by-step instructions has been developed.

Responsibilities

Decisions on treatment are made by the collections maintenance supervisor based on frequency of use, cost of treatment, intrinsic value and unique physical characteristics. In most cases, it is more cost effective and expedient to treat an item in-house rather than to rebind commercially. Cosmetic repairs are seldom made. The local bindery handles approximately 1250 items per month: 50% are book repair (tighten hinges, recase); 45% are general maintenance (pambinds, insertions); 4% are protective encasement (box-making, encapsulation); and 1% is conservation rebinding. Work done for special collections makes up 5% of the workload and is confined mostly to encapsulation, matting and box-making. Requests from special collections are generally handled on a project basis.

Binding preparation, with a staff of one paraprofessional and five student assistants, processes approximately 19,000 items annually at a cost of about $100,000.* Detailed contract specifications are written so that the vendor is able to provide a number of products suitable to the particular needs of the collection. The bulk sent are multiple-issue serials. One of the most important categories with respect to conservation is new case. These are typically signature-sewn items with the sewing intact (either the original hard cover has deteriorated or the book was originally purchased as a paperback). The binder does not disturb the original sewing; endsheets are replaced, the book is rounded and backed and a new buckram case is attached. The advantage is that the signatures are not lost (as in oversewing), which thereby increases the life expectancy of the book. The disadvantage is that it costs an additional $2 per item for special handling. Eighteen percent of the monographs to be bound are sent new case, while 7% are commercially pambound, 16%

———
*Unit cost including staff is $6.18; for binding alone is $4.92.

are bound in the ordinary book category (generally oversewn) and 59% are double-fan adhesive bound.

In keeping with the policy statement, books that are too embrittled to withstand further circulation enter a decision-making procedure designed to replace or reformat these materials. Options include withdrawal, replacement with commercial reprint or microform, photocopy or on-campus microfilm.* All searching is done by the conservation staff, but the ultimate decision on retention is made by the subject specialist in the divisional library.

Future plans and activities include the addition of a conservation technician who will act as shop foreman and train student personnel and thereby allow the collection maintenance supervisor to concentrate on administrative duties. There has also been discussion concerning increased centralization of stack maintenance activities, such as shelving and binding pick-up. Morris Library is in the process of converting to a statewide online circulation system (LCS) that will help to eliminate much of the paperwork associated with binding preparation.

An offshoot of the conservation program at Morris Library came with an October 1981 Library Services and Construction Act grant to develop an Illinois Cooperative Conservation Program (ICCP). Based at Morris Library and geared to serve all Illinois libraries, its initial objective is to coordinate disaster preparedness and to disseminate preservation information through workshops, correspondence and publications. (See Chapter IX.)

With its comprehensive program, Morris Library is able to set an example for other libraries that are developing programs. There is the opportunity to share resources through the ICCP and to coordinate preservation efforts. The key to Morris Library's successful conservation program is a strong commitment on the part of the library administration. Without continuing fiscal support the program cannot make full use of its facilities, let alone experience growth.

MILTON S. EISENHOWER LIBRARY, JOHNS HOPKINS UNIVERSITY

John F. Dean, Collections Maintenance Officer

In 1973 the Milton S. Eisenhower Library produced a basic staff study report on the existing, rather elementary, repair and preparation unit. The report posed several questions that prompted a much more detailed investigation of the library's needs. Three consultants' reports, produced in November 1973, May 1974 and April 1975, sought to resolve questions that seem essentially axiomatic to the preservation program problem.

• Is it possible to establish a preservation program designed to address a broad range of problems in a manner that is demonstrably responsive to the needs of the institution?

Microfilming is done by the University's micrographics operation, which conforms to standards for archival filming and processing.

• Given the enormous backlog of neglect and malpractice, is it possible to make a noticeable impact on the usability and appearance of the collections?

• Is it possible to combine a necessary, large-scale physical preservation approach with the seemingly irreconcilable piece-by-piece approach of the conservator/restorer?

• Can the establishment of an effective program be justified at a time of rapidly increasing costs and greater demands on the Library?

After six years of operating the program that resulted from the recommendations, it can be said that most of the basic objectives have been met, and full implementation of the program's scheduled development will occur within a short time.

Staff and Facilities

The first step in the program was the appointment of a collections maintenance officer in September 1975, with the general charge of "the planning and organization of conservation and preservation programs on a university-wide basis, and the development and management of the relevant mechanisms." The job description for the position specified four prime responsibilities: the development of library bindery specifications and binding preparation procedures, including the supervision of the commercial binding office; the development of an in-house bindery for the treatment of damage and deterioration evident in the retrospective collections; the direction of routine furbishing, surveying and collections maintenance operations, including standards for optimum storage conditions; and long-range planning and development for preservation of the university's collections, including the integration of preservation policies with collection development.

The Eisenhower Library administration was determined to integrate the program fully with conventional library services and to place the responsibility for funding firmly with the university, rather than a granting agency. The early studies of the collections maintenance officer were soon articulated in the form of a four-phase development schedule; the first phase was the establishment of the commercial binding office to set appropriate standards for commercial library binding. Four use surveys were conducted, which produced data for the design of a new binding specification.[1] Since most of the library binding budget was spent on periodicals, the design was tied directly to this established pattern of use, and its implementation resulted in a large cost saving. More than 50,000 volumes have been bound to date, without an instance of structure failure, at an approximate saving of $162,500. Significant improvements were also made in binding preparation procedures. The commercial binding office was established with real managerial authority to control preparation and documentation systems. The commercial binding office is also responsible for some minor repair and routine typing for the collections maintenance office.

The second phase of the development plan was the establishment of an in-house bindery capable of dealing with the damage and deterioration in the research collections, focusing in particular on the expeditious treatment of the more than 300,000 items published prior to 1850 and in daily use. The size and variety of the problem required a highly skilled, professional staff, capable of working quickly and efficiently on groups of routine materials yet able to perform with intelligence and sensitivity the complex restoration of rare, high-value items. Given the general unavailability of binders with the necessary combination of skills, an apprenticeship program was created, based upon the City and Guilds of London Institute model but modified to meet the special needs of the United States. The five-year program is certified by the U.S. Department of Labor, Bureau of Apprenticeship and Training and based upon on-the-job training bolstered by study and related classwork. The first three apprentices were appointed in June 1976, followed by periodic additions to a planned maximum of six.

Responsibilities

The bindery occupies an area of 4300 square feet and is equipped to provide the full range of book restoration services. One-third of production time is spent on *routine* binding—batch rebinding, usually in cloth, of pre-1850 books. In most cases, the original sewing is preserved and the structure, while simple, is conservationally sound. Lots are processed on an individual basis, each binder taking 50 or so volumes at a time through to the finishing stage. There are considerable advantages to scale, even for traditional hand processes, and unit times can be reduced while quality is increased. For example, all books have their headbands sewn with unbleached linen thread, a significant improvement in strength over any other method, yet unit time for sewing them is 3.5 minutes. Clearly, the degree of dexterity needed to produce headbands in so short a time is partially a function of the numbers sewn; by the same token, the bindery can afford to have all sewn headbands because the unit cost is low.

Another third of production time is spent on *special* work—work that cannot be conveniently batched because of the need for a detailed approach. The bindery produces 12 basic binding styles, which range from a simple cloth casebinding to a tight joint leather binding, and simple rebacking in cloth or leather to complicated restoration, and uses a standardized nomenclature to aid specification and other record keeping. Variations of the basic binding styles are frequently necessary. All books that must be resewn are washed and deacidified. Nonbook items (prints, manuscripts, maps, etc.) are also included in the special category, and the treatment is quite conventional, consisting of cleaning, washing, matting and encapsulation.

The remaining one-third of production time is divided equally between finishing and box making. Finishing is the blocking of gold on cloth bindings and the hand finishing of other bindings. Box making is the production of clam-shell type boxes, portfolios and other enclosures.

Each day staff fill out a daily docket of time spent on routine items. Nonroutine items that are restored have a record slip lightly tipped into the inside of the back board, which identifies the binder and provides a pointer to the permanent restoration record. Average monthly production of routine bindings is 328 volumes. The one-third of total time spent on special work is accounted for on an hourly basis; roughly 15 leather and vellum bindings and restorations per month are produced, and work on nonbook materials is done.

The bindery liaison assistant selects materials for treatment after they return from circulating. Brittle books are routed to the collection development center for retention or replacement decisions; books published after 1850 with damaged bindings but sound text blocks are sent for minor repair to the preparations department or commercial binding office; post-1850 books with loose text blocks are sent for a commercial library binding; and pre-1850 books that are damaged or deteriorated are sent to the university bindery. The bindery liaison also selects materials for restoration from the shelves as a result of survey data and coordinates the three teams of furbishers. During the systematic oiling and cleaning of the collection through furbishing, survey data are gathered and damaged materials are examined and noted for possible treatment by treatment codes.

Total annual salary costs for the collections maintenance office, 1981-1982, were $187,185; this included bindery, bindery liaison, collections maintenance, commercial binding office, preparation unit, and student help, with a 21% fringe benefit factor added. The 1980-1981 expenditures for commercial library binding were $22,600.

In addition to the tasks noted for the collections maintenance officer's three main departments, staff are engaged in other peripheral but vital duties. Temperature and humidity levels are monitored constantly by six hygrothermographs located throughout the library; advice and guidance are provided to other libraries and archives of the university and to other libraries in the region; workshops on basic techniques are conducted; and a manual guide series of publications is issued to provide practical guidance.

A third phase in the collections maintenance officer's 1976 development program was the establishment of a paper conservation department. Work is currently in progress to construct and equip a laboratory, adjacent to the bindery, to concentrate on the preservation of a wide range of nonbook materials (prints, drawings, manuscripts, etc.). The establishment of a paper conservation department will enable the bindery to devote full attention to the binding and restoration of books. A paper conservator and assistant were appointed early in 1982, and a teaching program of internship, workshops and publications began in autumn 1982. This phase of the program has been funded by a grant from the Andrew W. Mellon Foundation.

The fourth phase, the establishment of a preservation reprography department, is in the planning stage and is scheduled for implementation by July 1983.

The preservation program at Johns Hopkins is working well: large numbers of books and their bindings are being rescued from certain destruction, curricular support materials are being processed in a timely manner and the university's rarities are receiving skilled and sensitive treatment.

THE RESEARCH LIBRARIES, NEW YORK PUBLIC LIBRARY

John P. Baker, Head, Conservation Division

The Research Libraries of the New York Public Library, established in 1895 as the reference department, are a conglomerate of special libraries covering almost every subject field—with the exception of law, medicine, theology and pedagogy. The Research Libraries, one of the two main components of the library (the other is The Branch Libraries), are, for the most part, privately supported and comprise single-copy collections that now total over 22 million objects cataloged for use. Included in the collections are 5.6 million printed books and serials, 150,000 rare books, over 11 million manuscripts, 170,000 prints and drawings, 1.6 million microform units and more than 6 million other objects in a wide variety of formats including sheet maps, posters, broadsides, sound recordings, photographs (negatives and prints), scrapbooks and music scores.

Efforts to preserve the research collections on a systematic basis began in 1912, a short time after they were moved into the new building erected at city expense at the corner of Fifth Avenue and Forty-Second Street. It was not until 1972, however, that the library established the conservation division for the purpose of centralizing and coordinating all preservation efforts. The new division began as an asemblage of previously existing units within technical services plus the bindery, which for many years had reported to the business manager. Along with the acquisition and the cataloging divisions, the conservation division is part of an administrative group headed by the associate director for preparation services.

The conservation division now does the following:

• Provides and contracts for preservation services for the 21 public divisions and research centers that comprise The Research Libraries; these services include binding and repair, microrecording, restoration, fumigation;

• Plans and coordinates budgetary and fiscal support for existing preservation programs, monitors expenditures and assists in planning new programs, including preparation of funding proposals for submission to potential private donors, foundations and government agencies;

• Reviews library policies and procedures that have a bearing on the preservation, protection and security of the collections and recommends new ones when appropriate:

• Assists in the inspection and monitoring of environmental conditions in all storage areas of the four buildings that house the research collections:

• Assists, when needed, in the recovery of water-damaged materials and in the treatment of materials that are threatened by vermin, insects and mold;

• Assists with in-house staff training and development programs and in developing favorable attitudes toward conservation of the collections among members of the staff and the library's users;

• Represents the library in local, state and national forums pertaining to the conservation of research and archival materials.

Staff and Facilities

The division has a staff of more than 36 full-time positions; these are divided among three administrative units that comprise the division at the present time: the shelf and binding preparation office, the custom binding and restoration office and the preservation microfilming office. The staff includes two professional librarians, an administrative assistant, a specialist in binding and physical treatment, a conservator, nine conservation technicians, and several clerical, clerk-typist and technical workers. In fiscal year 1980-1981, salaries and salary-related items (i.e., fringe benefits) amounted to $550,000, or slightly more than $15,000 average per worker. In the same year, $650,000 was spent for contractual services, including binding, microrecording, restoration and miscellaneous preservation work, and $15,000 for supplies—overall, a total of more than $1.2 million. This was equivalent to 7% of The Research Libraries' general operating budget for that year. The amount spent for contractual services ($650,000) was approximately one-fifth of the total expenditure for acquisition of new materials (about $3 million).

Responsibilities

The first-time binding of recently acquired publications is one of the major programs administered by the conservation division. For the past several years, between 45,000 and 55,000 pieces a year have been sent to commercial firms specializing in library binding. Three firms are used at the present time; two are located in the New York City area and the third is some 500 miles away. In common with other research libraries, the New York Public Library must bind many different categories of publications for storage and use, each category requiring separate specifications with respect to the binding materials used and methods of affixing leaves and covers. To the extent possible, the way any given publication is bound is determined by the particular characteristics of that publication, including its physical structure at the time it was acquired, the quality of the paper, the type and extent of use it is likely to receive, how it will be stored, and the way the selection officer *wants* it bound or otherwise preserved. For purposes of drafting future budget requests, detailed statistics on quantities bound and average unit costs per category are maintained, and an average unit cost covering all categories bound during the year is derived. In 1980-1981, $282,000 was spent for binding about 45,000 volumes, yielding an average unit cost of $6.27.*

The collections maintenance and repair program is concerned with treatment of material that is already part of the cataloged collections. The objective of this program is to extend for as long as possible the useful life of books and other objects in the collections that are beginning to show signs of physical wear and deterioration. Under this program, the services of the in-house custom binding and restoration office, as well as outside binding firms and restoration facilities, are used.

Selection of material for rebinding and other forms of preservation treatment is done

---

*This figure does not include the cost of salaries for binding preparation activities.

in the public service units. Each division has a staff member who is designated conservation librarian, with a number of specific responsibilities including selecting material for treatment or replacement; deciding on the type and extent of treatment; monitoring stack conditions; and serving as liaison to the conservation division.

This arrangement provides an administrative framework for the collections maintenance program. The guidance and advice that the conservation division provides to the staff in identifying treatment options and determining the most appropriate treatment in terms of cost and other factors is a key element in the success of the program. Another important feature is the quota system, under which each division is permitted to send a specified number of pieces each month for rebinding or other preservation treatment. Routine printed materials in need of simple rebinding or recasing are sent to an outside binding firm on a regular monthly schedule. More specialized materials, such as older imprints and most nonbook formats, are routed to the in-house facility, which accepts materials requiring anywhere from one to 10 hours of production time for adequate treatment. Rare and unique materials of important cultural or historical significance are sent on a highly selective basis to outside restoration facilities.

For large research libraries, microrecording is the only economically viable means of dealing with the huge quantity of deteriorating publications in their collections. Microrecording began at the New York Public Library in the early 1930s, but it was not until the 1950s that a large-scale filming program was initiated. Since that time, 110,000 reels of master negative microfilm have been produced. Master negatives are created under conditions that meet current nationally recognized standards for the production, processing and storage of archival microforms.

In the past 10 years alone, The Research Libraries have spent $2.6 million on preservation microrecording. The current annual expenditure is about $280,000, which permits production of 1.4 million frames (exposures). Day-to-day management of the program is assigned to the division's preservation microfilming office; filming, processing and quality control are provided on a contractual basis by the photographic services division.

Major categories of materials filmed on an on-going basis include (1) current pamphlets that are acquired for the collections (about 3000 titles per year); (2) current foreign national gazettes from 79 countries (a joint program with the Library of Congress); (3) current serials on low-grade paper that are filmed in lieu of binding (over 800 titles are filmed on a continuing basis); (4) serials, monographs and pamphlets from the cataloged collections that are too fragile to rebind and are unavailable from outside sources; and (5) manuscript collections. Standards and procedures for attaining full bibliographic control of master microforms, utilizing the member-owned-and-operated automated data base of the Research Libraries Group, Inc., are being developed under a 1979 grant from the Andrew W. Mellon Foundation.

FOOTNOTES

1. John F. Dean, "The Binding and Preparation of Periodicals: Alternative Structures and Procedures," *Serials Review* 6 (July/September 1980): 87-90.

VII

The Protection and Physical Treatment
of Rare and Unique Library Materials

An apparent dichotomy exists between preserving the intellectual content of a physical object and preserving the physical object itself for its value as an artifact. An answer to the preservation challenge raised by this dichotomy is to preserve in the original format all that needs to be and to transfer the intellectual content of everything else to a stable medium. Although it is not always clear what "needs to be" preserved in the original, libraries have simplified the process of decision making by designating some items as "rare," "unique," "archival," "historical" or part of a "special" collection. Standards of practice and a library conservation profession have emerged to meet the need of libraries to preserve materials so designated.

STORAGE, USE AND EXHIBITION

Storage

The single most important aspect of the preservation of rare and unique library materials is ensuring a proper storage environment that will retard deterioration inherent in the materials, prevent needless deterioration and reduce the necessity for later conservation treatments. Even the most ethical and sound conservation treatment interferes with an item's artifactual value or historical evidence. Since deterioration is an inescapable process, libraries must largely content themselves with slowing down the chemical reactions that degrade *all* organic materials and lead to their eventual demise. Conservation treatment, by virtue of the time and expense involved, is possible for only a small percentage of those items deserving of treatment.

Use

Materials are designated as "special" so that their use may be restricted and supervised and they may more easily be preserved. Materials that are used are subject to increased wear and tear and may even be used up. Special collections departments ordinarily have rules concerning use by patrons and routinely orient new patrons to proper handling practices. It is not uncommon, for example, to forbid the use of pens for note taking, deny the photocopying of fragile materials and restrict access to the original if a microform or facsimile copy exists.

Exhibition

The "use" of materials by the repository itself during exhibitions holds the most potential for serious damage. Institutions generally exhibit their most treasured, valuable and unique items. Further, the expense and time involved in planning, designing and mounting an exhibit and producing a printed catalog usually ensures that items are exhibited for extended periods. Some items may even remain on "permanent" exhibit. If an institution has a full-time conservator on staff and an ambitious exhibit program, much of the conservator's time will be devoted to ensuring that items to be exhibited are in stable condition and that once exhibited, they are properly protected. In fact, a common reason for commencing conservation treatment is in anticipation of an exhibit. Conservation consultants are frequently involved in exhibit installation, especially in the transport of materials to other institutions for exhibit.

The principles governing safe exhibition of rare and unique library materials are the same as those that apply to museum materials. In some instances, exhibit cases may be transformed into elaborate microenvironments to control and monitor temperature, humidity and exposure to light. (Because of the particular sensitivity of photographic materials to light, many collections forbid the exhibition of original photographs and exhibit copies instead.) Exposure to light is the most challenging exhibit problem and the subject of numerous articles. The best exhibit situations minimize light exposure by allowing the person viewing the exhibit to turn on the light instead of leaving light on continuously. In no instance should exhibit lighting be left on when the library is closed.

The potential for *physical* damage to library materials during exhibition is great. Flat paper items such as manuscripts and maps must be mounted flat so that they do not sag. No pins, tacks, staples or clips should ever pierce a document. All materials used in the construction of an exhibit case and its linings, backdrop, and the mounting and support materials in contact with the artifacts must be totally inert and of the highest quality.

Bound volumes are particularly susceptible to structural damage. If a book that is held open for extended periods is not properly supported, a severe strain is put on the binding. Vellum bindings and texts are particularly sensitive to manipulation; combined with too dry an environment, they will become severely warped or distorted. Custom book cradles, which match the size of the book and the particular angle at which it is exhibited, can be constructed to support books properly. For tight back bindings, the use of mirrors to reflect the design is often the only reasonably safe solution. If custom book cradles are not economically feasible, books can still be exhibited relatively safely if care is taken to support their structure properly. A conservation-conscious institution will have an exhibit policy that stipulates environmental parameters, establishes guidelines for installation and mounting and sets limits on the time period that items may be exhibited.

THE ETHICS OF CONSERVATION TREATMENT

The conservation profession has advanced a number of ethical principles and standard practices that address the protection of cultural objects during treatment.[1] The American Association for Conservation of Historic and Artistic Works' (AIC) *Code of Ethics and Standards of Practice* succinctly outlines the professional responsibilities of the conservator toward the object, the owner or custodian, colleagues and students, and the public. It also describes standard practices for examination, reporting and treatment. This professional code and standard places primary emphasis on the *appropriateness* of treatment (which in many cases may mean simple protective encasement) and on *restraint* rather than excessive modification. There is no room for trade secrets or clever refabrication in a profession that promulgates unswerving respect for the aesthetic, historic and physical integrity of the object and full disclosure of the composition and properties of all materials and techniques employed. An increasing reluctance to use the word "restoration" is reflective of the stance that conservation is first, action taken to *prevent* deterioration, and only second, action taken to *correct* deterioration.

Conservation treatment begins with an examination of the object(s) to determine original structure and composition and the causes of deterioration or alteration. Analytical or technical services may be needed to supplement observations. A condition report that concludes with a proposal for treatment is ordinarily prepared. Often several options are listed and the benefits or outcomes of each explained. Following treatment, a report is prepared to document the object's condition before treatment and describe treatment procedures, methods and materials. Documentation frequently includes photographs taken before and after treatment—and during treatment, if needed—to reveal information about structure that cannot ordinarily be seen or to supply information that may be destroyed or obscured through steps taken to preserve the object.

The preservation of library materials is such a complex and mammoth task that continuing basic and applied research is vital to elucidate the causes of deterioration and to test new conservation methods and materials. Standards for treatment, and for materials used in treatment, are developed to promote consistent, high-quality work and to protect conservators from the unjustified claims of manufacturers.

TREATMENT DECISION MAKING FOR RARE AND UNIQUE MATERIALS

Conservation treatment is the application of methods and materials to retard or prevent deterioration or to repair damage to a structure that is weakened and thereby hastens further damage. It is justified when an item cannot withstand even careful use without being damaged, when its physical condition is unstable, or if it has been subjected to inappropriate or unaesthetic treatment in the past. In most cases, treatment for the sake of cosmetics cannot be justified.

Conservation treatment of rare and unique materials differs from the treatment of general collections in a number of important areas. Since general collections are maintained primarily for the textual or graphic information they contain, treatment emphasizes keeping items in usable condition so that they can continue to transmit information for as long as they are needed. The physical vehicle for the information may be altered without losing anything. The information contained in materials designated as "rare," however, may be *dependent* on the physical object itself, as well as on minute details of composition or structure.[2]

Treatment decisions for rare and unique materials should be made jointly by the curator who is most knowledgeable about an item or collection and the conservator who will be executing the treatment. Curatorial staff are responsible for determining treatment priorities for an entire collection and for providing insight into the bibliographic and scholarly significance of an item or collection for which treatment is indicated. Conservation staff members are responsible for determining condition, describing treatment options and clearly elucidating the benefits and implications of special treatments.

There are many important issues in treatment decision making. Should an item be restored to its original or near-original appearance or merely stabilized? Is it necessary to preserve original bindings? Should missing materials be replaced? Most collections can establish policies to guide decision making for general categories of materials, but each specific item designated for treatment will require additional individual attention. The final decision will be affected by the category of materials and the type and amount of use an item will receive, its value, the possible effects of treatment on artifactual evidence and the cost or time involved in treatment. No collection will ever be able to provide the best treatment for every item that deserves it, so the difficult task of priorities must be addressed.

EDUCATION AND TRAINING OF CONSERVATORS

Library and archives conservation, which has emerged as a specialty within the conservation profession only during the last 20 years, is still in the process of defining professional competence. In fact, the conservation profession in general is moving only gradually toward certification of practitioners—the first step being the development of standards for education and training. There are presently four academic programs for training museum conservators and a certification process within AIC for paper conservators.

Hand bookbinders and book conservators have traditionally been trained by apprenticeship to an established binder. However, the realities of the workshop situation and the pressures of production can sometimes interfere with the learning process. To provide an academic setting for training, a graduate program to train library conservators was established in the fall of 1981 as a joint program of the School of Library Service, Columbia University, and the Conservation Center of the Institute of Fine Arts, New York University (see Chapter IX for details). The Columbia program also includes a curriculum for preservation administrators to train librarians to direct comprehensive programs that include the areas of environmental control, disaster preparedness, collections maintenance, library binding and information preservation, as well as the conservation of rare and unique materials.

PROFESSIONAL SPECIALTIES

Cultural objects are composed of such a variety of materials and structures that conservators, of necessity, specialize—concentrating on the treatment of categories such as paintings, works of art on paper, textiles, books, photographs or wooden artifacts. In fact, the AIC *Code of Ethics* states that a conservator should "only work within the limits of his [or her] professional competence or facilities."

In large conservation workshops associated with libraries, conservators usually specialize in the treatment of bound volumes, flat paper items or photographs. Since these are broad categories, many individuals develop expertise in very defined areas such as illuminated manuscripts, daguerreotypes, Victorian cloth bindings or vellum. Combinations of specialties are also common: the fine binder who designs and executes original and unique bindings may also be a book conservator; the conservator specializing in works of art on paper may also treat paper manuscripts and maps.

LABORATORIES AND WORKSHOPS

Well-equipped conservation laboratories, workshops and studios contain equipment and instruments that enable conservators and conservation scientists to perform sophisticated tests and treatments.[3] The definition of "well-equipped" varies depending upon the purpose of the operation and the institution(s) it serves. A well-equipped workshop for a small college library would include a simple work area for cleaning, mending, book repair, polyester encapsulation and portfolios. Its most complicated testing equipment might be pH strips to test the acidity of paper.

Sophisticated conservation workshops and studios contain frequently needed items of scientific equipment (pH meter, hygrothermograph, photographic documentation set-up); conservation equipment that enables or facilitates treatment (vacuum suction table, leaf caster, board sheer, fume hood, stamping press, light table); and a wide variety of tools and inexpensive equipment. Work space will be suited to the type of work performed, but it usually includes work stations for individuals, large work tables and custom storage for supplies.

As technology for conservation grows, so does the list of expensive and sophisticated equipment. Many libraries and archives need to have access to treatment services but do not have the funds to support an elaborate in-house workshop. Testing laboratories, therefore, ordinarily serve from several to many institutions. Regional treatment centers are formed for the purpose of cost-sharing—equipment as well as staff. Further, for some types of treatments, it is decidedly more cost effective for a single facility to arrange to provide a sophisticated service for a number of libraries.

CASE HISTORIES

The following six case histories illustrate the complexity of conservation treatment for rare and unique library materials and the modus operandi of the professional conservator. Each was written by the conservator who executed the treatment. A range of materials and settings in which conservators work is represented. Although the case histories are specific, they are illustrative of the broad conservation treatment issues that confront the librarian, the curator, the scholar and the conservator as they work together toward the preservation of materials with historic and artifactual value.

CONSERVATION OF ORIGINAL BINDING ON A RARE BOOK

Laura S. Young*

Sechs Bücher vom Wahren Christenthum (1750) is in the rare book division of the United States Military Academy Library at West Point, NY. It was a gift to the Academy in the early part of the 19th century and is one of many historical and cultural items in this collection. It was nicely printed on good paper and attractively bound. It measures 24 cm x 20.2 cm x 9 cm. It is one of many items from West Point that we have treated (restored, rebound or boxed) and its case history illustrates a variety of interesting conservation techniques.

Condition

As the photograph on page 143 shows, the volume has not withstood the ravages of time, fire and water unscathed. The binding was full calf (brown) with front and back covers heavily tooled or embossed in blind. The leather was in bad condition, stained, cracked and loose in part from the boards; a few fragments were missing. The lower portion of the spine was missing entirely; the upper portion was scuffed, torn and somewhat brittle. The spine was untitled and undecorated. There were brass bosses on all eight corners of boards and brass clasps, but the lower halves of both clasps were missing and there was evidence that these were attached to the back board with leather straps. All the brass was badly tarnished and somewhat corroded. The wooden boards were badly warped. Large portions of the board papers were missing, and the remaining portions were dirty and badly stained.

Laid paper used for the text was in good condition, for the most part, with some yellowing from age or the sizing. Flyleaves were missing, and the frontispiece was dirty and stained. There was some water staining on the first few signatures. The book was sewn on five double cord raised bands, and the sewing in general was sound. The edges of the text were trimmed and stained black, seemingly with intent and not from smoke. Headbands were worked with linen thread on vellum strips and pasted on. The one at the head was broken and about half of it missing; the tail one was missing entirely.

Treatment

West Point requested that the volume be restored, preserving as much of the original binding as possible. Other options might have been to discard the original binding and put on a brand new binding (thus destroying the character of the book and much of its interest)

---

*Laura S. Young is an independent hand bookbinder and conservator. She trained from 1935 to 1944 under Gerhard and Kathryn Gerlach and subsequently taught hand bookbinding and conservation in the Graphic Arts Department of Columbia University and at the Pratt Institute. Since 1955, she has owned and operated a studio in New York City that accepts private commissions and private students. She is a fellow of the International Institute for Conservation and the American Institute for Conservation and was President of the Guild of Book Workers from 1958 to 1974. She is the author of *Bookbinding and Conservation by Hand: A Working Guide* (New York: R. R. Bowker, 1981).

Condition of the rare book before treatment.

or leave the book in its deteriorated state and simply put it in a suitable protective case. Its condition, however, was such that any handling at all would have caused further destruction or deterioration. The decision to conserve the original binding seemed most appropriate.

First, the boards and the spine of the binding were removed and safely stored. The spine of the book was then cleaned. (It needed very little cleaning.) The first 20 signatures were detached (the signatures consisted of four leaves—two folded sheets), and surface dirt and finger marks were removed with a pink pearl eraser and/or an Opaline bag. The water-stained and wrinkled pages were then soaked in lukewarm tap water for an hour, removed from the water, laid on paper toweling for a few minutes, then put between absorbent blotters and under a light weight to dry. When dry, necessary page repair and guarding was done with Usugami (a light-weight Japanese paper) and thin wheat starch paste.

New end sheets and flyleaves were made of Cockerell royal paper which matched the text paper very well in both color and texture and has a near neutral pH. Hinges of the same paper, reinforced with airplane linen, were attached to this made-up signature. The cords on the spine were extended by splicing on new hemp cords. An inner hinge of Okawara (a heavy Japanese paper) was attached with a mixture of wheat starch paste and Promatco A1023 (a polyvinyl acetate adhesive) to both the first and last signatures of the book. The signatures that were previously removed and the new end sheet signatures were sewn on. Since most of the sewing was sound, it seemed unnecessary and undesirable to "pull" the entire volume and resew it. When the sewing was completed, the end sheet signatures were attached to the inner hinges with the mixture of pastes. The spine was glued with hot animal glue and, when dry, the book was rounded and backed. The spine was then lined with acid-free materials for a tight back binding. New headbands were worked with natural unbleached linen sewing thread (No. 12) around a hemp cord core. All edges were cleaned with a pink pearl eraser. This completed the work on the text.

The leather and all bosses and clasps were removed from the boards, marked as to their proper position on the binding and safely stored. The leather was loose enough so that its removal presented no particular problem. The bosses were originally attached with brads that had been bent on the inside of the boards and hammered flat. In order to remove them safely, it was necessary to pry them up, straighten them, and drive them gingerly out of the boards until they could be grasped with pliers and pulled out. They were iron or steel, which no doubt explains much of the corrosion on the brass.

The boards were then put between thoroughly wetted blotters and into a press under light pressure. As the moisture soaked into the boards the pressure was increased. When the boards were completely flat the blotters were replaced with dry pulp boards, returned to the press and allowed to dry under pressure for several days. All of the brass was cleaned with naval jelly, which left them with a nice aged patina rather than shiny and new looking.

The boards were then attached to the book with the cords. The cords were originally frayed out and attached to the inside of the boards (a somewhat unusual technique) so they were reattached in the same fashion.

The book was then covered in new Hewit calf skin, which was dyed with analine dye to match the original leather. The bosses were attached with brass escutcheon pins cut in length to conform to the thickness of the boards and fixed in position with epoxy glue. The missing portions of the clasps were replaced with new brass clasps attached to leather strips. The original covering leather was attached to the new leather covers with the paste mixture previously described. Because of its poor condition and characterless appearance, the fragmented original spine was not used. The new spine was left untitled, and blind lines were tooled at head, tail and on the sides of the raised bands—both in conformance with the original. The discolored areas on the original leather were touched up with Liquitex modular colors, and the whole binding oiled with a mixture of lanolin and neat's-foot oil. The volume was again in good condition and should easily withstand future use.

For added protection and storage, the volume was housed in a Solander case constructed of .082 thickness Davey red label binder's board, covered with Joanna Western's maroon starch-filled buckram, lined with brown acid-free paper, and titled with an indented leather label stamped in 22k gold.

The estimated time spent on this job, including the Solander case, was 55 hours. The work was done jointly by Laura S. Young and assistant, Jerilyn Davis.

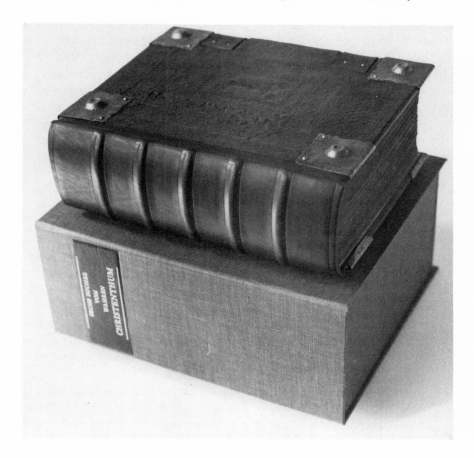

The rare book after treatment, with its protective box, underneath.

CONSERVATION OF THE SECRET BATTLE ORDER MAP

Thomas K. McClintock*

The Secret Battle Order Map is a large (7½'x 9') map that was used at the western front during World War I to record the location and movement of all allied and enemy forces in northwest Europe. It was kept at the Advance Post of Command of the Head-quarters, American Expeditionary Forces, Ligny-en-Barrois, France, and was designed to be easily transported between posts.

The object was composed of common lithographic road maps adhered with glue to four panels constructed of upsom board nailed to wooden frames. Over 1500 pins, thumb-tacks and tags of different designs and colors were pushed into the surface to represent significant pieces of information. Pins with red heads traced the front lines and pins with white heads designated the sectors of each army. Tags were stylized flags with variations that signified the location (by village), nationality, identification number, type (artillery, cavalry, etc.) and quality (enemy only) of each division. The thumbtack used to secure the tag was red or white, indicating whether it was a fresh or tired division, respectively. There were different tags to represent headquarters, army numbers, commanding officers and a summary of the status of allied and enemy divisions. The tags were moved about in response to official communiques and daily intelligence reports. The map illustrates the order of battle as of the hour of the armistice, 11 A.M., November 11, 1918.

The map was executed in March 1918 by Lt. Thomas North (retired major general). Allied staff officers considered it to be the most complete representation of the opposing forces, on which it was possible to determine at a glance where and what types of troops were massed. In 1919 it was presented to the West Point Museum by Gen. John Pershing. A stationary version of the map, used by the commander-in-chief of the A.E.F., is located at the National Museum of American History.

Condition

Each of the four panels measured 90"x 27" and contained 10-12 map sections that were adhered with a deteriorated glue to brown, pebbled upsom board sheets nailed to wooden frames (the mount). The map was on medium-weight paper (the support) that had darkened, discolored and become brittle. This condition was the result of the wood pulp stock used in the manufacture of the paper, its contact with poor quality mounting materials and adhesives and exposure to light and airborne pollutants. The surface was very irregular because of the poor adhesion of the paper support to the upsom and wood mount and the distortion of the mount itself. There were many tears and creases but relatively few losses except at the edges where the map sections were overlapped and where

*Thomas K. McClintock was trained in paper conservation at the Cooperstown graduate program of the New York State Historical Association. He is assistant conservator at the Northeast Document Conservation Center in Andover, MA, a regional center devoted to the conservation of books, historical artifacts and works of art on paper.

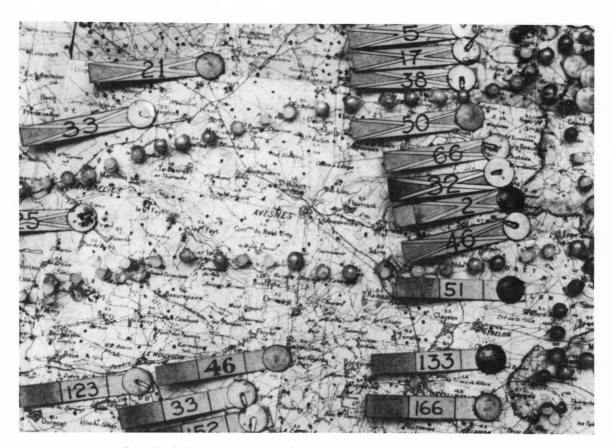

Detail of the untreated surface of the Secret Battle Order Map.

the panels butted against each other. Countless holes could be seen where pins and tacks had been placed and later removed in response to troop movements. The lithographic inks, particularly the red inks, had faded on some map sections. Because of their general differences in color and value, the map sheets resembled a patchwork.

The numerous pins, thumbtacks and tags were also damaged. The pins originally had glass heads painted red or white. On most of the pins the paint was partially or completely cleaved from the head. The glass heads themselves were often damaged and in some cases completely lost, leaving only small metal shafts stuck into the map. The metal thumbtacks had also lost much of their paint and were generally corroded. The paper tags were soiled, brittle and often torn. The inks used to color the tags had proven to be fugitive and, except for the blacks, were lost from exposure to light.

Because of its complex assembly and minimal protection during the years of exhibition, the deteriorated condition of the map was to be expected. The construction of the mounts had become insecure. The map had a generally faded and soiled appearance, robbing it of its immediate legibility and richness of information. These qualities were the cornerstone of the map's original value, and their loss was the cause for its conservation.

Treatment

The map could have been treated superficially, removing surface grime as the fragile pins, tacks and tags permitted, deacidifying the support with a nonaqueous spray, and mending the accessible damage to the support and mount. This would have been a stop-gap measure and the improvement in structure and appearance would have been only slight.

To improve the condition of the map significantly, the following treatment was proposed:

- Remove the pins, tacks and tags and record their locations;

- Remove the map sections from the upsom board mounts;

- Surface clean and wash the map sections and tags in water to clean and reduce the acidity in the paper and to remove the old discolored mounting adhesive;

- Deacidify and buffer the paper with an alkaline salt to guard against future exposure to acids;

- Mend and line (adhere a sheet of paper to the back of the support for reinforcement) the map sections and tags with long-fibered Japanese paper;

- Prepare four new panels to replace the insecure originals and mount the map sections on them;

- Treat the pins and tacks to remove corrosion products and replace those without heads;

- Return all pins, tacks and tags to their original positions.

The map could have been treated very satisfactorily with only its physical security in mind. The Northeast Document Conservation Center often has occasion to treat large maps in this way, and their appearance reflects their improved condition. All items are unique, however, and this was a particularly exciting and complex artifact. Unfortunately, it had changed considerably with time. In particular, the colors of the tags were lost because of the use of fugitive coloring materials, and the map's legibility had become confused. Therefore, in addition, it was proposed to return the colors to the tags, pins and thumbtacks and to tone the losses in the support by impainting. The treatment decision, reached in cooperation with the director of the museum, was to restore the physical condition and the appearance of the map with minimal compromise to the integrity of the artifact.

Before treatment was begun, detailed color slides were made of the entire object. With the aid of the quadrants originally printed on the map sections, the surface was divided into a grid pattern to record the locations of pins, thumbtacks and tags. Before removal, their color, number, name and locations in relation to each other were noted in detail.

This was time consuming but accuracy was absolutely necessary. Photographic enlargements were considered as an alternative to guide their replacement, but they were costly and less detailed and more difficult to use than the written record.

With all pins, tacks and tags removed, the map was cleaned of surface grime with eraser powder. Tests made during the condition examination confirmed that the colors used in the printing of the maps and in the manufacture of the upsom board were not soluble in water. Therefore, the mounts with the map sections attached were immersed in water and the paper and mount released from each other. The map sections were then separated, residual adhesive was wiped from their backs, and the maps were placed in trays of fresh water. After several hours of washing (until the water ceased to be discolored) the maps were immersed in an aqueous solution of magnesium bicarbonate to be deacidified. After drying, water soluble magnesium bicarbonate converts to insoluble magnesium carbonate, which remains in the paper structure to buffer it from future exposure to acids.

In preparation for mending and lining, the map sections were arranged by panel face down on a large light table. The quadrants were aligned and the edges squared. Tears in the paper and overlaps at the edges of sections were reinforced with strips of thin, long-fibered Japanese paper adhered with diluted wheat starch paste. After mending, two sheets of thick Japanese paper were adhered to the reverse of the entire panel with the same paste. The papers and paste used in this operation were traditional high-quality materials and the mends and linings, when properly prepared and executed, will remain secure, stable, flexible and easily reversible for years to come.

The original upsom board was not suitable for remounting because of its pebbled and distorted surface and its composition of poor-quality materials. Four new panels were constructed of dimensionally stable wooden lattice frames sheathed with rigid sheets of Fome Core and covered with several layers of buffered paper (see Figure VII.1). The lined maps were adhered to these individual mounts with wheat starch paste. The areas of loss in the map, most apparent at the edges where the panels butted together, were toned with the background color of the maps to provide continuity between them. Where the brown upsom board was left uncovered in the original mounting at the top left and right corners, the appearance was simulated by painting the same uncovered portions of the new panels.

The tags were surface cleaned, washed, deacidified and lined (because of their brittleness). In the course of their examination, it was discovered that they were originally colored but had faded. The coloring schemes were revealed under tack heads and overlapping tags where portions had been protected from exposure. An appendix about the companion map (provided by Donald Kloster of the National Museum of American History) confirmed the different coloring schemes. While it was known that enemy divisions' tags were colored (red, pink, white or blue) to signify the combat quality of the division (excellent, good, fair or poor), the classification of each division could rarely be determined from the tags themselves. Summaries of the original intelligence reports were located in the West Point Library, and the classification for each division was confirmed. With their accuracy assured, the tags were impainted in such a way as not to appear too new in comparison with the rest of the map, which had darkened and changed in tone with age.

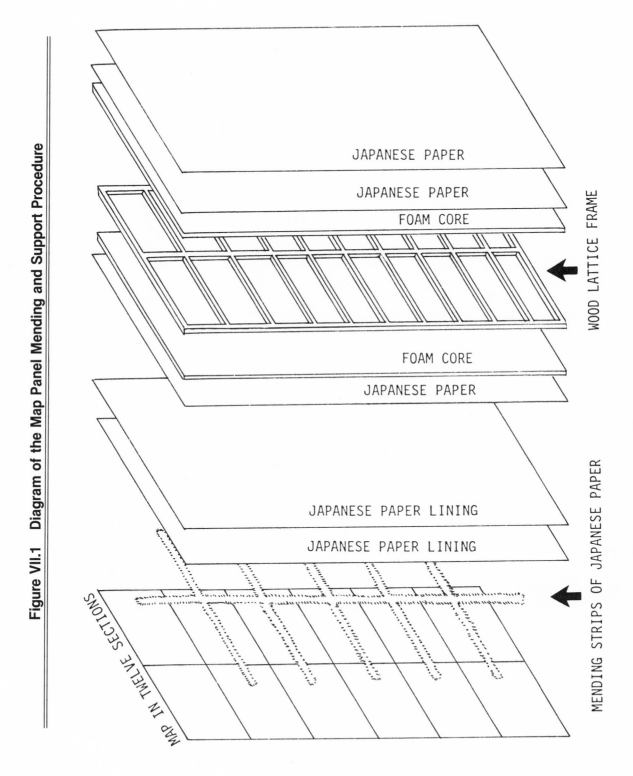

Figure VII.1   Diagram of the Map Panel Mending and Support Procedure

JAPANESE PAPER

JAPANESE PAPER

FOAM CORE

WOOD LATTICE FRAME

FOAM CORE

JAPANESE PAPER

JAPANESE PAPER LINING

JAPANESE PAPER LINING

MENDING STRIPS OF JAPANESE PAPER

MAP IN TWELVE SECTIONS

Flaking paint on the pins with glass heads could not be effectively reattached, so it was removed where necessary. The pins in sound condition were saved, and the rest were replaced by modern ones that were shaped, colored and abraded to resemble the originals. Examples of each type and color of pin and tack were left untreated to serve as references. The thumbtacks that held the paper tags were treated with oxalic acid to remove the corrosion products and were coated with a layer of rust-inhibiting paint. With the written documentation record as a guide, pins and tags were replaced in their original locations.

All treatment procedures were documented, and materials from the original that were not reused (e.g., upsom board) were returned to West Point. Each step in the treatment procedure was executed so that it could be reversed if necessary without damage to the object. After cleaning, remounting and impainting, the map was physically sound and improved in legibility and appearance but retained a feel for the original. The project took approximately 250 hours to complete. The conservator was assisted by Bucky Weaver and Allan Thenen.

The Secret Battle Order Map was returned to the museum with recommendations for display conditions of 65°F and 55-65% RH and a design for a compatible exhibition case and frame. The case would protect the map and its delicate surface from airborne pollutants, exposure to ultraviolet light and visitors.

PREPARATION OF A CALOTYPE WAXED PAPER NEGATIVE FOR PATRON USE

Siegfried Rempel*

The Calotype negative in this case history is an architectural landscape attributed to H.P. Robinson. The Calotype process, one of the first paper photographic processes, used a paper negative generated in the camera, which ultimately produced a positive paper print. The intrinsic value of these types of images is considerable, but even more important is their popularity with researchers. This, coupled with the desire of patrons to view the image by transmitted light, requires the print to be prepared in such a way as to minimize the possibility of damage.

Condition

The negative is a horizontal image measuring 20.1 cm x 16.6 cm. The waxed areas on the back were confined to the pictorial areas, the fore and middle grounds, and just beyond the sky. The negative shows a yellow-gold discoloration in association with those waxed areas. Dirt from physical abrasion is apparent on the back, but there are no folds, tears or losses.

*Siegfried Rempel is conservation scientist in photography, Humanities Research Center, University of Texas at Austin. He was a conservator in training at the Canadian Conservation Institute 1975-1976, assistant paper conservator 1976-1977 and conservation scientist 1977-1981.

Treatment

Treatment options included archival methods such as encapsulation or sleeving, museum methods such as matting, or conservation methods such as backing or inlaying. Encapsulation and sleeving are, at best, stop-gap measures. Both methods employ a transparent plastic material that provides protection while still allowing both sides to be viewed, as well as allowing viewing by transmitted light. Through encapsulation or sleeving, however, the print is placed into a "restricted" environment and may require some other preliminary treatment to prevent a deterioration environment from being generated.

Matting methods are preferred over encapsulation or sleeving because they allow a free environment exchange, as well as viewing of front and back. The disadvantage is that, for this type of print, floating matts with V hinges are required. The matt window lies outside the edges of the print to eliminate irreversible matt burn. Also, to view the back side of the print, the edges must be handled.

Conservation methods such as backing or inlaying are used in conjunction with the matting techniques. Backing is not recommended unless the support is structurally unsound. The application of a layer of water-based adhesives such as starch paste or modified cellulosics is undesirable because of the sensitivity of this type of photographic imagery to moisture. High relative humidities or excessive moisture contents in this paper support will accelerate the rate of chemical deterioration.

The inlay technique exemplifies the proper preparation of early photographic artifacts for use by patrons in a research center. Handling problems are often alleviated by matting, but the photograph's physical limitations may minimize the security obtained by matting alone. In this case, the image area of the photograph runs close to, or to the very edge of, the paper support. The print is loose, neither mounted nor backed, so that use by patrons, particularly while turning over, lifting and sorting, would lead to physical damage of the photograph. The inlay provides a protective outer skirting of paper, which will sustain the damages likely to occur during examination.

A mouldmade Fabriano paper was chosen for the inlay in a color to complement the tonality of the print. A high-quality handmade or mouldmade rag content paper is preferred for the inlay technique as machine-made and chemical wood pulp papers, even those with high alpha cellulose content, are less satisfactory in their workability. The thickness of the paper should approximate that of the photograph (or be a little thicker if an ideal match cannot be made). A minimum of two-inches extension beyond the edges of the photograph was required for the inlay with the grain direction running parallel to the grain direction of the photograph.

To prepare the inlay, the outline of the print was traced on a light table. To protect the print during tracing, a sheet of mylar was laid on the glass, followed by the print laid face down and a second sheet of mylar. The inlay paper was placed over the mylar sandwich with chain and laid lines lined up with the print. The entire assemblage was lightly weighted to prevent shifting. Tracing was done with a light pencil and light pressure to avoid embossing the photograph. The light table was turned on only when required. Tracing followed the print's exact contours about one-eighth inch into the photograph.

The pencil-outlined window on the inlay paper was cut out with a sharp scalpel. The inlay was then chamfered by carefully shaving down the front edge of the inlay paper to ensure a more exact fit between the photograph and the inlay paper.* *The photograph was not chamfered.* After chamfering, remaining traces of graphite were removed with a vinyl eraser. The overlap fit of the inlay to the photograph was checked on the light table.

To adhere the inlay to the photograph, the photograph was laid face down on a blotter and the cut out mask of the inlay piece positioned on its back—leaving only the very outer edges of the photograph showing. Using a Japanese paste brush, the exposed edges were pasted with a medium consistency wheat starch paste,† and the masking piece was removed. The photograph was then transferred face down to the light table and placed on a sheet of silicon release paper. With the light turned on, the inlay was carefully positioned on the back of the photograph. Using the silicon release paper as a support, the inlaid photograph was transferred to a thick package of soft blotters interspersed with sheets of four-ply mat board. A second sheet of silicon release paper was laid down over the photograph and covered with another set of blotters. The sandwich was placed in a press and nipped under light pressure for a minute or two. The blotters were removed, the adhesive bond checked and the seam of the inlay pressed lightly with a bone folder. After removing the silicon release paper, the photograph in its blotter package was pressed lightly for 45 minutes.

For safe presentation, the inlaid photograph was matted using a T hinge and standard window mat. To ensure that the print could be safely viewed by transmitted light, a double mat was used. The back mat had a sheet of UF-3 ultraviolet filtering Plexiglas added to provide support for the photograph. The Plexiglas edges were buttressed with a sink mat and taped into place with Filmoplast P. Neither the Plexiglas edges nor the tape contact the photograph.

THE REBINDING OF A 1614 BOOK AND THE DESIGN BINDING OF ITS 20th CENTURY REPRINT

Jean Gunner**

Today, fine binding includes not only past styles in full leather with elaborately tooled, formal, decorative designs, but also design binding, in which the artist/bookbinder creates a cover design to reflect the contents of the book. A modern fine binding is generally one of a kind; although similarities of style occur, the technique and design

---

*If a thin inlay paper is used, the chamfering technique can be replaced by a water-tear method. A drawing pen filled with distilled water and ethanol (3:1) is used to trace the outline of the photograph. The paper can then be separated along the wet line and the resulting fibered edge used to connect the inlay to the photograph.

†The choice between starch paste and methyl cellulose is often a personal one.

**Jean Gunner is bookbinder and conservator at the Hunt Institute for Botanical Documentation, Carnegie-Mellon University, Pittsburgh, PA. She trained at the Epsom and Ewill School of Art and held positions as bookbinder at Carolyn Horton and Associates in New York City and as assistant conservator at the New York Public Library. The Hunt Institute is a research facility for botanical history.

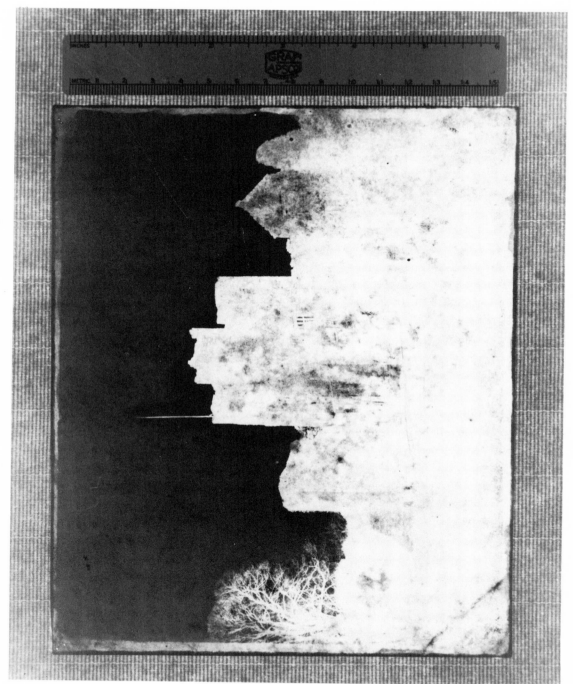

Inlaid photograph viewed by transmitted light.

reflect the skill and artistry of the individual binder. Unfortunately, until recent times little emphasis was put on the internal strength of the book, and inferior materials were often used, causing deterioration of both the text block and binding. Today, the competent bookbinder considers all aspects of the book, including paper treatment, book structure and cover decoration.

In 1979, the Hunt Institute assembled an exhibition entitled "The Tradition of Fine Bookbinding in the Twentieth Century." One of its primary purposes was to question how the modern binder should, or should not, rebind earlier works. Retrospective binding was practiced in the 18th century and became widespread in the 19th century, with binders copying the early styles but executing them with more precision and brilliance. Book collectors were primarily responsible for the vogue of retrospective binding, and today it is still often the collector's or curator's preference that dictates the style of a binding to be done. Now, however, some prefer to save original bindings, even dull run-of-the-mill calf bindings, at all costs. Other prefer more durable new bindings and a few want fine new bindings when books are of special value.

Condition

Two of the Hunt Institute's contributions to its 1979 exhibition were a *rebinding* of *Hortus Floridus* (1614) by Crispijn Van de Passe (1589-1670), a Dutch engraver, and a *design binding* of the two-volume reprint of that work by the Cresset Press (London, 1928-1929).

The Institute has two copies of the 1614 *Hortus Floridus,* one bound by John F. Grabau (1878-1948) in full-green levant, with simple blind and gold tooling and Dutch printed endpapers similar to those used in the late 18th century. Unfortunately, the edges of the text block were trimmed to neaten the edges after resewing, a common practice until recently, resulting in the loss of some manuscript writing on one page. The second copy, which was the one exhibited after rebinding, is especially valuable because about half the pages are handcolored and seven of its leaves contain the beginning of a manuscript written in Dutch by an early hand. The second copy was in its original binding of plain vellum over boards. The binding was badly warped, and the vellum had split in many places and had pulled away on the turn-ins, cutting through the board papers. The text block, apart from some minor water stains on the edges and broken sewing in several places, was in fairly good condition. Although the binding was contemporary, we decided that it was of no significant value and that to repair it would not have been very satisfactory. Since vellum is quite susceptible to changes in temperature and humidity, it is very possible that repairs would be "rejected" in time by the original material.

Treatment: The Rebinding

The curators of the collection and the bookbinder/conservator discussed several options for rebinding this book. Should it be rebound in new vellum? Should it be treated in a manner similar to that of the Grabau rebinding? Or should the new binding be designed to reflect the style of the period and place of publication? We chose the latter since the book was worthy of such treatment and it would add to its value. The time involved would not be significantly more than would be required for either of the other options; the treatment of the text block and the structure of the binding would have been equivalent on all three options.

The book was completely disbound and the spine folds reinforced with thin strips of Japanese tissue. No attempt was made to remove the water stains; they were not disfiguring the plates or text and there was no sign that they were weakening the paper, so they were left to reflect part of the book's history. The book was resewn on three flattened linen cords using the herringbone stitch and incorporating a continuous guard of acid-free paper. Bookbinding adhesives can become unstable, particularly under certain environmental conditions, and the continuous guard is used to prevent any adhesive from coming into contact with the text block. It also creates a very flexible binding, which allows the leaves to lie flat more easily when the book is opened. Plain handmade endpapers, compatible with the text block and reinforced with linen, were also sewn on. After the book had been jogged up on the head and spine to even the pages, a light coat of glue was put onto the spine.

Generally, the next step would have been to round and back the book, but in this case that step was eliminated. In the backing process the first and last few folds are forced into shape and can further weaken already weak paper. As the previous glue had penetrated some of the folds, thus weakening them, we felt it desirable to avoid the backing process. Instead, after the book boards were cut to size, the spine edges of the boards were beveled to compensate for the swelling produced by the repairs, sewing and continuous guard. The boards were then laced onto the book, "pulling" the book into a natural gentle curve (see Figure VII.2). Single red and gold endbands were sewn on, and the spine was lined with acid-free paper. Light-brown oasis goatskin was prepared, and the book was covered.

A great deal of research went into decorative styles used in the 17th century. No attempt was made to copy an early design; the new binding is clearly a 20th-century binding, but it is reminiscent of that earlier time. (See photograph, page 158.) After finishing, the binding was tooled with the binder's name and date on the turn-in of the back cover. For proper documentation a full description of the conservation treatment was written up and filed.

Treatment: The Design Binding

Rebinding the two-volume reprint of *Hortus Floridus* involved a completely different approach. In such cases the modern design binder can be more creative than in retrospective binding, where the structure and design are guided by older established modes.

The volumes were one of 30 sets printed on handmade paper and bound in plain vellum over boards, and they were in excellent condition. The decision was made to remove the 20th-century bindings in order to add design bindings. The books were taken apart completely and the covers discarded. The same forwarding techniques used with the 1614 edition were employed, with a few modifications and additions. Leather hinges replaced the linen ones, the text blocks were rounded and backed, and the heads of the text blocks were gilded. The covering leather was pared thinner at the turn-ins to give a streamlined appearance.

Figure VII.2   Schema of the Rebinding of *Hortus Floridus* (1614)

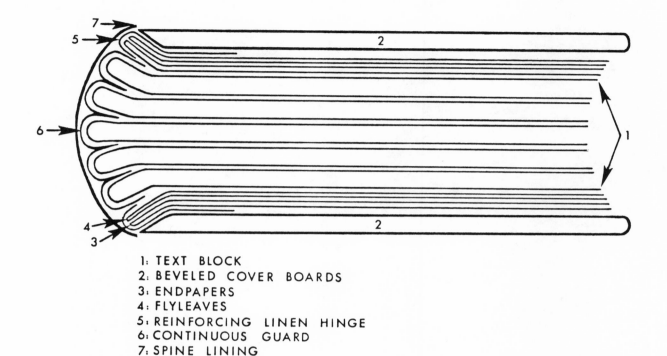

```
1: TEXT BLOCK
2: BEVELED COVER BOARDS
3: ENDPAPERS
4: FLYLEAVES
5: REINFORCING LINEN HINGE
6: CONTINUOUS GUARD
7: SPINE LINING
```

Source: Courtesy of the Hunt Institute

Previous to the forwarding, a design based upon the subject of the work had been worked out and all materials chosen. The subject of the work is bulbous plants; one volume describes spring-flowering bulbs, the other bulbs that bloom in summer, fall and winter. In traditional styles, the front design, or part of it, is generally repeated on the back cover. Modern designs, however, are often continuous across the spine from front to back cover. When the book is closed, the front and back should each be able to stand as an individual design; when open, the entire cover should present one integrated design, as illustrated in the photographs of the finished bindings.* (See photograph, page 159.)

An inlay technique, where cover leather is removed and replaced with a different color of the desired shape, was used for the background color representing the flowers' shapes. An onlay technique, where pieces of leather are pared thin and pasted and pressed onto the surface of the cover, was used for the multicolored shapes representing the petals and shading. A little gold and blind tooling was added to give extra texture to some of the petals. A great deal of accuracy is required when cutting out inlays and onlays as all the pieces must fit together perfectly. On these two volumes together, there are approximately 30 inlays and 250 onlays.

---

*A color reproduction of the binding is published in the catalog of the Hunt's 1979 exhibition, "The Tradition of Fine Binding in the Twentieth Century."

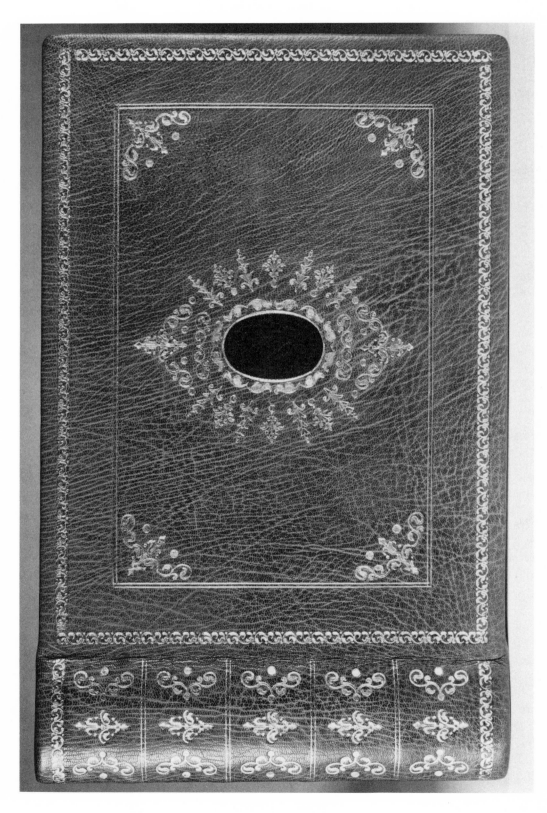

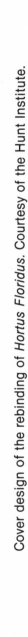

Cover design of the rebinding of *Hortus Floridus*. Courtesy of the Hunt Institute.

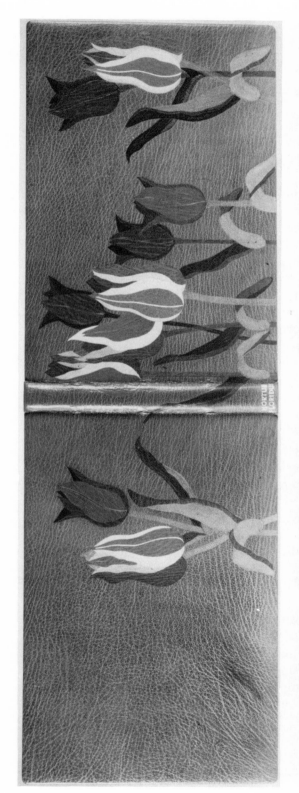

Cover design of the fine binding of the *Hortus Floridus* reprint, Volumes I (top) and II (bottom). Courtesy of the Hunt Institute.

The Hunt Institute is a noncirculating library, so use of these books is restricted to researchers in-house. However, there is no hesitation in allowing their handling by interested scholars; the books were bound with use in mind. Individual felt-lined clamshell boxes were made for all three bindings to protect them from scratches, dust and dirt.

CONSERVATION TREATMENT OF TWO VOLUMES OF EZRA STILES' *LITERARY DIARY*

Jane Greenfield*

The following case history describes the conservation treatment of two volumes of Ezra Stiles' *Literary Diary*. Ezra Stiles (1727-1795), a Yale College graduate, was a lifelong student and teacher and Yale's president from 1778 until his death. The value of his writings lies in his tremendous intellectual curiosity and the diversity of his interests— astronomy, meteorology, silk worm culture, Oriental languages, demography and the American Revolution, to name a few—and his extensive correspondence with scholars here and abroad. His papers contain a wealth of information on American intellectual history of the Revolutionary period and are the most frequently used material in the general collection of the Beinecke Rare Book and Manuscript Library at Yale.

Condition

The collection, left to Yale by Stiles himself, consists of over 70 volumes and bundles of diaries, notebooks and correspondence, as well as a mass of loose papers. Stiles had original and eccentric ideas about binding. For example, one signature would be inserted inside another in such a way that two sewings were needed inside a single outer fold; samples of silk (from his silk worms) were pinned into the "silk" volumes; and letters were folded in half and made into a signature of several letters placed one within the other so that the first half of a letter was several pages away from its ending, often with a central line of writing lost in the binding. He wrote to the edges of the pages, in gutter margins and, in fact, on almost any available blank area, so that notes on the curriculum of Yale College might be found on a blank half page of the volume on silk worm culture.

The quality of the paper varies greatly—strong and flexible in some volumes and breaking at a touch in others, and fragmenting edges have caused some slight text loss. Iron gall ink and a fine pen point were used so that in most cases the ink has not eaten through the paper. The bound volumes are not uniform in size but average about 210 mm in height and 165 mm in width. Most of them are bound in quarter sheepskin with marbled paper sides and are, to a large extent, falling out of their bindings.

*Jane Greenfield is the head, conservation department, Yale University Library. She studied at the New York School of Applied Design and the Art Students League and trained with conservators Paul Banks and Laura Young. She is a Fellow of the American Institute for Conservation. From 1965 to 1974 she operated her own bindery and taught bookbinding. She then established the Conservation Studio at Yale.

Treatment: Volume I

In 1974 the conservation of the Stiles collection was very high on Yale University Library's list of priorities, so the *Literary Diary,* Volume I, was sent to the then newly established Conservation Studio. Gutter margins and the edges of pages had broken or were close to doing so, leaves were breaking out of the binding and the paper was highly acidic. In view of the very heavy use the book received, it was decided that it should be deacidified, mended, encapsulated in polyester film and postbound. Following this decision, it was tacitly assumed that the rest of the collection would eventually be similarly treated.

Post binding of
Volume I of the
Literary Diary.

Treatment: Prior to Microfilming

In 1975 the Yale University Library received a grant from the National Historical Publications and Records Commission to issue a microfilm edition of the Stiles papers. This decision to microfilm caused us to reconsider the order and type of treatment for the collection.

Conservation treatment of materials to be published in microform or facsimile (as the first step toward their preservation) differs from that needed for materials to be conserved at one time for, we hope, all time. Preparing an archive for a good deal of handling and photographing should be a first step to the final conservation. The necessary pause between the first and second treatment steps allows time for reconsideration of conservation options with a firmer knowledge of the state of the material.

Those volumes of the *Literary Diary* with very brittle and fragmenting papers were sent to the conservation department for strengthening before they were photographed. Deacidification, which slows down paper deterioration, was done before any repairs were made. Thin, transparent Japanese paper (Tenjugo) and a clear, starch paste (a hydroxyethylated corn starch paste developed by the Library of Congress) was used for all repairs. Edges that were breaking or might do so were reinforced.

The microfilm edition of the *Literary Diary* has been an impressive conservation measure because it has cut down dramatically on the handling of the materials. However, scholars do often need to see the originals.

Treatment: Volume IV

Volume IV of the *Literary Diary* was one of the few diary volumes that needed treatment before it could be microfilmed, and so it had been disbound, deacidified and mended —still with the assumption that it would eventually be encapsulated and postbound like Volume I. In 1981 it nearly succumbed to the human fondness for uniformity. However, since the collection had been microfilmed subsequent to the treatment of Volume I, the treatment decision for Volume IV did not need to be based on the assumption that the original would receive heavy use.

At a meeting of two Beinecke Librarians and the head of the conservation department, the following treatment options were considered for Volume IV;

• Encapsulation and postbinding;

• Rebinding, using the original cover;

• Leaving the book disbound with each signature in an acid-free folder and the whole volume in a standard storage box.

The rationale was that the first option would prevent further mechanical damage and the second would preserve, to some extent, the integrity of the object. In both cases the text would be easily accessible. There were no objections to either treatment, other than perhaps the time needed, which was not a consideration. The third option would not eliminate the first two. It had the advantage that watermarks could easily be studied on a light table, and ink could be studied under a microscope. Objections to it were possible misplacement, loss or damage by mishandling.

After consideration, a modified version of option three was chosen. This decision would not have been reached independently by any one of the three people involved or perhaps would not have been the same if we had taken less time for reflection on the actual conservation needs of the collection in light of the expected amount and type of use. An acid-free folder was designed that allows one or two signatures to be held in place or easily removed and replaced. These folders will be used for the already disbound material in the collection. If the Beinecke Library finds the folder satisfactory in practice, it can be mass-produced for other volumes in the Stiles Collection.

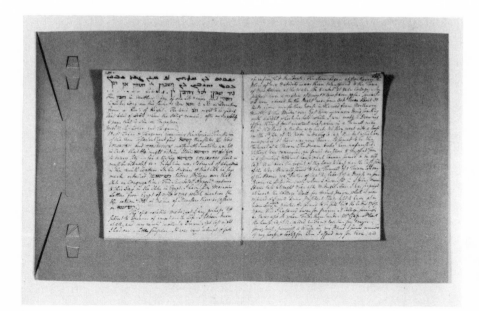

Acid-free folder designed for protection of Volume IV of the *Literary Diary.*

CONSERVATION OF THE LINCOLN MANUSCRIPT COLLECTION

Roger Bridges and Robert Wiest*

The Illinois State Historical Library (ISHL) has been in existence since 1889 collecting materials on the political, physical, religious and social history of Illinois. In 1970, the library moved into a new subterranean building underneath the renovated Old State Capitol in downtown Springfield. The unique design—a central core of five stacks surrounded by three levels for offices, reading rooms, storage and physical plant—allows multiple activities and easy access to the collections.

The Lincoln Manuscript Collection at ISHL is the largest collection of pre-presidential Lincoln materials anywhere. Assembled piecemeal from other collections, the manuscripts are arranged chronologically in two groups—those materials in Lincoln's own hand (approximately 1300 items) and the family papers (approximately 1200 items). Complementing the manuscript collection is a separate Lincolniana section containing published materials and collections of artifacts, photographs and memorabilia.

Discovery of the Storage Problem

Twenty-five years ago the graphic conservation department of R.R. Donnelley, Chicago, recommended use of a cellulose acetate folder (Markilo Transparent Envelopes; Lumarith L-B22 cellulose acetate) to house the Lincoln manuscripts. The folder, marketed under the brand name Lumarith, was thought to be safe and appropriate for the protec-

---

*Roger Bridges is head librarian, Illinois State Historical Library. Robert Wiest was formerly the manager, graphic conservation department, R.R. Donnelley and Sons.

tion of the collection.* The manuscripts were stored in metal file cabinets in a fireproof vault.

By 1978, the staff began to detect a slight odor in the vault but could not trace it directly. It was not until the spring of 1981 that Lincoln curator James T. Hickey opened two drawers of Lincoln material, all stored in Lumarith folders, and was startled by the nearly overwhelming odor coming from the drawers. At first staff thought it smelled like cellulose nitrate film breaking down and contacted R.R. Donnelley for advice. The consensus from Eastman Kodak and the research engineering lab at Donnelly was that the vault should be disarmed, for if the plastic were in fact cellulose nitrate, spontaneous combustion was a distinct possibility. The recommendations were to keep the vault air moving and cool, to empty the vault of the suspect material, then to empty the plastic envelopes in a well-ventilated area. Donnelley's graphic conservation department suggested the library store the manuscripts in paper folders while conservation of the collection was being discussed.

The staff who removed the folders at ISHL complained of being nauseated and losing their appetites during the two days required to unload the 2500 items. In the meantime, the library had also contacted the Research and Testing Laboratory of the Preservation Office at the Library of Congress. Scientists indicated that in the past Lumarith was considered to be chemically stable, but obviously those predictions were not holding up. It has since been discovered that cellulose acetate (especially when sulfuric acid catalysts are not completely washed out) will hydrolyze to give acetic acid. Hydrolysis is also catalyzed by contact with acid (pH 5.0) paper and promoted by storage in high temperature and humidity.[4] In this case, as the folders began to deteriorate, the products of degradation were trapped in the file cabinet and degradation was accelerated exponentially. The library staff moved quickly to complete the first stage of conservation by removing the manuscripts from the Lumarith folders.

While some records and memories suggested that in 1968 Donnelley had deacidified many of the early letters in preparation for a major exhibition, the graphic conservation department was unable to confirm any deacidification. Approximately one-third of the entire collection had been "silked,"† however. The question of prior deacidification was moot; the pH of the manuscripts was 3 to 4, and deacidification was definitely indicated. Although it could not be proven, it was assumed that the degradation of the Lumarith folders had significantly contributed to the deterioration of the paper.

Treatment

Donnelley proposed to stabilize the collection chemically by deacidification and protect it against further physical damage by polyester film encapsulation. Polyester film is a clear, dimensionally stable film that has no plasticizers to break down. *By today's standards* it should remain unchanged for an indefinite period and transfer no harmful products to the paper. It was further proposed that pressure sensitive tape be removed from

---

*The graphic conservation department (until 1980 the extra bindery) of R.R. Donnelley treated valuable books, manuscripts and works of art for 60 years until 1981.

†Silking is a method of strengthening fragile paper by application of silk gauze to both sides. It was introduced as early as the 1860s and continued to be used until the late 1960s.

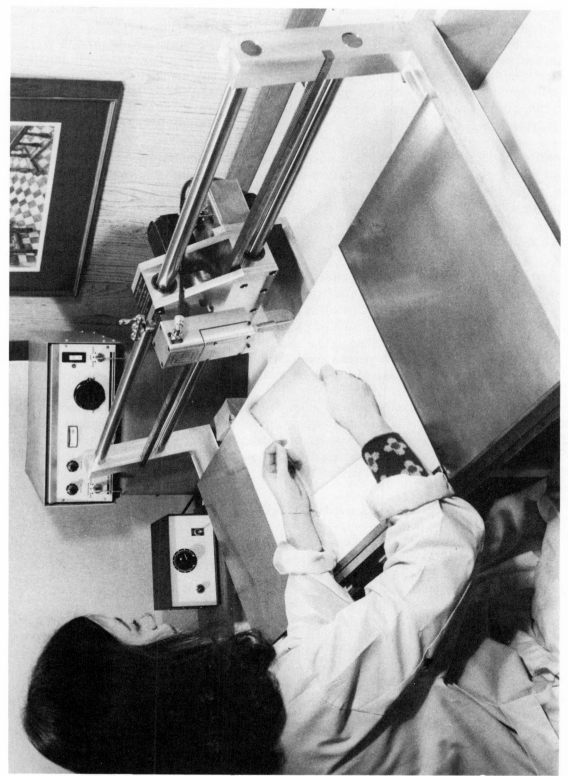

Minter ultrasonic welder in use. Courtesy William Minter.

approximately 30 items and any long tears be mended. At first, the library asked that one edge of the envelope be left open to make access to the item possible, but it was deemed too risky. Since the item is held quite firmly in place by static electricity, removal or attempted removal could cause severe damage to a document. Donnelley suggested that all four sides be sealed; should it be necessary to gain access to an item, three sides could be carefully trimmed and the document lifted out. A new envelope could be made on the spot. Removal was pictured as a very doubtful activity, so it was decided that all four sides would be sealed.

After the initial discovery of the storage problem, conservation treatment was straightforward, with no special difficulties. Before work could begin, however, a method of accounting for each physical piece had to be devised. The time and cost involved in the essential preliminary documentation and physical inventory prior to conservation treatment can be considerable and should be discussed by the curator and the conservator as treatment is discussed.

The Lincoln manuscripts were accepted for treatment in two halves—first, the Lincoln letters, second, the family letters. Nonaqueous deacidification using Wei T'o solution No. 2* was performed. There were no difficulties in deacidifying the silked items. After deacidification, each item was encapsulated in 3 mil Mylar, a Du Pont product, using a leased Minter ultrasonic welder.[†] The welder is quiet, easy to adjust and run, and hazardless. The weld produced is narrow, unobtrusive and smooth, with no additional thickness other than the thickness of the Mylar and no edge build-up.

The conservation treatment of nonaqueous deacidification combined with encapsulation using ultrasonic welding is one approach to archival preservation that is safe, effective and economical—especially in shops that are organized to handle material in quantity. The conservation of the Lincoln Manuscripts was a straightforward job, regardless of the significance of the papers and their unique nature.

FOOTNOTES

1. Hanna Jedrzejewska, *Ethics in Conservation* (Stockholm: Kungl. Konsthöskolan, Institutet för material kûnskap, 1976).

2. Gaylord Brynolfson, "Book as Object," in J. Russell, ed., *Preservation of Library Materials* (New York: Special Libraries Association, 1980), pp. 45-49.

3. National Conservation Advisory Council, *Conservation Treatment Facilities in the United States* (Washington, DC: National Conservation Advisory Council, 1980).

4. Correspondence. Peter Sparks (Chief, Preservation Office, Library of Congress) to Roger Bridges, April 22, 1981.

---

*A commercial nonaqueous deacidification solution.

†Developed by William Minter. See Chapter XIII for details.

VIII

Technological Solutions to Preservation and Conservation Problems

The application of science and technology to the fields of preservation and conservation alters the way libraries view their physical collections. Basic research into the causes of deterioration elucidates the dynamic nature of the organic materials collected by libraries and used by their patrons. Technology developed by conservators, scientists and engineers results in improved or new mass treatment methods, conservation and restoration techniques, and permanent and durable record materials. Finally, the application of sophisticated management tools, such as quantification studies of deterioration, lays the groundwork for long-term planning for preservation. The success of preservation efforts—both to retain and disseminate the intellectual content of deteriorating library resources and to protect artifactual evidence—depends on the continued application of science and technology to the preservation and conservation problems confronting libraries now and in the future.

IMPORTANCE OF BASIC RESEARCH

There are many levels of scientific support for conservation. On the simplest level, *analytical testing services* are frequently needed by conservators to determine the specific composition of an artifact or to test the quality of a conservation material. Such routine services are in contrast to *basic research* conducted over a period of years and often involving many conservators and scientists.[1] Although the results of basic research are usually long in coming and may not even lead to practical applications, basic research is vital to progress in the conservation field. Priorities established by conservators, curators and librarians help to determine the direction of basic research, and the results of research, in turn, influence planning for preservation and conservation programs.[2]

Basic research is carried out in laboratories as an investigative tool to understand the causes of deterioration. It is conducted in conjunction with applied research for the development of conservation techniques and materials, as well as to evaluate the effectiveness of such treatments. Since W.J. Barrow's landmark studies in the 1950s on the causes of paper deterioration, scientists and conservators have increasingly cooperated in efforts to define the mechanisms of deterioration and to work toward solutions. Examples of recent basic research projects include exploring the role of metal impurities in the degradation of paper, testing the effectiveness of methods of drying water-damaged library materials, determining rate of fading of dyes in color photographic materials, and studying the effect of bleaching on the physical and chemical properties of paper. A detailed description of one research topic as an example of the nature and complexity of basic research follows.

ACCELERATED AGING TESTS FOR PAPER

Studies of the validity of accelerated aging as a predictive test of paper permanence have occupied researchers for nearly 100 years.[3] Answers have not always been forthcoming, and problem solving has involved researchers working for many different institutions.

The purpose of accelerated (heat) aging is to predict paper permanence based on the fact that chemical activity proceeds faster when the temperature is raised. A high temperature for a short time period is used to simulate the effect of a lower temperature over a long time period. During an accelerated aging test, paper samples subjected to physical (folding endurance and tear resistance) and chemical (pH) tests are left in a heated oven for a specific time period, removed, and subjected to the same tests. Because paper is hygroscopic, the maintenance of a constant temperature and humidity in the test room is critical to test results.

While accelerated aging tests have been widely used in applied research to develop specifications for permanent/durable paper and to compare the effectiveness of deacidification methods, scientists have remained basically skeptical about the validity of accelerated or artificial aging to predict paper qualities after natural aging or to predict the effect of temperature on the *rate* of deterioration. The validity of the accelerated aging test was at the heart of the controversy over what constituted permanent/durable paper. If chemically purified wood pulp papers could not be accurately tested for permanence, then only all-rag fiber content papers could be trusted.

W.J. Barrow relied heavily on accelerated aging in his research. His 1959 "Tentative Specifications for Durable, Non-Coated, Chemical Wood Book Papers" included performance after accelerated aging as part of the standard.[4] After Barrow's applications of the accelerated aging test, questions concerning the validity of the test continued to prompt basic research throughout the 1960s. Major issues concerned the effect of humidity (moisture in the oven) on test results and the methods of interpreting results. The usefulness of the test was also questioned because of the effect of variables such as air pollution, temperature and relative humidity associated with *actual* storage conditions over a long period of time.

No fewer than seven papers on aspects of accelerated aging—such as use of the Arrhenius equation for extrapolating test results, the application of empirical equations to describe changes in paper properties after aging and the effect of varying relative humidity conditions on the folding endurance of aged paper samples—were presented at 1976 and 1979 symposiums on the preservation of paper and textiles sponsored by the American Chemical Society.[5] Scientists involved in basic research did agree on the *relative* and *general* usefulness of the test to compare paper samples or to evaluate the effectiveness of de-acidification processes and procedures. The sustained interest in accelerated aging was primarily a result of the importance of the test to other research projects, as well as a result of the challenge of designing a fully accurate test rather than accepting its limitations.[6]

Studies on the validity of accelerated aging tests continue to be conducted. A recent study at the Battelle Laboratories for the Library of Congress has explored the use of chemiluminescence, or light emitted from organic materials during oxidation (degradation) reactions, that can be measured by appropriate instruments and plotted to predict deterioration under actual use conditions.[7]

APPLIED RESEARCH IN CONSERVATION TECHNOLOGY

The application of technology to the conservation treatment of library materials, especially to their mass treatment, has been the most exciting and promising response to the preservation challenge facing libraries. Mass preservation "treatment" in the form of environmental control has been in the thinking of conservators and librarians since Gordon Williams' landmark study for the Association of Research Libraries (ARL) in 1964.[8] The disastrous flood in Florence, Italy, in November 1966 forced conservators, accustomed to the extensive treatment of single items of great value, to consider the application of traditional techniques to masses of material in need of immediate treatment.[9] It was just one step further to contemplate the treatment needs of whole collections of deteriorating single items.

The alliance of book conservators and their professional counterparts in the museum world[10] has been a major influence on the development of conservation techniques. Aided by the conservation scientist, a cross fertilization of techniques has resulted in the application of new technology to conservation procedures for library materials.

The recent development of conservation techniques has emphasized both the development of technology for the mass treatment of materials and the improvement and streamlining of single-item treatment procedures. Without compromising the quality of treatment, mass treatment is a solution to the extremely high per-item cost of treatment by traditional methods. Likewise, the scale of the conservation problem has encouraged a reevaluation of priorities for single-item treatment, and a philosophy has emerged that stresses protection and stabilization over extensive restoration or refabrication.[11]

FREEZING AND VACUUM DRYING OF WATER-DAMAGED MATERIALS

The experience of book and paper conservators assisting in salvage and restoration activities following the 1966 Florence flood emphasized the inadequacy of conventional methods for salvaging large numbers of water-damaged books and manuscripts.[12] Air drying and interleaving were not only extremely time-consuming operations, but they did little to prevent cockling of paper, blocking of coated papers, warping of book covers and distortion of book spines. Additionally, rampant mold and mildew growth was associated with slow drying methods.

In the early 1970s, following disasters involving the St. Louis Military Records Center and the Temple University Law Library, it was demonstrated that wetted books and documents could be successfully and efficiently dried and sterilized in large vacuum chambers.[13] Since then, and with the lamentable assistance of frequent library disasters, freezing and vacuum drying techniques have steadily improved[14] and a cadre of conservators and consultants with experience in salvaging materials now exists. (See Chapter IV.)

The challenge associated with a successful salvage operation is to act quickly, yet methodically. Libraries of every size should have individual disaster preparedness plans so that they will be able to respond quickly and appropriately. When large quantities of library materials have been wetted—by flood, burst pipe, sprinkler system or fire-fighting hoses—they must be removed quickly and frozen within 48 hours to avoid mold growth; they must also be handled carefully to avoid further damage. Quick freezing at -20°F produces the smallest possible ice crystals, prevents "blocking" or sticking of coated papers and stabilizes the condition of wet materials, with respect to both mold growth and warping and cockling.[15] Frozen materials can then be dried in vacuum chambers. These chambers, which are usually associated with scientific research, food processing and aerospace industries, have been made available by General Electric's Valley Forge (PA) Space Center, McDonnell Douglas Corp.'s McDonnell Aircraft Co. in St. Louis (MO), and Lockheed's STARS Space Simulation Chamber in Sunnyvale (CA), among others.

During vacuum drying, frozen water passes from a solid state directly to a gaseous state. This sublimation process helps prevent cockling and blocking and is critical to successful salvage. To speed the drying process, heat is often applied to the materials, usually by direct contact with a heated panel on the shelving. A condensing panel is used to collect water vapor evaporating from the frozen materials. Temperature sensors inserted into the center of materials monitor the drying process. A fumigation cycle using ethylene oxide may be called for in cases where extensive mold growth began before materials were frozen. A drying cycle in a chamber holding 5000 items requires approximately three days. Some very large or very dense materials must be dried in a second cycle, but this is preferable to overdrying the majority of materials.

After freeze drying, materials are *very* dry (2% moisture) and thus brittle and fragile. Before use, they must be allowed to reacclimate, that is, to regain an ideal moisture level of 5-7%. Freeze drying will not restore warped covers or distorted bindings. Materials will be in the same configuration after drying as before freezing. The length of time materials remain wet before being frozen will relate directly to the amount of damage. Using a large vacuum chamber allows many books to be treated in one four-day cycle; however, many people are still needed to unpack frozen books and shelve them in the chamber by size, to check individual items for dryness after the cycle is complete and to repack dried materials for transport to a holding area. After drying, many materials will also require restoration by traditional methods such as surface cleaning, hand sewing and recasing.

DEACIDIFICATION

Both basic and applied research relating to the deacidification of paper have been undertaken steadily since the mid-1940s.[16] The technique of aqueous deacidification (i.e., using water-based solutions) was first developed by William J. Barrow as a method of arresting chemical deterioration by neutralizing acids that were present in the paper either from its manufacture or from absorption from adjacent acid materials or polluted environments. The strength of the deacidification solution and the specific agent used determine the percentage of alkaline buffering left in the paper to protect against future acid attack. Aqueous deacidification methods continue to be used by conservators to treat many paper artifacts and the text blocks of rare books. Aqueous deacidification is a labor-intensive procedure requiring continuous skilled supervision. Most conservators recommend a prior step of washing to remove soluble dirt and products of acid degradation. When aqueous deacidification is indicated for bound volumes, they must be disbound and the sheets treated flat.

Research into aqueous deacidification as a conservation technique has concentrated on the long-term effects on the physical and chemical qualities of paper and on devising improved procedures for handling and processing materials. The seemingly simple technique of washing sheets of paper in an alkaline bath has actually raised a number of important issues. The penetration of alkaline compounds into deacidified paper was reported on by Kelly and Fowler of the Library of Congress (LC).[17] The effect of "overpure" (distilled or deionized) water on the aging properties of paper was explored by Tang and Jones of LC,[18] and an article by Hey discussed the wash water issue, as well as other factors influencing the success of aqueous deacidification.[19] Wilson et al. of the Preservation Services Laboratory of the National Archives and Records Service (NARS) published a detailed report in 1979 on the preparation of deacidification solutions.[20] Further research on the preparation of deacidification solutions was conducted for the Illinois State Archives by Richard D. Smith of Wei T'o Associates, Inc. He developed a system to prepare solutions in a pressure tank—minimizing the problems of variable solution strength and partial insolubility of basic magnesium hydroxide powder.[21]

Conservation facilities engaged in large-scale aqueous deacidification operations have, of necessity, devised techniques for streamlining procedures. Espinoza of the Conservation Office at LC reported in detail the sequence of operations for wet processing of book leaves standardized at LC for the Book and Paper Speciality Group at the 1981 annual meeting of the American Institute for Conservation.[22] At the same meeting, William Minter, a private book conservator, described his process for wet processing text blocks by immersing suspended signatures into a deep tank for washing and deacidification.[23]

Nonaqueous Methods

Both liquid and gaseous nonaqueous deacidification methods have been explored since the 1960s.[24] These methods have been applied in situations where aqueous methods are unacceptable because of the fragility of the paper support or the solubility of inks and colors in water. Nonaqueous methods appear most adaptable to the treatment of large quantities of materials at one time or to mass deacidification.

Of the three mass deacidification methods currently being tested, two—using either diethyl zinc vapor or a magnesium alkoxide as a liquified gas—hold promise for practical application. (The third, the morpholine vapor phase method developed at the Barrow Research Laboratory and tested for two years at the Virginia State Library,[25] has been reported to be unsatisfactory because there is no buffer left in the paper to guard against future acid attack.[26])

The liquified gas mass deacidification and buffering process using a magnesium alkoxide as the deacidification agent was developed by Smith of Wei T'o Associates, Inc. and tested in a pilot plant in Canada.[27] The system is located in the Records Conservation Office which jointly serves the Public Archives of Canada and the National Library. In December 1981, the system became fully operational and can treat 5000 books per week based on a 24 hour-per-day, seven-day-a-week schedule.

In the Wei T'o process, previously vacuum dried materials are loaded into the process chamber and the air is evacuated. Deacidification solution is pumped into the chamber and, following impregnation of the materials with the pressurized solution, excess solution is drained off and returned to the storage tank for reuse. Flash drying recovers additional solvent vapors for reuse, and drying using a vacuum pump removes most of the residual solvent from the materials. The process chamber atmosphere is raised to normal to complete the treatment cycle. Treated materials must be allowed to regain moisture before they can be handled. An adequate alkaline reserve is left in the paper to guard against future acid attack.

Mass deacidification using Wei T'o solvents appears to have both commercial and local applications. Although only the largest libraries or cooperative treatment facilities would be able to afford to set up their own facilities, the process could be made available to many more libraries at a reasonable cost by the commercial sector.

Mass deacidification using diethyl zinc as the deacidification agent was developed in the Preservation Research and Testing Laboratory at the Library of Congress.[28] The process has been successfully tested in large scale runs using facilities at the General Electric Space Center and more recently at the NASA Goddard Space Flight Center in Greenbelt, MD. Because diethyl zinc is pyrophoric, exploding on contact with air, it must be shipped in a 50/50 mixture with mineral oil, separated from the mineral oil before use, and used in a zero-leak-rate vacuum chamber.

During preparation for deacidification, materials are loaded loosely into the chamber, warmed to 45°C to speed drying, and dried completely by evacuation of the chamber. Liquid diethyl zinc (approximately 3% of the weight of the material to be treated) is introduced into the chamber, where it volatilizes completely and deacidifies materials over a three-to-four day period. After removal of excess diethyl zinc, moist carbon dioxide is added to the chamber to hydrolize ethyl zinc carbonate deposited in the paper to a 2% zinc carbonate alkaline reserve. The entire cycle lasts eight days. After further testing and the construction of a pilot plant to treat materials in federal repositories, LC hopes to encourage a commercial concern to build plants and offer deacidification services to libraries around the country.

Practical Issues

The two mass deacidification processes described above have been shown to be viable; their commercial and practical application for libraries, however, remains to be demonstrated. Deacidification is a conservation technique best applied to combat *future* deterioration of book stock that is acidic but not yet embrittled or weakened by acid degradation of the cellulose fibers; it does not restore lost strength or flexibility to paper. At approximately $5 per item plus the costs of transportation and record keeping, it is still considerably less expensive than microfilming, but deacidified books can not be inexpensively duplicated for distribution to other libraries with deteriorating copies.

Perhaps the most important issue for libraries contemplating mass deacidification is an exploration of the decision-making process that must precede incorporation of the procedure into comprehensive preservation programs. The Public Archives/National Library of Canada is concentrating on Canadiana first, while the Library of Congress will institute a program to deacidify books with acid paper as they are acquired.

COLD STORAGE OF COLOR PHOTOGRAPHIC MATERIALS

Many large collections of color photographic materials, such as collections held by the American Film Institute, Eastman Kodak Co., the Library of Congress, the Museum of Modern Art and Walt Disney Productions, are now being stored in low-temperature vaults to combat rampant dye fading and degradation of the film base and emulsion.[29] Color motion picture film and color transparencies are prepared for long-term storage by sealing in air-tight containers or bags following cooling in a staging area. The purpose of the staging procedure is to minimize dimensional stress by an intermediate step of cooling and drying.

Low-temperature storage is presently the only practical solution to color film preservation, although it may be financially feasible in the future to digitize three-color separations (see below). Even if a technical solution for color fading was available, economics would preclude large-scale conversion of all the color materials of permanent historic and research interest. Low-temperature storage is an interim "solution" until such time as a permanent color process is practically available and widely used.

The application of low-temperature storage, while considered necessary to meet the immediate and irreversible problem of color fading, is still an uncertain technique. The design and operation of cold vaults have been thwarted by a lack of data on the effects of storage at specific temperatures and relative humidities and a lack of communication among curators, architects, refrigeration engineers, contractors and maintenance people. Most important, there are no recognized standards for cold storage temperatures and humidities used vary from 0° to 50°F and from 20% to 52% RH. More raw data and real-time aging experience are needed to develop standards and evaluate the preservation effects of cold storage.

There are other issues to consider by those planning, managing and servicing cold storage vaults. Should cold storage be "dead" storage with service copies made for all materials? What are the preservation implications when materials are repeatedly removed from cold storage and used? Do originals need to be retained for their artifactual value, or should archivists and librarians concentrate on encouraging the development of improved technology to preserve the intellectual content of color photographic materials?

Optical Disk Technology

The application of optical disks in libraries will undoubtedly revolutionize systems for information production, storage, access, distribution and preservation.[30] Information from printed, graphic and photographic materials is optically scanned and recorded by laser beam, which produces pits or holes in the sensitive surface of an optical disk. The surface is "read" by reflection of light and displayed on high-resolution screens or printed in facsimile. The disk is manufactured with a protective coating, sealing or encasement, making the surface impervious to dust, chemical agents and oxidation.

Unlike analog systems of reproduction such as microfilm, where each subsequent generation suffers a loss of image resolution and tone quality, optical disks produce a virtual facsimile every time and "forever." The image information is encoded in digital format and thus is not subject to degradation. The archival quality of the digital storage medium, while important, is not critical to preservation because the image quality can be monitored electronically and the code transferred repeatedly without loss of information should the original disk begin to degrade. Further, by manipulation of the digital code, enhancement of degraded images is possible.[31]

Although the technology for optical *digital* storage of information exists, its practical application and cost efficiency in libraries have yet to be demonstrated. However, use of the more conventional optical *video* disks to store nonprint media and motion picture films (an offshoot of the home video entertainment market) has been researched in pilot projects in museums and libraries.[32] Despite the fact that the archival qualities of the medium are not well known, they are known to be better than motion picture film. Video disks enhance the accessibility of photographic materials when originals must be kept in cold storage for preservation purposes. Although the initial production cost of a video disk is from $2500 to $4000, the cost of disk duplication is only about $10. Commercial applications are already available.

The Library of Congress, through its Cataloging and Distribution Service, is using optical disk technology for storage and demand publication of catalog cards. The DEMAND system digitizes graphic (in some cases handwritten) information from catalog cards for storage on optical disk. A modified Xerox laser printer produces cards on demand. Through use of a multiple grey level digital scan, images on damaged or deteriorated cards are routinely enhanced. Beginning in 1983, an optical disk preservation project at LC will explore the use of optical *digital* disks for recording, storing and retrieving complex graphic and printed material, half-tones and color reproductions. A concurrent project will test an optical *video* disk system for storage of nonprint media and films.

The technology of optical disk is expanding rapidly, and manufacturers are developing systems for a variety of applications in science, business and libraries.[33] Not unlike the evolution of sound recording, optical disk technology is going through an intensive period of development and competition, and a standard format and recording material has yet to emerge.[34] An acceptable and even exceptional resolution and reproduction quality will also be necessary for widespread acceptance of the medium.

Other challenges confront application of optical disks to libraries, including cost and integration with existing systems. Not least of all, the political, financial and legal implications of information sharing and transfer will have to be addressed. However, the capabilities of the optical disk for image storage and preservation are almost limitless. The system could incorporate retrospective preservation microfilming efforts as well as provide an alternative to the archival, labor-intensive and qualitative problems of microfilm.[35] Finally, the possibility of immediate access to facsimile versions of originals through interactive computer data bases may revolutionize the direction and priorities of library preservation.

PHASED PRESERVATION

The concept of phased preservation, developed since 1971 by the Preservation Office at LC,[36] is a planned approach to deterioration that organizes treatment into stages, or phases, as a method of dealing with the masses of materials in need of sophisticated conservation treatment. Such a system allows LC to concentrate resources for extensive treatment on materials that are being used, while buying time for masses of lesser-used materials and for exploring technology that may result in more economical and improved techniques in the future. The phased program is based on the premises that (1) rapid deterioration of the collections occurred *before* the institution of environmental controls and has progressed very slowly and (2) further physical deterioration can be effectively eliminated by providing protection through reduction of handling and proper storage enclosures.

Phased preservation is an economical method of providing long-term protection that is essential for large collections. When masses of materials are treated in a like fashion, streamlining of procedures is possible. Examples of first-phase treatment are the production of high-quality service copies to reduce handling of unique scrapbooks and photograph albums, removal of damaging pressure-sensitive tape, polyester film encapsulation of embrittled and weakened flat paper materials, and the construction of protective boxes for vulnerable and fragile bindings. During this phase, additional needs can be recorded, perhaps in machine-readable format, so that items in need of similar treatment can be retrieved en masse in the future.

The institution of a system of phased preservation allows libraries to stabilize the condition of collections and to conduct treatment based on priorities. Phased preservation also allows libraries to solve the housekeeping problems caused by deterioration, while systematically planning for selection of materials with artifactual value for restoration and designation of other materials for transfer to another format. The realities of scarce preservation and conservation dollars make a phased approach a viable and practical method of controlling the deterioration of large collections containing many infrequently used, but historically important, materials.

POLYESTER FILM ENCAPSULATION

The technique of polyester film encapsulation was developed in the Preservation Office at LC in the early 1970s as an alternative to cellulose acetate lamination.[37] Fragile flat paper documents are provided with physical support by encapsulation in a sandwich of clear, inert polyester film. The sandwich is held together at the edges with double-sided tape. No adhesive touches the document, which is held in place by static electricity. Unlike lamination, no heat or pressure is applied, and the process is immediately and completely reversible.[38] Very large maps and posters as well as ordinary-sized documents are routinely encapsulated in both modest and sophisticated conservation facilities around the country. Encapsulation has also been used in the construction of post-bindings, such as the binding of encapsulated leaves of a scrapbook or individual brittle pages of a book or periodical.

Encapsulation is a widely applied simple conservation technique requiring only inexpensive materials and tools. However, the use of double-sided tape is both time-consuming and aesthetically unappealing. Two machines have recently been developed that join the polyester film envelope without tape. The machines use two different methods and have different advantages depending on the application. Because the machines are expensive, they are more likely to be purchased by larger institutions or cooperative treatment facilities.

Private conservator William Minter, in cooperation with engineer Peter Malosh, developed a method of welding polyester film using ultrasound. (See Chapter VII.) The ultrasound system has a special generator that changes standard 115 volt AC current at 60 cycles per second to 40,000 cycles per second. The electrical impulse is converted to mechanical vibration and the polyester film is welded together by friction. The weld produced is small and smooth and allows flexibility in positioning the document within an envelope. Conservation Resources International, Inc., a commercial supplier of conservation materials and services, developed the Model B50 Polyweld sealing machine that heat fuses the outer edges of a polyester film envelope. The machine can seal 100 inches per 3.5 second cycle and is particularly well-suited to the mass production of uniform-sized envelopes.[39]

LIMP VELLUM AND PAPER CASED BINDINGS

The need to replace deteriorated rebindings with historically sympathetic, permanent and durable book structures prompted the exploration and development of limp vellum and paper cased bindings. These experimental book structures borrowed features from early limp bindings of the 16th and 17th centuries. Book conservators involved in restoration activities after the Florence flood observed that early limp bindings survived the disaster in better condition than did rigid board bound leather volumes.[40] Other conservators noted that limp bindings had stood the test of time and provided simple, yet appropriate, protection of the text block of ordinary-sized books.[41]

Book conservators experimenting with limp structures improved on the historical models and placed the technique in the context of contemporary conservation theory. Standards evolved that specify the quality of materials (such as handmade paper and stable polyvinyl acetate adhesives), flexible sewing techniques (such as a concertina guard to protect the back of the signatures and bandless sewing), and efficient construction of the cover. Variations on the theme of limp binding are applied when appropriate for an individual item or category of materials.[42] The limp binding conservation technique is sophisticated in its simplicity because it combines the best that is known about sound binding structures with a quick and inexpensive procedure for applying conservation and restoration techniques.

MINI FREEZE DRYING

A 1981 grant from the Andrew W. Mellon Foundation to the Newberry Library in Chicago allowed Richard D. Smith to explore modification of a commercial refrigeration unit to salvage water-damaged library materials and to treat mold and insect-infested library materials.[43] Although the scope of some water disasters may warrant the use of enormous vacuum chambers, most disasters are small, involving dozens of books rather than thousands. The common disasters of a burst pipe, leaky roof or dripping air conditioner may affect only one or two shelf ranges of materials; in such cases, use of a large vacuum drying chamber is impractical and air drying is unsatisfactory. A modified refrigeration unit can be used to dry and disinfect small quantities of materials. The technique has some advantages over vacuum drying because it allows items to be dried slowly under observation and because the conservator can manipulate the materials during drying (e.g., to straighten cover boards) thereby reducing the amount of restoration work needed after salvage.

Over time, almost every library will experience a small-scale disaster involving water damage. Not every library will be able to purchase a refrigeration unit for salvage purposes, but the larger conservation facilities and certainly the regional conservation treatment centers could own units and operate them for the benefit of other libraries. A modified refrigeration unit with extra controls would cost under $15,000. The unit requires a one-month cycle to dry materials and a three-day cycle for disinfestation. Operation of the unit for one month would cost under $50.

QUANTIFICATION STUDIES AND PRESERVATION MANAGEMENT

Without a realistic assessment of the scope of the preservation problem, libraries are unable to plan effectively for the immediate and future preservation needs of their collections. Quantification studies provide insight into the cause and extent of deterioration and serve as an essential management tool both for planning purposes and, more critically, as justification for preservation funding.[44] Although most condition surveys have focused on books, the principles apply equally to other types of materials.

Practically speaking, only the wealthiest institutions will be able to address adequately even a quantified preservation problem through aggressive programs of duplication, reformatting, conservation and restoration of deteriorating collections. However, quantification studies can lead to cooperative projects among libraries to reduce the cost of preservation and avoid duplication of efforts. Cooperative projects are appropriate to the magnitude of the problem and the reality of scarce funding. Studies can help libraries determine where the problems lie in terms of collection location, date and place of publication, and subject areas. They can also help define ancillary problems such as acid pH and percentage of items having disfunctional bindings. The assessment of "brittleness" is the most immediately critical consideration since brittle books cannot be subjected to ordinary use without sustaining permanent damage and possible loss of information.

The following examples illustrate recent quantification studies.

University of California Libraries

In 1977 a survey was conducted of monographs in the circulating collections of the University of California (UC) libraries to determine physical and chemical qualities relating to strength and usability of book papers.[45] A random sample selection, drawn in 1974 from catalogs of each general library collection in the UC system, was later used for the survey. The entire monograph collection in 1974 was estimated at over 6 million volumes systemwide. A total sample size of 2280 was used for the survey.

Paper samples removed from each monograph in the survey were subjected to tests for folding endurance, tear resistance, pH and groundwood content. Testing methodology conformed to standards published by the Technical Association of the Pulp and Paper Industry (TAPPI). Results of the study were compared and contrasted to earlier quantitative studies conducted by the Barrow Research Laboratory in Richmond, VA.

Tests of folding endurance and tear resistance relate directly to the strength of paper—its ability to be used and rebound. In the UC study, 28% of the paper samples tested scored in the Barrow categories of weak or unusable on one or both tests. A test of pH is indicative of the future degradation and embrittlement of book paper, and 86% of the samples tested at a pH of 6.0 or less. Based on the study results, the conclusion was drawn that "monographs published between 1850 and 1944 should be the target group for any preservation program for the monograph collection." Additionally, it was estimated that "as many as 479,000 volumes in the UC collection in 1974 were in the Barrow categories of weak or unusable strength and were of high or very high acidity."

The survey of the UC collection resulted in an overall view of the condition of circulating monographs. Test results did not allow a prediction of which specific books were in need of preservation, but the survey technique was shown to be a useful and accurate tool for quantification of deterioration in individual collections.

Green Library, Stanford University

In 1979 a survey was conducted in the Green Library stacks (1.5 million volumes in the humanities and social studies research collections) to determine the percentage of deterioration of the collection based on accurate qualitative measurements.[46] Survey results have been used at Stanford to justify funding for the Brittle Books Program. The survey did not attempt to identify individual books nor to determine the cause of deterioration.

The survey was conducted by analyzing the condition of a random sample of 400 bound books in the collection. The sample size was based on a formula in an article by M. Carl Drott.[47] A computer program was used to generate random numbers to select level, range, section, shelf and book. The program automatically eliminated ranges and sections that might not hold books. Deterioration was measured for each sample by grading three categories—paper condition, binding condition and board and cover condition. The category of paper condition was weighted to reflect the more serious implications of paper deterioration. Each category was assigned three grades of condition, and the final score for overall deterioration of each sample was based on the grades assigned to each category. The percentage of deterioration for the whole collection was determined based on the scores established for all books in the survey.

A total of 195 hours was required to conduct the survey, including planning, supervision, pretest, survey and data compilation. To ensure consistency and accuracy, specific guidelines were written to help the survey team recognize each grade, and the survey team participated in a training workshop and pretest.

Data obtained in the Stanford survey indicated that of the 400 titles chosen by random sample from the humanities stack collections, 32.8% were in good condition, 40.8% were in moderate condition and 26.5% were in poor condition. The significance of the Stanford library survey (besides the obvious application to preservation planning in that institution) is the possibility for comparison surveys conducted in other libraries. Data generated by such a survey can be used by a library to plan and budget for the preservation of the intellectual content of deteriorating materials.

Sterling Memorial Library, Yale University

A sophisticated survey in the Sterling stacks was conducted beginning in 1980 to quantify book characteristics and to study possible causes of book deterioration.[48] The survey was carried out under the direction of the conservation and preservation departments by interns in training at Yale. The survey and training project was funded by a three-year grant from the National Endowment for Humanities (NEH).

The interns examined 18,340 items based on random number lists generated by a computer program. A series of 14 questions was answered for each volume. Several questions concerned book characteristics such as country and date of publication, the type of primary protection (type of binding, protective box or other support), covering material and method of page attachment (type of sewing or adhesive binding). Other questions were related to the condition of the paper (pH and folding endurance) and binding (condition of inner hinge, protection of text, broken text block). Final questions considered evidence of mutilation (underlining, marginalia, pressure-sensitive tape, stains), environmental damage (fading, mold or insect damage, water stains) and need for structural repair. Data were recorded by two-person teams on standard IBM machine-readable answer sheets. The survey was developed to give an accuracy of 3% and is applicable to the entire Sterling collection.

Preliminary manipulation of the data showed that 86% of all books examined had a pH *lower* than 5.4. The test of folding endurance showed that 45% of the sample broke off after two double folds of the corner of an inner page. Over 10% of the books examined had broken or missing bindings and over 15% were in need of immediate repair. There were 12% bound in highly acidic pamphlet binders that compromise preservation and should be replaced.

The value of the Sterling survey was in its comprehensive approach, large sample size and the fact that it was conducted by carefully trained conservation and preservation interns. Further manipulation of the data to compare some categories and merge others and to generate information relating to date and place of publication is planned.

American Theological Library Association

A survey concluded in 1980 established a realistic estimate of the number of religous monographs published in two time periods: 1800-1899 and 1860-1929.[49] The latter period includes items suspected to be in an advanced state of paper deterioration and embrittlement. The purpose of the survey was to arrive at a cooperative plan for preserving the intellectual content of theological monographs through microfilming and duplication.

The survey was conducted under the auspices of the American Theological Library Association with the cooperation of 82 member libraries. A multiple-part sampling methodology was used to estimate collection sizes for the two time periods in each separate library. From 40 to 100 hours were required to conduct the survey per library. The survey estimated that 998,000 monographic titles are held by the 82 participating libraries for the time period 1860-1929. The number of *unique* titles published between 1860 and 1929 was estimated at 218,000.

A second stage of the survey determined how many libraries would be required to provide 100% of the total titles targeted for preservation. From a preservation standpoint it was encouraging to find that significant percentages of the titles were held by relatively few libraries. One library would be needed to supply 60% of the titles, four libraries would supply 80%, 15 libraries would supply 95% and 39 libraries would supply 100%. Of course, some unique titles would be found in every library. A check of microforms available for the sample titles indicated that 13.3% of the titles had already been filmed.

The Association is presently exploring the possibility of a coordinated preservation microfilming project. The project would serve as a model for cooperative filming projects for other subject fields.

FUTURE NEEDS

Much has been accomplished by the application of science and technology to defining and solving preservation and conservation problems. However, more research is critically needed.[50] Basic research into the mechanisms of deterioration is still needed, especially for library materials other than paper and for new record materials. Until all the factors affecting deterioration and preservation are clearly understood, the development of preventive measures and conservation techniques will be hampered.

Libraries need simple and reliable testing methods for determining the composition of materials and predicting longevity, as well as quick diagnostic tests that can be conducted by a conservator to aid in treatment decision making and documentation. Perhaps most urgently needed, however, is research to establish the relative importance of different causes of deterioration and to determine the effect of altering the storage environment on the *rate* of deterioration. This knowledge could lead to a formula for relating dollars spent (on improving environmental conditions) to dollars saved (for the cost of replacement, reformatting and repair or restoration). The statistics and hard facts generated would be persuasive tools to justify preservation program funding to administrators.[51]

Preservation Management

Research into the management aspects of preservation will help libraries plan and execute efficient preservation programs. Management tools such as quantification studies to measure the deterioration of specific collections are a step in the right direction; however, more specific applications that can be directly related to a library's mission and budget are urgently needed. The cost analysis of specific preservation methods (such as microfilming and phase preservation) and conservation techniques (such as mass deacidification and rebinding) *combined* with quantification studies can give libraries the information they need to set their preservation course realistically.

A study being conducted by NARS to determine the costs associated with microfilming documents and providing archival storage for them is an example of the kind of costs research needed. The Policy and Research Committee of the Preservation of Library Materials Section (PLMS) of the American Library Association (ALA) is currently gathering data on the costs of specific conservation techniques to see if comparisons can be made among institutions or if costs are so tied to local conditions that other methods of analysis are necessary. The recent institution of a "point system" for allocating the efforts of conservators in the Preservation Office at LC is an example of the kind of in-house planning tool that will increase the effectiveness of a preservation program. At LC, each division in Research Services is assigned an annual point budget, and the selection of materials to be treated is made by the division based on estimates submitted by conservators for a large number of items. The system allows the division to make informed decisions based on priorities and focuses the efforts of the conservation staff.[52]

Research and Evaluation

Basic research to investigate and develop new record materials and methods such as optical disk may revolutionize preservation, but careful evaluation of new technologies and materials is also necessary if libraries are to avoid the same disturbing realities in the next century that they have faced in this century—the inherent impermanence of paper, leather, film and color photographic materials. Continual reevaluation of preservation and conservation methods and practices will also help libraries avoid unpleasant surprises. A multipart study is currently being conducted at NARS to reassess microfilming as a preservation technique; in addition to studying costs, study teams are examining the durability of polyester as a film base, inspecting a representative sample of the microform holdings for deterioration and investigating alternative methods of copying.[53]

An enormous number of research subjects could be addressed that would lead to improved methods of preservation. *Library Technology Reports,* a publication of ALA, has commissioned a consulting engineering firm to prepare a feasibility report on a device that would modify an ordinary photocopy machine for face-up copying. Research and development is also needed in areas such as rebinding books that are of permanent research value but not yet considered "rare," the application of computer programming to environmental control systems, the development of polyvinyl acetate adhesives that will bond permanently to coated paper stock and a mass method of strengthening brittle paper.

Communication

An important aspect of basic and applied research is *communication:* of research priorities to the scientific community by librarians and conservators, and among scientists involved in similar research projects. Publication of the results of research in an easily understood form (so that conservators, librarians and engineers can make use of the knowledge) is also critical. The ninth International Congress of the International Institute for Conservation of Historic and Artistic Works met in Washington in September 1982 with the theme "Science and Technology in the Service of Conservation." Papers focused on the dialogue between conservator and scientist, covering areas such as the application of new methods and materials, the scientific evaluation of existing practices and the formulation of unsolved problems in scientific terms.

As further indication of the importance of science and technology to conservation, the National Conservation Advisory Council (after nine years of planning) has published a *Proposal for a National Institute for Conservation of Cultural Property* .[54] The proposed Scientific Research and Development Division would conduct long-term research; encourage, coordinate and contract for research at established laboratories around the country; provide testing and analytical services; communicate technical information to the conservation community; and publish the results of research.

Standards

An oft-stated need in library preservation is for the development of standards—for storage environments, record materials, and conservation supplies and treatments. The development of standards usually follows basic research and requires the consensus of a cross section of experts and special interest groups. For example, elucidation of the causes of deterioration together with knowledge about how aspects of environmental control affect deterioration is a prerequisite to the development of standards for environmental control. Further, no one scientist will be an expert on all the environmental factors affecting deterioration and preservation, nor will the same standard be appropriate for all types of library materials or all types of libraries.

As a start in the right direction, the American National Standards Institute (ANSI) Committee Z39 has appointed a subcommittee to draft a standard for "environmental conditions for storage of paper-based library materials." ANSI standards already exist for the storage of microforms (see Chapter III). Professional associations such as the ALA/PLMS, the American Institute for Conservation (AIC) and the Guild of Book Workers (GW) are all actively addressing the topic of standards.

Written standards for record materials will make the task of preservation simpler for future generations; significant progress has already been made for paper and microforms. The ANSI PH5 committee has issued a number of standards for microforms. Specifications for permanent/durable book paper were developed by W.J. Barrow and restated in 1975 by the Barrow Research Laboratory, Inc.[55] The Council on Library Resources Committee on Production Guidelines for Book Longevity in 1981 issued an *Interim Report on Book Paper*[56] that included guidelines for paper to be used in books. In 1982, the committee also reported on publishers' bindings issuing a *Preliminary Report on Longevity in Book Binding*.[57] Organizations such as the National Historical Publications and Records Commission (NHPRC), ALA and the Library of Congress encourage the use of permanent/durable record materials. An ANSI subcommittee, "Permanent Paper for Library Materials," is in the process of drafting a standard which we hope will have an impact on publishers. Standards for conservation supplies and materials (such as adhesives and book board) and for conservation treatments (such as library binding and the percentage of alkaline reserve left in paper after deacidification) do not exist except in the practice of individual conservators or institutions.

With funding for preservation research scarce, careful planning, coordination of priorities and creative use of existing resources are paramount. Librarians, conservators, curators and scientists must continue to campaign for the funding needed to carry out vital research and development projects. Cooperation and progress in areas such as the development of standards and managerial tools will enable libraries to make intelligent use of conservation technology.

FOOTNOTES

1. Robert M. Organ, "Science for the Conservator and the Curator," *Journal of the American Institute for Conservation* 20 (1981):41-44.

2. National Conservation Advisory Council, *Report of the Study Committee on Scientific Support* (Washington,DC: National Conservation Advisory Council, 1979).

3. Verner W. Clapp, *Story of Permanent/Durable Book Paper 1115-1970.*(Copenhagen: Restaurator Press, 1972).

4. Randolph W. Church, *The Manufacture and Testing of Durable Book Papers, Based on the Investigations of W.J. Barrow* (Richmond, VA: Virginia State Library, 1960), p.31.

5. John C. Williams, ed., *Preservation of Paper and Textiles of Historic and Artistic Value, Volume I* and *Volume II* (Washington, DC: American Chemical Society, 1977; 1981) (Advances in Chemistry Series 164 and 193).

6. Wilson and Parks, "Comparison of Accelerated Aging of Book Papers in 1937 with 36 Years Natural Aging," pp. 46-48.

7. G. David Mendenhall, "What Light from Books Can Tell Us," *Library Scene* 9 (3) (September 1980):18-19.

8. Gordon R. Williams, *The Preservation of Deteriorating Books: An Examination of the Problem with Recommendations for a Solution* (Washington, DC: Association of Research Libraries, 1964). Reprinted in revised form in *Library Journal* 91 (January 1 and 15, 1966):51-56;189-94.

9. Sherelyn Ogden, "The Impact of the Florence Flood on Library Conservation in the United States of America: A Study of the Literature Published 1956-1976." *Restaurator* 3 (1-2)(1979):7-11.

10. Paul N. Banks, "The Scientist, the Scholar and the Book Conservator: Some Thoughts on Book Conservation as a Profession," *Atti Della XLIX Riunione della S.I. P.S.,* Siena, 23-27 Settembre, 1967 (September 1967):1213-1219.

11. Christopher Clarkson, "The Conservation of Early Books in Codex Form: A Personal Approach," *The Paper Conservator* 3 (1978):33-50.

12. Ogden, "The Impact of the Florence Flood on Library Conservation in the United States of America: A Study of the Literature Published 1956-1976," p. 20.

13. Martin G. Koesterer and John A. Geating, "Application and Utilization of a Space Chamber for the Drying of Books, Documents and Other Materials and Their Decontamination to Prevent Biodeterioration," *Journal of Environmental Sciences* 19 (5) (September/October 1976):29-33.

14. James N. Meyers and Denise D. Bedford, eds., *Disasters: Prevention and Coping* (Stanford, CA: Stanford University Libraries, 1981).

15. Peter Waters, *Procedures for Salvage of Water-Damaged Library Materials* (Washington, DC: Library of Congress, 1975), p.5.

16. William J. Barrow, *Manuscripts and Documents: their Deterioration and Restoration* (Charlottesville, VA: University Press of Virginia, second edition, 1972), pp.45-49.

17. George B. Kelly and Stanley Fowler, "Penetration and Placement of Alkaline Compounds in Solution-Deacidified Paper," *Journal of the American Institute for Conservation* 17 (1978):33-43.

18. Lucia C. Tang and Norvell M.M. Jones, "The Effects of Wash Water Quality on the Aging Characteristics of Paper," *Journal of the American Institute for Conservation* 18 (1979):61-81.

19. Margaret Hey, "The Washing and Aqueous Deacidification of Paper," *The Paper Conservator* 4 (1979):66-80.

20. William K. Wilson et al., *Preparation of Solutions of Magnesium Bicarbonate for Deacidification of Documents* (Washington,DC: National Archives and Records Service, 1979).

21. Richard D. Smith, "Operation Manual: Wei T'o Magnesium Bicarbonate Aqueous Deacidification Solution Preparation System," Illinois, Office of the Secretary of State, Archives and Records Department. Identification No. PC-61782, September 15, 1981.

22. Robert Espinoza, "Aqueous Treatment of Text-Blocks," *Proceedings of the Book and Paper Speciality Group, American Institute for Conservation 9th Annual Meeting* (Dayton, OH: Cassette Recording Co., 1981). Tape cassette.

23. William Minter, "Washing and Deacidification of Book Leaves: A New Approach," *Proceedings of the Book and Paper Speciality Group, American Institute for Conservation 9th Annual Meeting* (Dayton, OH: Cassette Recording Co., 1981). Tape cassette.

24. Richard D. Smith, "Paper Deacidification: A Preliminary Report," *Library Quarterly* 36 (October 1966):273-292.

25. Williams, *Preservation of Paper and Textiles of Historic and Artistic Value, Volume I,* pp.72-87.

26. Carolyn Harris, "Preservation of Paper-Based Materials: Deacidification Methods and Projects," Paper presented at the Twenty-Seventh Annual Allerton Park Institute "Conserving and Preserving Library Materials," November 15-18, 1981. Sponsored by the Graduate School of Library and Information Science, University of Illinois, Urbana, IL.

27. Richard D. Smith, "Progress in Mass Deacidification at the Public Archives," *Canadian Library Journal* 36 (6) (December 1979):325-334.

28. George B. Kelly, "Mass Deacidification with Diethyl Zinc," *Library Scene* 9 (3) (September 1980):6-7.

29. Lawrence F. Karr, ed., *Proceedings: Conference on the Cold Storage of Motion Picture Films* (Washington, DC: American Film Institute, August 1980).

30. Allen B. Veaner, "Permanence: A View from and to the Long Range," *Microform Review* 8 (2) (Spring 1979):75-77.

31. T. M. Cannon and B. R. Hunt, "Image Processing by Computer," *Scientific American* 245 (4) (October 1981):214-225.

32. Janice Sorkow, "Video and Optical Digital Disk Technology and Programs," Paper presented at the First Annual Preservation of Library Materials Conference, Philadelphia, PA, May 13-14, 1981.

33. R. Barrett, *Developments in Optical Disk Technology and the Implications for Information Storage and Retrieval* (Boston Spa, Wetherby, West Yorkshire, England: British Library, 1981) (British Library Research and Development Report No. 5623). Extracted in the *Journal of Micrographics* 15 (1) (January 1982):22-26.

34. Herb Brody, "Materials for Optical Storage: A State-of-the-Art Survey," *Journal of Micrographics* 15 (1) (January 1982):33-37.

35. Gerard O. Walter, "Will Optical Disk Memory Supplant Microfilm?" *Journal of Micrographics* 13 (6) (July/August 1980):29-34.

36. Peter Waters, "Phased Preservation," Paper presented at the Second Annual Preservation of Library Materials Conference, Washington, DC, February 22-23, 1982.

37. Frazer G. Poole, "Current Lamination Policies of the Library of Congress," *American Archivist* 39 (1976):157-159.

38. Library of Congress, Preservation Office, *Polyester Film Encapsulation* (Washington, DC: Library of Congress, 1981).

39. "Polyester Welding Machines," *AIC Newsletter* (American Institute for Conservation of Historic and Artistic Works) 7 (3) (May 1982):10-11.

40. Barbara Giuffrida, "Limp and Semi-Limp Vellum Bindings," *Designer Bookbinders Review* 4 (Autumn 1974):2-7 and (Spring):2-13.

41. Gary Frost, "Limp Paper Cased Binding for Small Printed Books," *Abbey Newsletter* 3 (1) (June 1979):5-6.

42. Linda K. McWilliams, "An Experimental Book Structure for Conservation," In-house document, Preservation Office, Library of Congress, May 1978.

43. Richard D. Smith, personal communication, April 5, 1982.

44. Christinger Tomer, "Identification, Evaluation, and Selection of Books for Preservation," *Collection Management* 3 (1) (Spring 1979):45-54.

45. Richard G. King, Jr, *Deterioration of Book Paper: Results of Physical and Chemical Testing of the Paper in 2280 Monographs in the Collections of the University of California Libraries* (Berkeley, CA: Office of the Assistant Vice President, Library Plans and Policies, November 24, 1981).

46. Sarah Buchanan and Sandra Coleman, "Deterioration Survey of the Stanford University Libraries Green Library Stack Collection," Stanford University Libraries, in-house publication, June 1979.

47. M. Carl Drott, "Random Sampling: A Tool for Library Research," *College and Research Libraries* (March 1969):120-125.

48. Unpublished survey instructions and preliminary results from the Sterling Survey of Book Condition. Yale University Libraries, October 1981.

49. Andrew D. Scrimgeour et al., "Collection Analysis Project, Final Report," Ad Hoc Committee for the Preservation of Theological Materials, American Theological Library Association, June 1981.

50. National Conservation Advisory Council, *Report of the Study Committee on Scientific Support* (Washington, DC: National Conservation Advisory Council, 1979).

51. Pamela W. Darling, "Will Anything Be Left? New Responses to the Preservation Challenge," *Wilson Library Bulletin* 56 (3) (November 1981):179.

52. Waters, "Phased Preservation."

53. "National Archives Reviewing Microfilming Program," *American Archivist* 44 (3) (Summer 1981):258-259.

54. National Conservation Advisory Council, *Proposal for a National Institute for Conservation of Cultural Property* (Washington, DC: National Conservation Advisory Council, April 1982).

55. Bernard F. Walker, "Specifications for Permanent/Durable Book Papers," *American Archivist* 38 (July 1975):405-416.

56. Council on Library Resources, Committee on Production Guidelines for Book Longevity. *Interim Report on Book Paper* (Washington, DC: Council on Library Resources, April 1981). Also published in *Publisher's Weekly* 219 (22) (May 29, 1981):19-22.

57. Council on Library Resources, Committee on Production Guidelines for Book Longevity. *Preliminary Report on Longevity in Book Binding* (Washington, DC: Council on Library Resources, 1982). Also published in *Publisher's Weekly* 222 (1) (July 2, 1982):37-38, 40.

IX

Preservation and Conservation in the Library Profession

The presence of preservation and conservation topics on the agendas of state, regional and national library associations are proof of increased awareness of the preservation challenge facing libraries and of the determination to seek solutions. Significant projects and progress by organizations devoted to preservation and conservation are indicative of increased maturity of the field and its progress beyond calls to action and statements of concern.

Descriptions of associations and organizations, cooperative efforts and educational opportunities that follow illustrate the phenomenal growth and activity of preservation and conservation in the library profession. Appendix 2 lists the addresses of the specific associations, organizations and programs that are mentioned here.

AMERICAN LIBRARY ASSOCIATION

In recent years the focus of the American Library Association's (ALA) concern with preservation has been determined by the activities of the Preservation of Library Materials Section (PLMS) of the Resources and Technical Services Division (RTSD). The section was established following the 1980 annual conference and succeeded the RTSD Preservation of Library Materials Committee, itself the successor of the RTSD Binding Committee. Through its standing committees and Discussion Group, PLMS addresses the preservation problems that all libraries face; encourages educational and research programs; disseminates information about preservation techniques, supplies and programs; and cooperates with groups such as paper manufacturers, publishers and binders, as well as with other organizations interested in preservation.[1]

Cooperation and coordination of activities with the Reproduction of Library Materials and Resources Sections has resulted in a stronger voice for preservation and less duplication of effort. The joint program, "Toward a North American Program of Preservation

Microfilming,'' at the 1981 annual conference created the agenda of the RTSD Preservation Microfilming Committee. Cooperation among the ALA, the American Association of Publishers and PLMS resulted in a cosponsored program on the quality of book paper at the ALA's 1982 annual conference.

PLMS standing committees include Education, Physical Quality of Library Materials, Policy and Research, and Library/Binders Relations. The committees have been active in such projects as publishing the *Preservation Education Directory,* encouraging the publication of standards for conservation materials, gathering information on the costs of conservation treatments and planning for a series of pamphlets on library binding. With PLMS, preservation has an official voice in the library world and the opportunity to attack priority problems identified by the profession. A preconference on library binding is planned for the 1983 annual conference, and a subcommittee of the Education Committee is developing plans for a series of regional workshops to be cosponsored with the Preservation Office of the Library of Congress (LC).

SOCIETY OF AMERICAN ARCHIVISTS

The Society of American Archivists (SAA) is a professional association of archivists, manuscript curators and records managers. From its headquarters in Chicago, SAA administers a variety of programs that address collecting and surveying historical records and their intellectual control, use, security and conservation. SAA is also concerned with professional training and continuing education for archivists. An active publications program includes the SAA's journal, *American Archivist,* a newsletter, the *Basic Manual Series,* directories, glossaries, bibliographies and republication of archival classics. Basic archival workshops on topics such as business archives, photographs, security and management are periodically offered.

The SAA has a history of strong support of conservation. In January 1977 a Conference on Priorities for Historical Records was sponsored by SAA to identify specific funding priorities. Conference participants rated conservation as the top priority for funding. Additional high-ranking priorities included experimentation with mass treatments, establishment of a network of regional conservation centers, a national conservation program and a formal training program for paper conservators.[2]

With funding from the National Endowment for the Humanities (NEH), in 1980 SAA initiated a two-year Basic Archival Conservation Program. The program is providing training and guidance to enable archivists to assess conservation needs and establish realistic programs. The emphasis is on a comprehensive approach, which integrates conservation practices with all other aspects of archival management.[3] Twelve workshops are being held throughout the country, and a consultant service is available for repositories on a cost-sharing basis. The program will reach approximately 350 staff members through the workshops and 50 institutions through the consultant service and will culminate with the publication of a basic conservation manual as part of SAA's *Basic Manual Series.* In 1982 NEH funded the Basic Archival Program II to extend the project to the preservation of photographic collections.

AMERICAN INSTITUTE FOR CONSERVATION OF HISTORIC AND ARTISTIC WORKS

The American Institute for Conservation (AIC) is a professional association of conservators and conservation scientists working both in private practice and for institutions. Its purpose is to exchange and disseminate information on conservation and conservation techniques and to encourage and maintain high standards among conservators. AIC constitutes a national resource of expertise in the conservation of cultural objects. Although its main orientation is museum objects, AIC also considers the conservation of books, maps, documents and photographs held in libraries. The affiliated Foundation of the American Institute for Conservation (FAIC) raises funds for the scientific and educational activities of AIC, promotes awareness of conservation among the general public and documents the history of conservation. AIC Fellows are members endorsed and elected by other Fellows following an examination or investigation that may be required by the membership committee to demonstrate the applicant's knowledge, skill and experience. AIC also has professional associate, associate and institutional members.

The *Journal of the American Institute for Conservation* is published biannually and contains refereed scholarly articles. The *Newsletter* keeps members informed about news, workshops, conferences, courses and seminars, new supplies and equipment, position openings, publications, technical information and the concerns of members. To meet the needs of members and in recognition of the diversity of cultural artifacts, speciality groups were organized in 1980 to provide both focused activities at the annual meeting and an opportunity for a less formal exchange of information, ideas and techniques. The groups include Book and Paper, Textiles, Objects, Wooden Artifacts and Furniture, Paintings, and Photographic Materials.

Major concerns of AIC are with the ethics of conservation treatment; the obligation to preserve the integrity of an object being treated; and the education, certification and professional standards of the membership. Each Fellow and Professional Associate agrees to abide by the *Code of Ethics and Standards of Practice.*[4] AIC is slowly moving toward professional certification by examination and currently has a Board of Examiners (BOE) for Paper Conservators. The examination procedure includes a written application describing qualifications, documentation of treatments on works of art or artifacts representing a variety of media and problems, a written examination, a visit by representatives of BOE to the applicant's workshop and an informal oral examination.

THE GUILD OF BOOK WORKERS

The Guild of Book Workers is a national organization representing the book arts. Founded in 1906 to encourage the hand book crafts in an era of mechanization, the Guild exists to foster communication between artists and craftsmen, to encourage high standards of book conservation and restoration, and to stimulate the commission of fine bindings by broadening a public awareness of book arts. Its members include hand binders, book conservators, calligraphers, private press printers and papermakers, as well as librarians and book collectors interested in bookbinding. The Guild sponsors programs and workshops on historical aspects of the book arts and current trends and technical aspects of book-making; it organizes exhibits of members' work and publishes a biannual *Journal* and quarterly *Newsletter*. Guild services include an extensive, periodic up-dated list of supply sources, an annotated membership list and a directory of *Opportunities for Study in Hand Bookbinding and Calligraphy*. The Guild's library is devoted to the book arts, with many items available on loan to members. In April 1982 the Standards Committee sponsored a Seminar on Excellence in Bookbinding where speakers presented papers to describe and il-lustrate personal standards in the specializations of conservation binding, artists' books, designer bindings, limited edition binding and restoration binding.

LIBRARY BINDING INSTITUTE

The Library Binding Institute (LBI) is a national trade association of library binders and suppliers. Certified library binders are LBI members who agree to adhere to industry standards and whose plants have been inspected for certification. LBI established the Book Testing Laboratory at the Rochester Institute of Technology to study the physical characteristics of library books. Besides serving as a training center, the laboratory can evaluate the performance characteristics of bound volumes and evaluate new materials and methods. LBI offers a free examination service for libraries to determine adherence to specifications.

LBI addresses both production and management aspects of library binding and acts as an advocate for its members with the library community. Three representatives of the in-dustry, including one non-LBI binder, serve as consultants to the Library/Binder Relations Committee of the ALA/PLMS. The dialogue between binder and librarian helps to clarify issues concerning topics such as the selection of appropriate binding methods, the role of the binder in preservation and specifications for library binding. In 1981 LBI issued a ma-jor revision of its 1971 *Standard for Library Binding* to specify materials and methods for a library bound product "to meet the requirements of libraries for an end product capable of withstanding library circulation and use, and to provide maximum reader usability."[5] The *Standard* details the so-called "Class A" binding—an oversewn volume capable of withstanding heavy use. An appendix contains specifications for alternative cover materials and other methods of page attachment not considered the industry standard, but often more desirable from a preservation point of view, such as sewing through the fold and double fan adhesive binding.

NATIONAL CONSERVATION ADVISORY COUNCIL/NATIONAL INSTITUTE FOR CONSERVATION

The National Conservation Advisory Council (NCAC) was created in 1973 with fund-ing from the National Museum Act to study the problems associated with the conservation of the nation's cultural resources and to make recommendations concerning present and future needs. From its inception, NCAC also served as a forum for discussion among organizations and institutions concerned with conservation practice. The membership of NCAC includes nine permanent members representing national organizations such as LC,

AIC and the National Trust for Historic Preservation, and approximately 50 associate members and official observers as representatives of regional conservation centers, training programs, major repositories of cultural materials, and national professional associations and granting agencies.

In NCAC's role as an advisory body, it established study committees and task forces to gather information on which to base policy recommendations. Besides publishing a preliminary analysis of conservation needs and possible corrective actions, NCAC also published reports on regional centers, conservation needs of libraries and archives, scientific support for conservation, education and training, architectural conservation and conservation facilities.[6] In addition to its fact-finding and advisory roles, NCAC was charged to consider the advisability of creating a national institute for conservation (NIC). Such an institute would advance the cause of conservation by working to increase public understanding and support; by providing sophisticated support services (such as information retrieval, continuing education and analytical testing) for existing preservation efforts and for practicing conservators; and by stimulating and coordinating research and development.

The general concept of a national institute was endorsed in 1977 by NCAC, and a *Discussion Paper on a National Institute for Conservation of Cultural Property* was published in 1978 and distributed widely for discussion and comment. In 1982 a specific and detailed *Proposal for a National Institute for the Conservation of Cultural Property* was published that incorporated the concerns and stipulations of the conservation community. The proposal outlines the organization of a NIC, describes possible functions of three divisions—information services, education services, and scientific research and development—and discusses a proposed staff, space requirements and projected budget. Following publication of the proposal, NCAC changed its name to NIC to reflect its directions more accurately. It is currently seeking funding to provide services to the conservation community.

ASSOCIATION OF RESEARCH LIBRARIES

The Association of Research Libraries (ARL) is an organization of 113 large research libraries in the United States and Canada dedicated to expanding national library cooperation and improving access to research materials. *ARL Statistics* is published annually and used to compare and rank research libraries in categories such as the size and composition of the collection and staff, interlibrary loans, expenditures and salaries. ARL's Office of Management Studies (OMS) plans and administers programs to help libraries assess their management, organization and operations through a formal assisted self-study process. Programs such as the Public Services Improvement Program, the Management Review and Analysis Program, and the Collection Analysis Project help libraries to examine aspects of their collection and services and plan for change, improvement or reorganization. *SPEC Kits* are published by the OMS Systems and Procedures Exchange Center on specific topics and consist of compilations of in-house documents from ARL members that reflect current practices. *SPEC Kits* on preservation include *No. 66 Planning for Preservation, No. 69 Preparing for Emergencies and Disasters* and *No. 70 Basic Preservation Procedures.*

ARL actively seeks funding to carry out special projects and also cooperates with other organizations to enhance communication between research libraries and the scholarly community and to improve bibliographic access to research library resources. The ARL Microform Project was established in 1981 to coordinate cooperative cataloging ventures that will provide bibliographic access to titles produced in large microform sets. ARL coordination will ensure that there is no duplication of effort, that standards are followed, that the work is evenly distributed and that the records are available to all libraries in convenient forms.[7]

ARL has been a strong voice for national preservation planning. In 1960 it established a committee on preservation, which in 1962 charged Gordon R. Williams with preparing a plan for dissemination and preservation of library materials. The Williams plan began by assessing the preservation problem and recommending the establishment of a central agency that would provide low-temperature storage for at least one copy of every deteriorating book and would make copies available on request. The plan was adopted by the committee and endorsed in principle by ARL members in January 1965.[8] The Williams report assumed that libraries would be willing to donate materials to a central agency for preservation. However, in the late 1960s the largest libraries had instead begun to develop in-house programs to grapple with the preservation problem. ARL published a second report in 1972 by Warren J. Haas that reviewed current preservation activities and recommended action in the areas of research, education and training, local preservation programs and collective action.[9] The important point that preservation is inseparable from the broader objectives of access to and dissemination of research resources was emphasized. In the 10 years since the Haas report, many of the projections and recommendations have in fact materialized.

In 1980 ARL addressed the preservation problem through a two-year project funded by NEH to design and test a self-study procedure that would enable academic libraries to identify and address their preservation problems. The Preservation Planning Program was based on a strategy that involves local library staff in the investigative and planning stages that are preliminary to increased preservation activities and that help build a broad base of support for preservation within the library. The *Preservation Planning Program Manual*[10] describes and illustrates the self-study process for preservation planning. A companion *Resource Notebook* contains important and often difficult to obtain materials and cites published materials to increase specific knowledge of preservation among the study team and task forces. Involvement in the formal program through OMS includes extensive consultation, training and assistance.

RESEARCH LIBRARIES GROUP

The Research Libraries Group, Inc. (RLG) was organized in 1974 and included the New York Public Library (NYPL) and the libraries of Yale, Columbia and Harvard universities (Harvard later withdrew). In 1980 RLG amended its charter and enlarged its membership; there are now 25 full members throughout the country. This increased membership considerably expands RLG's potential for effective cooperative action and coordinated activities.

The Research Libraries Information Network (RLIN) is RLG's automated bibliographic network. RLG addresses problems faced by larger libraries of rising costs and dwindling funds for resources. RLG has a standing Preservation Committee composed of a representative of each full member library. The committee addresses common concerns, potential cooperative preservation activities such as cooperative filming and preservation responsibility in conjunction with collection strengths, and topics such as specifications for binding.

Plans are underway to develop RLIN enhancements for preservation, including the ability to enter information on preservation microfilming and the physical condition of specific items in members' collections for lending/use purposes. The entering of item-specific information about the existence of master microform negatives and service copies and the *intent* to film specific items is a priority of RLG.[11] The basis of the project will be the preservation microfilming information currently entered from the New York Public Library's master negative file. Projected RLIN enhancements for preservation purposes will be compatible with MARC format so that information can be transferred among automated data bases. The system will be capable of producing an RLG list of microform masters. The implementation of RLG's Preservation Program has resulted in increased and upgraded preservation efforts in some of the largest research libraries in the country. The ability to share preservation information outside of RLG will be a valuable contribution to a national preservation program.

PRESERVATION OFFICE, THE LIBRARY OF CONGRESS

The preservation function at LC was reorganized in 1967 to provide a comprehensive program and greater emphasis on the application of scientific principles and sound administrative methods. The new Preservation Office replaced existing binding and restoration activities performed for LC by Government Printing Office employees and centralized all preservation and conservation activities (except those for motion picture films and sound recordings) under one office and budget.

The Preservation Office includes four subordinate offices and the National Preservation Program. The Restoration Office treats individual items in the collections and implements the phased preservation program (see Chapter VIII). The Binding Office coordinates all contractual binding done by commercial binderies for the general collections—about 200,000 items per year. The Research and Testing Office conducts sophisticated research into the mechanisms of deterioration and preservation and works to develop solutions to preservation problems. The research laboratory also provides limited testing and evaluation of conservation materials and supplies and performs analytical services. The Preservation Microfilming Office administers LC's program of microfilming brittle and deteriorated materials and encourages cooperative microfilming projects. Actual camera work is done by the library's Photoduplication Service to specifications.[12] Approximately $1 million is spent annually on preservation microfilming—40% on brittle books and 60% on serials, newspapers and special collections. The move to the Madison building in summer 1981 greatly expanded facilities for preservation and, for the first time, located the entire Preservation Office in adjacent quarters.

During the last 15 years, the Preservation Office has been a moving force in the preservation field. Its organization has served as a model (albeit large) for other libraries by defining separate but interconnected preservation functions. In the absence of an academic training program for library conservators (see below, Columbia University Program), LC provided in-house training for its own staff, advanced training for staff from other institutions and internships for graduates of museum conservation programs. The research laboratory has been responsible for important basic research and the development of improved conservation techniques. (See Chapter VIII for descriptions of LC contributions to research and development.)

The Preservation Office has served as a clearinghouse for preservation and conservation information and disseminated the results of its own research and development (see below, National Preservation Program). The official publications program, although modest, has produced several important works.[13-18] Some of the most useful written information has been LC's own in-house series, *Conservation Workshop Notes on Evolving Procedures.* Finally, the superior staff that has led the way continues to play a leadership role in national associations and frequently participates in conferences, seminars and workshops.

FUNDING AGENCIES

Grants for preservation and conservation projects from the Council on Library Resources (CLR), the NEH, the Office of Education Higher Education Act (HEA) and the Andrew W. Mellon Foundation have been vital to progress in the preservation field. Many other private and public sources have also contributed to the preservation cause by funding important and innovative programs and projects.

CLR, established in 1956 by the Ford Foundation, has supported basic and developmental research and pilot preservation projects from the first year of its operation.[19] CLR supported the work of the Barrow Research Laboratory for 16 years, ALA's Library Technology Project (1959-1973),[20] and research conducted by Richard D. Smith as a doctoral student at the University of Chicago (1966-1970).[21] Beginning in 1971, CLR provided funds over a five-year period to equip and support the Preservation Research and Testing Laboratory at LC. In 1972 CLR provided start-up funds for the New England (now Northeast) Document Conservation Center as a model regional center for library and archival materials. After two years the Center became self-supporting (see below, Regional Treatment Centers).

CLR has supported many smaller projects including Gordon R. Williams' 1964 report for ARL, the Brittle Books Project at LC, and a publication of the American Association for State and Local History, *Collection, Care and Use of Historical Photographs,* by Robert Weinstein and Larry Booth (1977). CLR supported the December 1976 National Preservation Program Planning Conference at LC—an invitational conference that brought together 60 individuals from the library, archival, scientific and conservation communities for discussion of the implications and implementation of a national plan for preservation.[22] In 1979 CLR formed the Committee on Production Guidelines for Book Longevity to enhance the dialogue among publishers, paper manufacturers and librarians and to form guidelines for reasonable permanence and durability of publishers' products based on criteria established for different categories of materials.

The Research Resources Program in the Division of Research Programs of NEH focuses on making research materials accessible to scholars. In addition to funding projects such as the microfilming of materials in foreign repositories and the development and publication of finding aids, NEH also funds model conservation and preservation projects.[23] In 1978 NEH awarded $190,000 to Yale University libraries for a three-year project to survey the collections, to develop workshop and training materials and to provide internships in bookbinding, conservation and preservation administration. NEH funds made possible the ARL/OMS Preservation Project to design a self-study procedure for academic libraries. NEH also made possible the planning study for Columbia University's preservation and conservation programs. A matching grant of $375,000 was subsequently made to establish the programs (see below). NEH's Challenge Grant program provides $1 for every $3 raised in the private sector and has stimulated many more preservation projects than would have been possible through federal funding alone.

Many grants awarded under the HEA Title II-C Strengthening Research Library Resources program have included a preservation or conservation component. Support for cataloging or processing rare materials has often been combined with support for their physical and intellectual preservation through microfilming, deacidification and restoration. A 1978 HEA grant of $550,000 went to NYPL to support preservation microfilming, the restoration of rare materials and the microfilming of a collection of deteriorating bound pamphlets. Title II-C funds were used by Columbia University libraries to bring the master microform negative collection under bibliographic control, to provide conservation treatment for over 1500 architectural drawings in the Avery Architectural and Fine Arts Library, to develop standards for the storage of drawings, to microfilm rare Chinese materials, to provide a range of treatments for rare books in the Health Sciences Library and to treat rare American and English literary and art posters. Such diversified projects are the heart of the Strengthening Research Library Resources program.[24]

Private foundations have provided funds for numerous preservation projects, often with more flexibility than is possible with federal funding agencies. Foundations have frequently supplied money for the restoration of specific collections and matching money for projects under NEH's Challenge Grant program. The Andrew W. Mellon Foundation, especially, has generously funded projects of a cooperative nature such as entering NYPL's master negative file into the RLG/RLIN data base, a training and workshop program at the paper conservation department at Johns Hopkins University library, and supporting the Conservation Center for Art and Historic Artifacts in Philadelphia (see below, Regional Treatment Centers).

The existence of external funding has been critical in bringing the preservation field to its present level of sophistication and activity. Grant funds have been particularly useful in stimulating cooperation and priming institutional support of preservation and conservation programs. Without the assistance of funding agencies at crucial moments, progress in solving preservation problems would surely have languished. External support, however, cannot be a substitute for local support. Funding agencies have increased their emphasis on the coordination of activities at the national level, nonduplication of effort, the cooperative nature of project proposals and assurances of institutional commitment.

COOPERATIVE PRESERVATION AND CONSERVATION EFFORTS

The concept of cooperative preservation is simple. By joining together, libraries can save resources and money, avoid duplication of effort and have access to services that would otherwise be inaccessible. The mechanisms of cooperation, however, are not very simple. Formal arrangements that take into consideration fiscal and personnel resources are complicated to arrange, and require equal levels of commitment on the part of all libraries involved. Progress in national preservation planning and coordination has been slow since libraries have only recently become more aware of the need for broad-based preservation programs and cognizant of the scope and complexity of the preservation problem. The work accomplished through ARL and RLG is reflective of a national preservation program and indicative of increased interest on the part of libraries in a coordinated effort. LC's National Preservation Program (NPP), christened after the 1976 planning conference, is beginning to define its role in the cooperative arena, and interest in regional conservation is burgeoning.[25]

NATIONAL PRESERVATION PROGRAM

From a slow start, the NPP is gearing up to serve as a nationwide information clearinghouse. The expanded NPP will have an active publications program and advanced internship opportunities. A planned technical consulting service will make expertise at LC more readily available. From the beginning, LC's preservation program has been, in a sense, nationwide; exploring theoretical and managerial solutions to the Library's own preservation problems has worked for the benefit of all libraries. NPP will enhance LC's nationwide role and provide direction and coordination to preservation by helping to define priorities, by actively communicating the methods and technology explored at LC and elsewhere, and by making models available from which other libraries can work.

REGIONAL PROGRAMS

Several projects have been aimed at developing regional interest in preservation. The Western States Materials Conservation Project funded in 1979 by the National Historic Publications and Records Commission began as a year-long project to determine conservation needs in the states west of the Mississippi River and to develop a coordinated plan for the West.[26] At 20 state meetings and a subsequent feasibility colloquium, librarians identified existing conservation programs, defined needs and suggested action. On a more modest scale, in 1982 the Midwest Regional Study for Materials Conservation held three regional colloquiums to determine interest in cooperative conservation. The Colorado Conservation Study in 1980-1981 combined a workshop and survey agenda to reach a representative sample of libraries in the state as a prerequisite to outlining a statewide conservation program.[27,28]

Three other regional projects are using grant funds to develop a package of specific services to encourage cooperation. The Book Preservation Center serving the New York metropolitan area is sponsored by the New York Botanical Gardens Library and is funded by a generous three-year grant from NEH. The Center holds workshops, distributes training materials and helps "librarians implement in-house preservation programs within the very real limitations of space, money, and staff."[29] The Illinois Cooperative Conservation Program (ICCP), using funds from the Library Services and Construction Act and operating from a base at Morris Library, Southern Illinois University, under the umbrella of the Illinois Library and Information Network (ILLINET), is conducting an 18-month project to develop a cooperative approach to preservation in a one-state region. ICCP is conducting workshops around the state, dispensing information in the form of focused information sheets and posters, and developing a modest package of other services.[30]

With start-up funds from NEH, the State Historical Society of Wisconsin will develop, over a two and a half year period, a Wisconsin Statewide Conservation Service Center. The Center will provide leadership and assistance to Wisconsin institutions to enhance the preservation of research materials. Activities will include on-site consultation, education, training and minimal treatment services.

An important concept in cooperative conservation is that, whatever services are available cooperatively, they must be *in addition* to activities taking place at individual libraries.

Also vital to the preservation effort are library administrators who are willing to commit staff time and funds to reorganize and upgrade the preservation and conservation function within their own libraries. Cooperation is not a substitute for local action, but an enhancement. Preservation knowledge and action (however modest) on the local level are prerequisites to effective cooperative action.

REGIONAL TREATMENT CENTERS

The most notable development in the area of regional conservation for library materials has been the experience of the Northeast Document Conservation Center (NEDCC). NEDCC was formed in 1973 but was conceived as early as 1965 by Walter Muir Whitehill and George Cunha at the Boston Anthenaeum. The Center was established under the New England Interstate Library Compact with start-up funds from CLR.[31] Today, a staff of 30 serves a clientele of several hundred members ranging from small historical societies to large university libraries. NEDCC provides professional conservation treatment for a wide variety of materials including flat paper (maps and manuscripts), books and art on paper. A microfilm service produces master negatives and service copies and specializes in hard-to-film materials. NEDCC, which began as a treatment center, expanded to include field services such as mobile fumigation, disaster assistance, on-site consulting, surveys and collection evaluations, and workshops.[32]

The Conservation Center for Art and Historic Artifacts (CCAHA) in Philadelphia is an independent, nonprofit treatment laboratory specializing in the treatment of works of art on paper but also involved in survey and workshop activities. The center serves a varied membership in the mid-Atlantic region and is organized solely for the purpose of providing conservation services to its membership. A new archival treatment section has been added, and the center is contemplating the addition of book conservation facilities.

The Kentucky Department of Libraries and Archives offers document restoration services for Kentucky institutions—primarily for flat paper documents. The document preservation section also provides information services for the state and acts as a clearinghouse for information. Workshops are given for libraries and historical societies. The Public Records Division provides disaster assistance for any repository with records relating to Kentucky history and stocks an inventory of equipment and supplies needed in disaster situations.

From its inception, it was hoped that NEDCC would serve as a prototype for other regional centers serving libraries and archives around the country. In 1982, nine years after its start, NEDCC is still the only major regional treatment center devoted *primarily* to library and archival materials. The development of a treatment center is a complicated and expensive undertaking, and experts have vigorously warned against the too rapid rise of multiple treatment centers before there are enough qualified people to staff them.[33]

Treatment centers are essentially devoted to highly specialized item-by-item treatment of art works, rare books and unique materials. Raising the conservation consciousness of curators, librarians and administrators has resulted in a shift in focus toward the long-term maintenance of *whole collections* and preservation of the intellectual content of deteriorating library and archival materials. Can an institution support a regional treatment center when it can only afford to send a few special items for treatment each year and when the bulk of the collection is in desperate need of preservation attention? NEDCC and CCAHA have responded to this shift in focus by expanding consulting and training activities and by working closely with clients to help them select materials for treatment within the framework of a rational overall plan. Fledgling cooperative and regional efforts around the country are emphasizing those activities that help libraries develop viable local programs to cope with the preservation problem.

TYPES OF COOPERATIVE SERVICES AND ACTIVITIES

All libraries need to preserve the *mass* of deteriorating materials as well as to arrange for the physical treatment of special items. Based on the experience in cooperation to date, it may be that the best arrangement for providing conservation services is a regional treatment center that can also dispense information, provide workshop and consulting activities, and coordinate regional cooperative projects. The question still remains, however: Can all these needs be met by a network of nationally linked regional centers?

Information and Training

Information services have as their goal the dissemination of specific information to those people who need it. Examples of specific preservation information are recommended standards for environmental control, how to air dry a damp book, a source for alkaline paper and box board, and specifications for archival processing of microfilm. Conservators would need specific technical and scientific information from a national center such as an expanded National Institute for Conservation (see NCAC/NIC above). Regional centers dispensing information and libraries with preservation programs would need reliable technical information through the clearinghouse function of the National Preservation Program. Workshops are also a type of information service and can be offered regularly or periodically. Short, intensive courses to teach simple conservation procedures can also be offered by a cooperative center, regional group or national professional association.

Consulting and Surveying

Shared expertise in the form of a consultant service can help members of a cooperative venture identify problems and determine directions. Collection surveys define and quantify individual situations, and accompanying reports can suggest improvements and serve as a basis for justifying increased funding for the local preservation effort. An inspection of the building might reveal the most economical plan for improving air exchange, upgrading systems for filtration of airborne pollutants or adapting existing air-conditioning systems for humidity control. A consultant could survey present treatment practices and make recommendations for upgrading and expanding routine repair operations. A specific, valuable collection might warrant piece-by-piece examination by a conservator with recommendations for protection, treatment options and costs. Consultation can be a routine service offered by a conservation center; or a cooperative center could serve a liaison function and arrange for a consultant or put libraries in touch with appropriate experts.

Cost Sharing

The dictionary definition of cooperation stresses economic cooperation and mutual profit. Conservation services that are financially unfeasible for the individual library or infrequently needed can be made available through cost sharing or a pooling of resources. For example, there is no reason for every library to own a $7000 fumigator that may be used only a few times a year. Likewise, large batches of polyester film encapsulation may be performed more efficiently and less expensively at a cooperative center that owned a machine to seal the edges of the envelope neatly and quickly. It is cost efficient for a cooperative center to invest in technology that will improve the efficiency of preservation services for large quantities of materials and make the technology available to many small institutions through a shared facility.

Coordinated Preservation Microfilming Projects

Coordination of large-scale preservation microfilming projects is a logical role for a formal cooperative organization or center to assume. Libraries that are already cooperating for interlibrary loans, cataloging, or coordinated purchasing of materials can also plan preservation microfilming projects that will reduce costs by eliminating duplication of effort and achieve greater preservation of information by combining resources. Cooperative filming projects can also allow specific libraries to concentrate on their strengths, thereby enhancing bibliographic control of discrete subject areas.

Treatment

For a number of very valid reasons, the literature of cooperative conservation is replete with warnings about the establishment of treatment centers. First, fully trained conservators are still scarce, and there are simply not enough qualified people available to direct the workshops of many regional centers. Second, technical support staff must be trained in-house—a time-consuming and costly undertaking. Third, the cost of equipping a full-scale treatment facility is great. And fourth, even "at-cost" treatment is very expensive.

Some economies of scale are possible for some types of treatment, but many operations take a given number of hours to be completed satisfactorily, regardless of whether the work is done on a profit or not-for-profit basis. A center normally charges for services on an hourly basis. Overhead is included in the billing rate. There cannot be "fixed" costs for certain treatments because of the wide range of damage that can accrue to materials, as well as variations in the physical properties of materials, the environment in which the item was stored, and the use or abuse to which the item was subjected. The success of a center may depend on the ability of its conservators to estimate accurately the cost of each individual job and the willingness of its members to pay large sums for the treatment of individual items.

EDUCATIONAL OPPORTUNITIES IN PRESERVATION AND CONSERVATION

In 1976, ALA's Preservation of Library Materials Section *Preservation Education Directory* began as a two-page description of 12 academic courses in preservation. The latest edition, in 1981, is a 30-page listing of three extensive programs, 25 regular courses taught at library schools, 37 library schools that teach preservation as parts of other courses, and 25 other institutions offering courses or workshops on preservation on a continuing basis. Preservation and conservation are also the topics at numerous seminars, colloquiums, workshops and institutes; in addition, pioneers in the field and noted conservators have received repeated requests for speaking engagements.

Special Programs and Workshops

Educational opportunities in preservation are sponsored most frequently by library schools, universities as part of a continuing education curriculum, and libraries with comprehensive preservation programs of their own. National organizations, state library associations, state libraries, and regional consortiums and networks also frequently sponsor special programs on preservation. Indicative of the infiltration of preservation into professional librarianship are the programs being presented as part of the *regular* meetings of state and regional library associations.

Workshops are also held in conjunction with cooperative and regional programs. Regional planning studies such as the Colorado Conservation Study, the Midwest Regional Conservation Study and the Western States Materials Conservation Project have all held regional workshops as a way of informing participants of the need for preservation, as well as for eliciting discussion of issues in a regional context. Many others are following this pattern. The Northeast Document Conservation Center regularly holds workshops as part of its education and field services programs. SAA's Basic Archival Conservation Program supports a nationwide series of workshops to focus on the needs of small archival repositories, and the Illinois Cooperative Conservation Program held a series of eight workshops to disseminate basic conservation knowledge to a diverse library audience.

A wide range of topics is covered at workshops and seminars, including causes of deterioration; preventive measures such as environmental control, maintenance and housekeeping; preservation management and administration; disaster prevention and preparedness; library binding, mass treatments, simple repairs and protective measures; preservation microfilming and information preservation programs; and ethical considerations in the treatment of rare materials.

Some of the most successful program agendas are those that focus on a particular audience or type of material. The month-long Columbia Institute on the Development and Administration of Programs for the Preservation of Library Materials was taught in summer 1978 to prepare 12 experienced librarians to administer preservation programs. A Conference on Preservation Management of Performing Arts Collections was sponsored by the Theater Library Association in spring 1982 to address the special problems of collections containing everything from audiovisual material and paper ephemera to set designs and costumes. The University of Texas at Austin offers a series of courses on a continuing basis on the preservation and restoration of photographic images. Courses that focus on a specific topic provide an opportunity for more in-depth coverage than is possible with courses for a general audience.

Many preservation librarians and conservators have lamented that workshops and seminars are attended by those people that are already convinced of the need for preservation. Increasingly, workshop planners are attempting to tailor their programs to meet the interests of library administrators—those people in a position to have a real impact on the implementation and success of broad preservation programs. Administrators are interested in topics such as staffing for preservation, costs, staff and patron education, and cooperative efforts.

Likewise, many people who attend programs to learn "how-to-do" preservation are disappointed by the theoretical nature of the presentations. These attendees are interested in specific treatments, the organization and equipping of work areas, and demonstrations of hands-on techniques. In recognition of the need for interest, participation and action on many levels and from different perspectives, ALA's Preservation of Library Materials Section is planning a series of regional workshops in cooperation with LC's Preservation Office beginning in the spring of 1983. A one-day workshop will be held for library administrators, a two-day workshop will be held for middle management librarians with preservation responsibilities, and two five-day hands-on workshops will be held to teach simple remedial and protective conservation techniques.

Continuing Courses

Workshops and seminars aimed at library administrators and librarians alert them to preservation problems and administrative and managerial solutions, while workshops demonstrating basic conservation techniques are a method of preventing deterioration by teaching people very simple hands-on procedures that are conservationally sound. There are also continuing courses to provide more intensive training. For example, for years LC accepted interns from other libraries and helped fill a gap in conservation education. LC staff also held summer continuing education courses through the University of California at Santa Cruz. Yale's internship program for bookbinders taught simple hands-on techniques over a five-month period in addition to more general preservation topics. More recently, nine three-month internships at Johns Hopkins University library have been funded by the Mellon Foundation for staff from other libraries. The Illinois Cooperative Conservation Program accepts staff engaged in repair activities at academic libraries for three-to-five-day training sessions geared to the particular library. Workshops held by the New York Botanical Gardens Book Preservation Center have focused on teaching simple hands-on techniques. Bookbinding courses are taught with conservation and restoration components at the Center for Book Arts in New York City and Capricornus School of Bookbinding and Restoration in Berkeley, California.

These hands-on training opportunities stop short of formal apprenticeship training and cannot be considered as a substitute for the extensive on-the-job training under a conservator that is required of conservation technicians. However, they are an opportunity for staff employed in library repair or mending units to learn simple, sound techniques that can be applied to general collections or protective measures for special collections materials. Perhaps the most useful aspect of hands-on training is to *re*train, that is, to instill conservation consciousness in people who are doing hands-on work anyway and to teach them what they should *not* do along with what they can safely do.

Conferences

Major conferences for conservation professionals, in addition to the regular conferences and preconferences of professional associations, are periodically held. They are often focused on a broad topic, and the papers presented examine different viewpoints as a preliminary to the discussion of issues. The Seminar on Fine Bookbinding in the Twentieth Century, sponsored by the Hunt Botanical Institute Library in November 1979, brought together over 150 bookbinders, conservators, curators and collectors. The Cambridge International Conference on the Conservation of Library and Archive Materials and the Graphic Arts, sponsored by the Society of Archivists and the Institute of Paper Conservation in September 1980, was attended by 460 book, manuscript and paper conservators and conservation scientists. Four days of tightly organized sessions were devoted to special topics such as scientific developments in paper conservation, leaf-casting, repair and relaxation of vellum and parchment, and priorities in book conservation. In April 1982, the Guild of Book Workers' Seminar on Excellence in Hand Bookbinding brought together 125 bookbinders and book conservators. Conferences such as these are an opportunity for the field to examine itself and to engage in intensive professional dialogue.

COLUMBIA UNIVERSITY CONSERVATION AND PRESERVATION PROGRAMS

Workshops, institutes, seminars and courses on preservation and conservation are useful and enlightening experiences for library staff, but the complexity of the preservation problem and the breadth of knowledge and skills needed to apply solutions are best taught through a formal academic program—for both preservation administration and library conservation. Even long-term apprenticeship training of conservators does not always provide the kind of theoretical and experimental situation most conducive to learning because of the production pressures of an active workshop.

By the late 1950s, the museum profession recognized the need for formal academic training in conservation to promulgate professional standards and ethics and to teach conservation applications of science and technology. In the 1960s, the first degree-granting museum conservation program was established at the Institute of Fine Arts of New York University; three other programs were established in the 1970s (Cooperstown, Queens University and Winterthur). A few library and archive conservators emerged from these programs, but the majority of students stayed in the museum world. Through the 1970s, planning studies called for the establishment of a similar program for library conservators, as well as for a specialist program within library science for preservation administrators. Finally, in 1981 programs were established at the Columbia University School of Library Service.[34]

The Preservation Administration Program is designed to prepare people to manage comprehensive preservation programs. Academic work includes those courses normally required for a library degree plus extensive work in preservation and library administration. The program also includes a laboratory course in conservation treatment and a supervised field work project. The two-year program leads to a master of science degree and an advanced certificate in library preservation administration. Graduate librarians can complete the certificate program in a single year. Graduates are prepared for positions with responsibility for activities such as monitoring the environment, disaster preparedness and staff and patron awareness of preservation; library binding and collections maintenance; preservation microfilming, brittle books replacement and cooperative filming projects; and in-house repair and protective encasement.

The Conservator Program is a three-year program designed to train "workbench" conservators; it is offered in cooperation with the conservation center of the New York University Institute of Fine Arts. Academic work includes courses in the history, structure, manufacture and composition of library materials; preservation administration, conservation philosophy and ethics; and the protection and care of collections. Six laboratory courses in book and paper conservation treatment are offered. Two summer field projects expose students to the real world of libraries; the third year of the program is a formal internship at a recognized conservation laboratory. The program is intended as extensive training in both the scientific aspects of treatment and the development of sophisticated manual skills and leads to a master of science degree in library science and an advanced certificate in library conservation.

At present, the Columbia University School of Library Service is the only institution which offers full-scale academic programs specifically in the field of library preservation and conservation. Other educational opportunities in this area are provided by related course work in library schools and specialized workshops. However, as mentioned earlier, while such programs are certainly valuable, they are not a substitute for a formal academic program.

As the role of preservation and conservation in libraries becomes increasingly important, it is hoped that more academic programs in this area proliferate.

FOOTNOTES

1. American Library Association, Resources and Technical Services Division, Preservation of Library Materials Section, *Bylaws* (Chicago, IL: American Library Association, 1980).

2. Mary Lynn McCree and Timothy Walch, eds., "Setting Priorities for Historical Records: A Conference Report," *American Archivist* 40 (3) (July 1977).

3. Society of American Archivists, Basic Archival Conservation Program, *A Basic Bibliography for Conservation Administration* (Chicago, IL: Society of American Archivists, May 1981).

4. American Institute for Conservation of Historic and Artistic Works, *Code of Ethics and Standards of Practice* (Washington, DC: American Institute for Conservation, 1982).

5. Library Binding Institute, *Library Binding Institute Standard for Library Binding* (Boston, MA: Library Binding Institute, April 17, 1981), p. 1.

.6. National Conservation Advisory Council, *Conservation of Cultural Property in the United States* (1976). *Report from the Regional Centers Study Committee to the National Conservation Advisory Council* (1976). *Report of the Study Committee on Libraries and Archives: National Needs in Libraries and Archives Conservation* (1978). *Report of the Study Committee on Scientific Support* (1979). *Report of the Study Committee on Education and Training* (1979). *Conservation Treatment Facilities in the United States* (1980) (Washington, DC: National Conservation Advisory Council).

7. Richard Boss, *Final Report of the Bibliographic Control of Materials in Microform Project* (Washington, DC: Association of Research Libraries, 1981). Jeffrey Heynen, "The ARL Microform Project," *Research Libraries in OCLC: A Quarterly* 6 (3) (April 1982).

8. Gordon R. Williams, "The Preservation of Deteriorating Books; Examination of the Problem and Recommendations for a Solution," *Library Journal* 91 (January 1, 1966):51-56 and (January 15, 1966):189-94.

9. Warren J. Haas, *Preparation of Detailed Specifications for a National System for the Preservation of Library Materials* (Washington, DC: Association of Research Libraries, 1972). Reprinted in *Information—Part 2: Reports, Bibliographies* 2 (1-2) (1973):17-37.

10. Pamela W. Darling and Duane E. Webster, *Preservation Planning Program: An Assisted Self-Study Manual for Libraries* (Washington, DC: Association of Research Libraries, Office of Management Studies, 1982).

11. Nancy E. Gwinn, "Preservation Planning at RLG," *Conservation Administration News* 10 (5-6) (July 1982).

12. Library of Congress, Photoduplication Service, *Specifications for the Microfilming of Books and Pamphlets in the Library of Congress* (1973). *Specifications for Microfilming Manuscripts* (1981) (Washington, DC: Library of Congress).

13. Library of Congress, Preservation Office, *Selected References in the Literature of Conservation* (1975). *Environmental Protection of Books and Related Materials* (1975). *Preserving Leather Bookbindings* (1975). *Marking Manuscripts* (1977). *Preserving Newspapers and Newspaper-Type Materials* (1977) (Washington, DC: Library of Congress) (Preservation Leaflets Series, no. 1-5.)

14. Peter Waters, *Procedures for Salvage of Water-Damaged Library Materials* (Washington, DC: Library of Congress, 1975) (LC Publications on Conservation of Library Materials).

15. Library of Congress, Preservation Office, *Polyester Film Encapsulation* (Washington, DC: Library of Congress, 1980) (LC Publications on Conservation of Library Materials).

16. Merrily A. Smith, *Matting and Hinging Works of Art on Paper.* (Washington, DC: Library of Congress, 1981) (LC Publications on Conservation of Library Materials).

17. Matt Roberts and Don Etherington, *Bookbinding and the Conservation of Books: A Dictionary of Descriptive Terminology* (Washington, DC: Library of Congress, 1982) (LC Publications on Conservation of Library Materials).

18. Margaret R. Brown, Don Etherington and Linda McWilliams, *Boxes for the Protection of Rare Books: Their Design and Construction* (Washington, DC: Library of Congress, 1982) (LC Publication on Conservation of Library Materials).

19. Nancy Gwinn, "CLR and Preservation," *College and Research Libraries* 42 (2) (March 1981):104-126.

20. Verner Clapp, "LTP—The Rattle in an Infant's Fist," *American Libraries* 3 (7) (July-August 1972):795-802.

21. Richard D. Smith, "New Approaches to Preservation," *Library Quarterly* 40 (January 1970):139-171. Also published in *Deterioration and Preservation of Library Materials* (Chicago, IL: University of Chicago Press, 1970), pp. 139-171.

22. Library of Congress, Preservation Office, *A National Preservation Program: Proceedings of the Planning Conference* (Washington, DC: Library of Congress, 1980). Planning Conference held December 1976.

23. National Endowment for the Humanities, Division of Research Programs, *Research Resources Program Guidelines and Application Instructions* (Washington, DC: National Endowment for the Humanities, 1982).

24. Columbia University Libraries, *Research Materials Preservation and Access,* ca. 1981. A report of activities conducted under the Strengthening Library Resources Program sponsored by the U.S. Department of Education.

25. Carolyn Clark Morrow, "National Preservation Planning and Regional Cooperative Conservation Efforts," Paper presented at the Twenty-Seventh Annual Allerton Park Institute "Conserving and Preserving Library Materials," November 15-18, 1981. Sponsored by the Graduate School of Library and Information Science, University of Illinois, Urbana, IL.

26. Karen Day, "A Conservation Plan for the West," *Conservation Administration News,* 6 (February 1981):1, 6-8.

27. Howard P. Lowell, *Toward a Cooperative Approach to the Preservation of Documentary Resources in Colorado* (Denver, CO: Colorado State Library, 1981).

28. David Alexander, "Mile High Conservation," *Conservation Administration News,* 9 (April 1982):8-10.

29. Judith Reed, "A Nucleus for Guidance, A Center for Preservation," *Library Scene* 9 (3) (September 1980):12-13.

30. "Preservation News: Re Illinois Cooperative Conservation Program," *Conservation Administration News,* 9 (April 1982):17.

31. George M. Cunha, "A Regional Restoration Center for New England," *Bulletin of the American Institute for Conservation of Historic and Artistic Works* 13 (2) (1973):6-16.

32. Ann Russell, "Regional Conservation: a New England Example," In John C. Williams, ed., *Preservation of Paper and Textiles of Historic and Artistic Value II* (Washington, DC: American Chemical Society, 1981), pp. 25-31.

33. Ann Russell, Director of NEDCC, has suggested a sum of $500,000 to establish a treatment center. Comment made during a lecture to the Pittsburgh Colloquium of the Midwest Regional Study for Materials Conservation, April 2, 1982.

34. Paul N. Banks, "Education in Library Conservation," *Library Trends* 30 (2) (Fall 1981):189-201.

Afterword

Libraries contain resources in many different formats and composed of many different materials. Library materials on paper, film, magnetic tape and vinyl chloride—to name a few—all have *physical,* as well as bibliographic, requirements. Library materials are not static objects, but are affected by an environment created by the library building and its systems and inhabited by library patrons and staff. Furthermore, library materials are used, and not always under ideal circumstances.

Fortunately, the preservation field is no longer uncharted territory. Comprehensive programs appropriate to a variety of library models are in place and functioning. Many preservation and conservation needs have been identified. Membership in the preservation and conservation profession is steadily growing, and individuals, institutions and organizations are vigorously pursuing research and development. Perhaps most satisfying, however, is that there are practical steps that can be taken today (without great expense) to extend the useful life of materials. With a little more effort, we can ensure continued access to information no matter how impermanent the original medium.

The preservation challenge calls for professional librarians to become interested in the physical packages that transmit information to users. Although taking care of what we already have may seem much less interesting than collecting and arranging new materials, it is just as integral a part of collection development. Online bibliographic systems to enhance access to library resources and sophisticated sleuthing for patrons in search of obscure information are pointless if significant portions of collections are rendered useless through disrepair and deterioration.

In an era of standstill budgets for library materials and services, and when new positions are at a premium or nonexistent, it is easy to understand why many librarians turn away from the preservation challenge. But, as Pamela Darling pointed out in her introduction to this book, an informed library profession capable of cooperative action, and commitment from library administrators, are crucial to the preservation effort. Without direction and support from library leaders and involvement of library staff on all levels, the preservation challenge cannot be met.

Appendix 1: Sample Job Descriptions for Preservation and Conservation Personnel

PRESERVATION LIBRARIAN*

Summary of Responsibilities

The Preservation Librarian is responsible for the organization of all preservation and conservation activities for the research collections. He/she is directly involved in preservation planning and assists the library administration in determining preservation policies, facilitating their implementation and promoting their acceptance library-wide.

Specific Duties

1. Coordinates disaster prevention activities, drafts the disaster preparedness plan and serves as the disaster salvage team leader.

2. Arranges for the monitoring of the library's environment including temperature, humidity, light exposure and atmospheric pollution.

3. Organizes the information preservation program including bibliographic searching for replacements and reformatting of deteriorated/vulnerable originals.

4. Develops specifications for contract binding, mass deacidification and preservation microfilming, and directs the preparation of materials.

5. Acts as preservation liaison/advocate with other department heads, bibliographers and departmental librarians.

6. Organizes collection surveys, as appropriate, to determine preservation and conservation priorities.

---

*Typical job titles also include Preservation Officer; Conservation Librarian; Conservation Officer; Head, Preservation Department; Head, Conservation Department.

7. Develops preservation training and consciousness-raising programs for staff and patrons.

8. Specifies maintenance schedules for equipment such as magnetic tape players, microfilm readers and film projectors. Monitors storage and shelving conditions and makes recommendations.

9. Develops in-house physical treatment activities appropriate to the collection and directs codification of treatment standards and specifications.

10. Directs preservation and conservation supervisory personnel and fosters effective working relationships and staff development within the department.

11. Reviews and evaluates the preservation program in light of new technology and changing needs.

12. Maintains contact with preservation agencies and organizations and cooperates, as appropriate, with other libraries and state, regional and national programs.

13. Determines the overall physical arrangement of the department and prepares a budget and an annual report.

Qualifications

Demonstrated competence in administration and management. Ability to communicate effectively and be persuasive.

In-depth knowledge of preservation issues and concerns, technological and managerial solutions to preservation problems, and current directions in the preservation and conservation fields.

Graduate degree in librarianship and additional advanced training/experience in library preservation and conservation.

CONSERVATOR

Summary of Responsibilities

The Conservator is responsible for the physical treatment of rare/unique library materials in the research and special collections. He/she assists in the development of preservation and conservation policies and is primarily responsible for determining standards and specifications for treatment that conform to professional conservation practices and ethical concerns.

Specific Duties

1. Performs sophisticated and complex individual treatments on rare and unique library materials.

2. Performs analytical and chemical tests, as appropriate, to determine treatment and provides detailed documentation of all treatments performed.

3. Arranges for/consults about the treatment of artifacts not within his/her area of expertise.

4. Conducts condition surveys and consults with subject specialists/curators and recommends treatment for specific items and whole collections.

5. Designs and organizes the conservation treatment facility and specifies equipment and supplies.

6. Supervises the installation of exhibits of materials from the research collections.

7. Recommends repair and treatment procedures for nonrare materials and trains and supervises conservation technicians.

8. Cooperates with other conservators to advance research and development in the conservation field.

Qualifications

Advanced academic degree in a related subject is normally expected.

Demonstrated knowledge of the physical and chemical nature of library materials and the causes of deterioration.

Advanced training in library conservation through a recognized academic training program or formal apprenticeship.

Demonstrated competence in the physical treatment of library materials.

CONSERVATION TECHNICIAN

Summary of Responsibilities

Under the direction of the conservator/preservation librarian, the conservation technician performs conservation procedures for a variety of materials from the research collections to enhance their continued use and preservation. He/she follows predetermined standards and specifications to ensure quality and consistency.

Specific Duties

1. Repairs books from the general collections including procedures such as rebacking, recasing and simple rebinding.

2. Performs simple conservation treatments for flat paper materials including surface cleaning, mending, encapsulation and matting.

3. Constructs custom protective enclosures for rare/fragile materials.

4. Participates in phase conservation and collections maintenance activities such as storage containerization, refurbishing, stack surveys, environmental monitoring, inspection of microfilm holdings, and cleaning of phonograph records and magnetic tape.

5. Performs routine maintenance on playback equipment and microfilm readers.

6. Assists the conservator in executing complex conservation procedures for rare or unique materials.

7. Contributes to the functioning of the treatment facility by stocking and preparing supplies, servicing equipment and helping to maintain an orderly workshop.

Qualifications

Bachelor's degree or equivalent experience in a library, academic or educational environment.

Demonstrated understanding of and respect for research materials and the role of the library.

Superior manual dexterity and willingness to learn new techniques.

Training in library conservation with a qualified conservator or experienced preservation administrator.

Appendix 2: Preservation and Conservation Associations, Organizations and Programs

American Institute for Conservation of
  Historic and Artistic Works
The Klingle Mansion
3545 Williamsburg Lane
Washington, DC 20008
(202) 364-1036

American Library Association
50 E. Huron St.
Chicago, IL 60611
(312) 944-6780

Andrew W. Mellon Foundation
140 E. 62nd St.
New York, NY 10021
(212) 838-8400

Association of Research Libraries
1527 New Hampshire Ave., N.W.
Washington, DC 20036
(202) 232-8656

Columbia University
Conservation and Preservation Programs
School of Library Service
516 Butler Library
New York, NY 10027
(212) 280-2241

Conservation Center for Art and Historic
  Artifacts
260 S. Broad St.
Philadelphia, PA 19102
(215) 545-0613

Council on Library Resources, Inc.
1785 Massachusetts Ave., N.W.
Washington, DC 20036
(202) 483-7474

Guild of Book Workers
663 Fifth Ave.
New York, NY 10022

Illinois Cooperative Conservation Program
Morris Library, Southern Illinois University
Carbondale, IL 62901
(618) 453-5122

Kentucky Department of Libraries and
  Archives
Document Restoration Services
300 Coffee Tree Rd.
PO Box 537
Frankfort, KY 40602-0537
(502) 875-7000

Library Binding Institute
50 Congress St., Suite 633
Boston, MA 02109
(617) 227-7450

Library of Congress
National Preservation Program
Washington, DC 20540
(202) 287-5213

Library of Congress
Preservation Office
Madison Building
Washington, DC 20540
(202) 287-5213

National Endowment for the Humanities
Research Resources Program
Mail Stop 350 NEH
806 15th St., N.W.
Washington, DC 20506
(202) 724-0341

National Institute for Conservation
c/o A&I 2225
Smithsonian Institution
Washington, DC 20560
(202) 357-2295

New York Botanical Gardens Library
Book Preservation Center
Bronx, NY 10458
(212) 220-8754

New York University
Conservation Center
Institute of Fine Arts
1 East 78th St.
New York, NY 10021
(212) 988-5550

Northeast Document Conservation Center
Abbott Hall
School St.
Andover, MA 01810
(617) 470-1010

Queens University
Art Conservation Programme
Kingston, Ontario, Canada K7L 3N6
(613) 547-5950

Research Libraries Group, Inc.
Jordan Quadrangle
Stanford, CA 94305
(415) 328-0920

Rochester Institute of Technology
Book Testing Laboratory
School of Printing
One Lomb Memorial Drive
Rochester, NY 14623
(716) 475-2698

Society of American Archivists
330 S. Wells St., Suite 810
Chicago, IL 60606
(312) 922-0140

State University of New York at Oneonta
Cooperstown Graduate Program,
   Conservation of Historic and Artistic
   Works
Cooperstown, NY 13326
(607) 547-8768

U.S. Department of Education
Office of Libraries and Learning Technologies
Division of Library Programs
Library Education and Postsecondary
   Resource Branch
400 Maryland Ave., S.W.
Washington, DC 20202
(202) 245-9601

University of Delaware
Winterthur Art Conservation Program
301 Old College
Newark, DE 19711
(302) 738-2479

Wisconsin Statewide Conservation Service
   Center
State Historical Society of Wisconsin
816 State St.
Madison, WI 53706
(609) 262-8975

Selected Bibliography

Adelstein, Peter Z. "Preservation of Microfilm." *Journal of Micrographics* 11:333-37 (July/August 1978).

American Institute for Conservation of Historic and Artistic Works. *Code of Ethics and Standards of Practice.* Washington, DC: American Institute for Conservation, 1979.

American National Standards Institute. *American National Standard Practice for Storage of Processed Photographic Plates.* New York: American National Standards Institute, 1972 (ANSI PH1.45-1972).

American National Standards Institute. *American National Standard Practice for Storage of Processed Safety Photographic Film.* New York: American National Standards Institute, 1979 (ANSI PH1.43-1979).

American National Standards Institute. *American National Standard Specifications for Photographic Film for Archival Records, Silver-Gelatin Type on Cellulose Ester Base.* New York: American National Standards Institute, 1976 (ANSI PH1.28-1976).

American National Standards Institute. *American National Standard Specifications for Photographic Film for Archival Records, Silver-Gelatin Type on Polyester Base.* New York: American National Standards Institute, 1976 (ANSI PH1.41-1976).

American National Standards Institute. *American National Standard Specifications for Stability of Ammonia-Processed Diazo Photographic Film.* New York: American National Standards Institute, 1979 (ANSI PH1.60-1979).

American National Standards Institute. *Method for Comparing the Color Stabilities of Photographs.* New York: American National Standards Institute, 1969 (ANSI PH1.42-1969).

American National Standards Institute. *Method for Evaluating the Processing of Black-and-White Photographic Papers with Respect to the Stability of the Resultant Image.* New York: American National Standards Institute, 1980 (ANSI PH4.32-1980).

American National Standards Institute. *Methylene Blue Method for Measuring Thiosulfate and Silver Densitometric Method for Measuring Residual Chemicals in Films, Plates, and Papers.* New York: American National Standards Institute, 1971 (ANSI PH4.8-1971).

American Paper and Pulp Association. *Dictionary of Paper.* 3rd ed. New York: American Paper and Pulp Association, 1965.

American Society for Testing and Materials. *Paper and Paperboard: Characteristics Nomenclature, and Significance of Tests.* Philadelphia: ASTM, July 1963 (Special Technical Publication No. 60-B).

Bach, Wilfred and Anders Daniels. *Handbook of Air Quality in the United States.* Honolulu, HI: Oriental Publishing Co., 1975.

Ballou, Hubbard ed. *Guide to Microreproduction Equipment.* Silver Spring, MD: National Microfilm Association, 1971. *Supplement,* 1972.

Banks, Paul N. "Education in Library Conservation." *Library Trends* 30:189-201 (Fall 1981).

Banks, Paul N. "Environmental Standards for Storage of Books and Manuscripts." *Library Journal* 99:339-343 (February 1, 1974).

Banks, Paul N. *A Selective Bibliography of Materials in English on the Conservation of Research Library Materials.* Chicago, IL: The Newberry Library, 1978.

Barger, Susan M. *Bibliography of Photographic Processes in Use Before 1880.* Rochester, NY: Graphic Arts Research Center, Rochester Institute of Technology, 1980.

Barr, Pelham. "Book Conservation and University Library Administration." *College and Research Libraries* 7:214-19 (July 1946).

Barrett, R. *Developments in Optical Disk Technology and the Implications for Information Storage and Retrieval.* Boston Spa, Wetherby, West Yorkshire, England: British Library, 1981 (British Library Research and Development Report No. 5623). Extracted in the *Journal of Micrographics* 15:22-26 (January 1982).

Barrow Research Laboratory. *Permanence/Durability of the Book; Volume 7: Physical and Chemical Properties of Book Papers, 1507-1949.* Richmond, VA: W.J. Barrow Research Laboratory, 1974.

Barrow Research Laboratory. *Permanence/Durability of the Book; Volume 5: Strength and Other Characteristics of Book Papers, 1800-1899.* Richmond, VA: W.J. Barrow Research Laboratory, 1967.

Barrow, William J. *Manuscripts and Documents: Their Deterioration and Restoration.* 2nd ed. Charlottesville, VA: University Press of Virginia, 1972.

Belanger, Terry. "The Price of Preservation." *Times Literary Supplement,* no. 3947: 1358-59 (November 18, 1977).

Boehm, Hilda. *Disaster Prevention and Disaster Preparedness.* Berkeley, CA: University of California, April 1978.

Brill, Thomas B. *Light: Its Interaction with Art and Antiquities.* New York: Plenum Press, 1980.

Britt, Kenneth W., ed. *Handbook of Pulp and Paper Technology.* 2nd ed. New York: Van Nostrand Reinhold Co., 1970.

Brock, JoAnn. *A Program for the Preservation of Library Materials in the General Library.* Berkeley, CA: University of California, 1975.

Brown, Margaret. *Boxes for the Protection of Rare Books: Their Design and Construction.* Washington, DC: Library of Congress, 1982.

Browning, B.L. *Analysis of Paper.* New York: Marcel Dekker, 1975.

Buchanan, Sally. "The Conservation Program at Stanford University Library." *Conservation Administration News* 7:6-7, 10 (June 1981).

Buchanan, Sally and Walter Henry. *Users Guide to the Conservation of Library Materials.* Stanford, CA: Stanford University Libraries, 1980.

Byrne, Sherry. "Columbia University: Pioneer in Preservation." *Conservation Administration News* 7:4-5 (June 1981).

Casterline, Gail Farr. *Archives and Manuscripts: Exhibits.* Chicago, IL: Society of American Archivists, 1980 (Basic Manual Series).

Church, Randolph W., ed. *Deterioration of Book Stock: Causes and Remedies. Two Studies on the Permanence of Book Paper Conducted by W.J. Barrow.* Richmond, VA: Virginia State Library, 1959 (Virginia State Library Publication No. 10).

Church, Randolph W. *The Manufacture and Testing of Durable Book Papers, Based on the Investigations of W.J. Barrow.* Richmond, VA: Virginia State Library, 1960.

Clapp, Verner W. *The Story of Permanent/Durable Book Paper, 1115-1970.* Copenhagen: Restaurator Press, 1972 (Restaurator Supplement, no. 3). Also in *Scholarly Publishing* 2:107-24;229-45; 353-67 (January, April, July 1971).

Clarkson, Christopher. "The Conservation of Early Books in Codex Form: A Personal Approach." *The Paper Conservator* 3:33-50 (1978).

Columbia University Libraries. Preservation Department. *The Preservation of Library Materials: A CUL Handbook, Guidelines, and Procedures.* New York: Columbia University Libraries, Fall 1980.

Comparato, Frank E. *Books for the Millions: A History of the Men Whose Methods and Machines Packaged the Printed Word.* Harrisburg, PA: The Stackpole Co., 1971.

Conrad, James H. "Copying Historical Photographs." *History News* 36:21-28 (August 1981) (Technical Leaflet 139).

Council on Library Resources. Committee on Production Guidelines for Book Longevity. *Interim Report on Book Paper* and *Preliminary Report on Book Bindings.* Washington, DC: Council on Library Resources, April 1981 and May 1982. Also published in *Publisher's Weekly* May 29, 1981 and July 2, 1982.

Craft, Meg and Sian Jones. *Written Documentation.* Washington, DC: American Institute for Conservation, 1981.

Cunha, George M. *What an Institution Can Do to Survey Its Conservation Needs.* New York: New York Library Association, Resources and Technical Services Section, 1979.

Darling, Pamela W. " 'Doing' Preservation, with or without money: a lecture on carrying on a preservation program." *Oklahoma Librarian* 30:20-26 (October 1980).

Darling, Pamela W. and Sherelyn Ogden. "From Problems Perceived to Programs in Practice: the Preservation of Library Resources in the U.S.A., 1956-1980." *Library Resources and Technical Services* 25:9-29 (January/March 1981).

Darling, Pamela W. "Microforms in Libraries: Preservation and Storage." *Microform Review* 5:93-100 (April 1976).

Darling, Pamela W. and Duane E. Webster. *Preservation Planning Program: An Assisted Self-Study Manual for Libraries.* Washington, DC: Association of Research Libraries, Office of Management Studies, 1982.

Darling, Pamela W. *Preservation Planning Program: Resource Notebook.* Washington, DC: Association of Research Libraries, Office of Management Studies, 1982.

DeCandido, Robert. "Preserving our Library Materials: Preservation Treatments Available to Librarians." *Library Scene* 8:4-6 (March 1979).

Diaz, Albert. *Microforms in Libraries: A Reader.* Weston, CT: Microform Review, Inc., 1975.

Diehl, Edith. *Bookbinding, Its Background and Technique, Volume I and II.* New York: Hacker Art Books, 1979 (Reprint of 1946 edition).

Eastman Kodak Co. *Preservation of Photographs.* Rochester, NY: Eastman Kodak Co., 1979 (Kodak Publication No. F-30).

Eastman Kodak Co. *Storage and Preservation of Microfilms.* Rochester, NY: Eastman Kodak Co., 1976 (Kodak Publication No. D-31).

Eastman Kodak Co. *Video Film Notes: Care and Handling of Television Film.* Rochester, NY: Eastman Kodak Co., 1976 (Kodak Publication No. H-40-9).

Edwards, Stephen R., Bruce M. Bell and Mary Elizabeth King. *Pest Control in Museums: A Status Report.* Lawrence, KS: Association of Systematics Collections, 1981.

Elliott, R.G.H. "Leather as a Bookbinding Material." *Designer Bookbinders Review* 2:2-8 (Autumn 1973); 3:11-16 (Spring 1974); 3:11-15 (Autumn 1974).

Ellsworth, Susan. *Handbook of Motion Picture Film Care.* Lake Bluff, IL: Kinetronics Corp., 1978.

Feller, Robert L. "Stages in the deterioration of organic materials." In Williams, John C., ed. *Preservation of Paper and Textiles of Historic and Artistic Value I.* Washington, DC: American Chemical Society, 1977, pp. 314-35 (Advances in Chemistry Series 164).

Feller, Robert L. "Thermochemically Activated Oxidation: Mother Nature's Book Burning." *Pennsylvania Library Association Bulletin* 28:232-42 (November 1973).

Frost, Gary. "A Brief History of Western Bookbinding—Without One Mention of Decoration." *The Abbey Newsletter* 2:39-43 (February 1979).

Gill, Arthur T. *Photographic Processes, A Glossary and a Chart for Recognition.* London: Museums Association, 1978. (Museums Association Information Sheet, no. 21).

Greathouse, Glenn A. and Carl J. Wessel. *Deterioration of Materials: Causes and Preventative Techniques.* New York: Reinhold Publishing Corp., 1954.

Haas, Warren J. *Preparation of Detailed Specifications for a National System for the Preservation of Library Materials.* Washington, DC: Association of Research Libraries, 1972. Reprinted in *Information—Part 2: Reports, Bibliographies* 2:17-37 (1973).

Hagenmeyer, R.W. "The Impact of Increasing Paper Consumption and Resource Limitations on Alkaline Papermaking." In Williams, John C., ed., *Preservation of Paper and Textiles of Historic and Artistic Value II.* Washington, DC: American Chemical Society, 1981, pp. 241-49 (Advances in Chemistry Series 193).

Haines, Betty M. "Deterioration in Leather Bookbindings—Our Present State of Knowledge." *British Library Journal* 3:59-70 (Spring 1977). See also discussion in *The Abbey Newsletter* 2:28 (December 1978).

Hall, David. "Phonorecord Preservation; Notes of a Pragmatist." *Special Libraries* 62:357-62 (September 1971).

Hannigan, Mary V., J. Naghski and W. Windus. "Evaluation of the Relative Serviceability of Vegetable and Chrome Tanned Leathers for Bookbinding." *Journal of the American Leather Chemists Association* 60:506-18 (1965).

Haylock, E.W., ed. *Paper, Its Making, Merchanting, and Usage.* 3rd ed. London: National Association of Paper Merchants, 1974.

Horton, Carolyn. *Cleaning and Preserving Bindings and Related Materials.* 2nd ed. Chicago, IL: American Library Association, 1969 (Library Technology Program Publication No. 16).

Hunter, Dard. *Papermaking: the History and Technique of an Ancient Craft.* 2nd ed. New York: Alfred A. Knopf, 1947 (Unabridged Dover edition published in 1978).

Illuminating Engineering Society. *IES Lighting Handbook.* 5th ed. New York: Illuminating Engineering Society, 1972.

Jedrzejewska, Hanna. *Ethics in Conservation.* Stockholm: Kungl. Konsthöskolan, Institutet för material°kunskap, 1976.

Karr, Lawrence F., ed. *Proceedings: Conference on the Cold Storage of Motion Picture Films.* Washington, DC: American Film Institute, 1980.

Keck, Caroline. "The Position of the Conservator in the Last Quarter of the Twentieth Century." *Journal of the American Institute for Conservation* 18:3-7 (Autumn 1978).

Keyes, Keiko Mizushima. "The Unique Qualities of Paper as an Artifact." *The Paper Conservator* 3:4-8 (1978).

Knight, G.A. "Factors Relating to Long Term Storage of Magnetic Tape." *Recorded Sound,* 66-67:681-92 (April-July 1977).

Koda, Paul S. "The Analytical Bibliographer and the Conservator." *Library Journal* 104:1623-26 (September 1, 1979) (LJ Series on Preservation, no. 6).

Kushel, Dan. *Photodocumentation for Conservation: Procedural Guidelines and Photographic Concepts and Techniques.* Washington, DC: Foundation for the American Institute for Conservation, 1980.

Lafontaine, Raymond H. *Recommended Environmental Monitors for Museums, Archives, and Art Galleries.* Ottawa, Canada: Canadian Conservation Institute, 1978. rev. ed. (Technical Bulletin no. 3).

Lafontaine, Raymond and Patricia A. Wood. *Fluorescent Lamps.* Ottawa, Canada: Canadian Conservation Institute, 1980 (Technical Bulletin no. 7).

Library of Congress. *A National Preservation Planning Program: Proceedings of the Planning Conference.* Washington, DC: Library of Congress, 1980.

Library of Congress, Preservation Office. *Polyester Film Encapsulation.* Washington, DC: Library of Congress, 1981.

Library of Congress, Preservation Office. *Preserving Leather Bookbindings.* Washington, DC: Library of Congress, 1975 (Preservation Leaflet Series, no. 3).

Library of Congress, Photoduplication Service. *Specifications for the Microfilming of Books and Pamphlets in the Library of Congress* (1973); *Specifications for the Microfilming of Newspapers in the Library of Congress* (1971); *Specifications for the Microfilming of Manuscripts in the Library of Congress* (1981). Washington, DC: Library of Congress.

McCrady, Ellen. "Research on the Dressing and Preservation of Leather." *The Abbey Newsletter* 5:23-25 (April 1981).

Macleod, K.J. *Museum Lighting.* Ottawa, Canada: Canadian Conservation Institute, 1975 (Technical Bulletin no. 2).

McWilliams, Jerry. *Preservation and Restoration of Sound Recordings.* Nashville, TN: American Association for State and Local History, 1979.

Martin, John H., ed. *The Corning Flood: Museum Under Water.* Corning, New York: The Corning Museum of Glass, 1976.

Materazzi, Albert. *Archival Stability of Microfilm—A Technical Review.* Washington, DC: United States Government Printing Office, August 4, 1978. Also published in *Microfilm Techniques* 7:24, 26-28 (November/December 1978); 8:8-11 (January/February 1979); 8:12-15 (March/April 1979).

Metcalf, Keyes D. *Library Lighting.* Washington, DC: Association of Research Libraries, 1970.

Meyers, James N. and Denise D. Bedford, eds. *Disasters: Prevention and Coping.* Stanford, CA: Stanford University Libraries, 1981.

Mezher, Glenham and Jeffrey Turner. *Micrographic Film Technology.* Silver Spring, MD: National Micrographics Association, 1979.

Morris, John. *Managing the Library Fire Risk.* 2nd ed. Berkeley, CA: University of California, 1979.

Morrow, Carolyn Clark. *Conservation Treatment Procedures: A Manual of Step-by-Step Procedures for the Maintenance and Repair of Library Materials.* Littleton, CO: Libraries Unlimited, Inc., 1982.

Morrow, Carolyn Clark. "A Conservation Policy Statement for Research Libraries." University of Illinois, Graduate School of Library and Information Science *Occasional Papers Series,* no. 139 (July 1979).

Morrow, Carolyn Clark and Steven B. Schoenly. *A Conservation Bibliography for Librarians, Archivists, and Administrators.* Troy, NY: Whitston Publishing Co., 1979.

National Bureau of Standards. *Evaluation of Archival Stability of Copies from Representative Office Copying Machines.* Washington, DC: National Bureau of Standards, 1974. [NBSIR 74-498(R)].

National Conservation Advisory Council. *Conservation Treatment Facilities in the United States.* Washington, DC: National Conservation Advisory Council, 1980.

National Conservation Advisory Council. *Report of the Study Committee on Libraries and Archives: National Needs in Libraries and Archives Conservation.* Washington, DC: National Conservation Advisory Council, November 1978.

National Conservation Advisory Council. *Report of the Study Committee on Scientific Support.* Washington, DC: National Conservation Advisory Council, 1979.

National Fire Protection Assocation. *Recommended Practice for the Protection of Libraries and Library Collections.* Boston, MA: National Fire Protection Association, 1980 (NFPA, no. 910-1980).

National Micrographics Association. *Guide to Micrographic Equipment: User Equipment.* Silver Spring, MD: National Micrographics Association, 1979.

National Micrographics Association. *Practice for Operational Procedures/Inspection and Quality Control of First-Generation, Silver-Gelatin Microfilm of Documents.* Silver Spring, MD: National Micrographics Association, 1979 (NMA MS23-1979).

Noble, Richard. "Archival Preservation of Motion Pictures: a Summary of Current Findings." *History News* 35:21-30 (April 1980) (Technical Leaflet 126).

Ogden, Sherelyn. "The Impact of the Florence Flood on Library Conservation in the United States of America: A Study of the Literature Published 1956-1976." *Restaurator* 3:1-36 (1979).

Orraca, Jose. "Shopping for a Conservator." *Museum News* 59:60-66 (January/February 1981).

Ostroff, Eugene. *Conserving and Restoring Photographic Collections.* Washington, DC: American Association of Museums, 1976. First published in *Museum News* 52:42-45 (May 1974); 53:40-42 (September 1974); 53:42-45 (November 1974); 53:34-36 (December 1974).

Parker, Albert., ed. *Industrial Air Pollution Handbook.* London: McGraw Hill Book Co., 1978.

Patterson, Robert H. "Organizing for Conservation: A Model Charge to a Conservation Committee." *Library Journal* 104:1116-19 (May 15, 1979) (LJ Series on Preservation, no. 2).

Patton, Frank and Pamela W. Darling. "The Bee Wing Case: A Preservation Travesty." *Library Journal* 102:771-75 (April 1, 1977).

Pickett, A.G. and M.M. Lemcoe. *Preservation and Storage of Sound Recordings.* Washington, DC: Library of Congress, 1959.

Poole, Frazer, et. al. "The Preservation Program of the Library of Congress." In *A National Preservation Program: Proceedings of a Planning Conference.* Washington, DC: Library of Congress, 1980.

Powers, Sandra. "Why Exhibit? The Risks Versus the Benefits." *American Archivist* 41:297-306 (July 1978).

Rempel, Siegfried. *The Care of Black-and-White Photograph Collections: Cleaning and Stabilization.* Ottawa, Canada: Canadian Conservation Institute, 1980 (Technical Bulletin no. 9).

Roberts, Matt and Don Etherington. *Bookbinding and the Conservation of Books: A Dictionary of Descriptive Terminology.* Washington, DC: Library of Congress, 1982.

Saffady, William. *Micrographics.* Littleton, CO: Libraries Unlimited, Inc., 1978.

Sargent, Ralph. *Preserving the Moving Image.* Washington, DC: Corporation for Public Broadcasting and the National Endowment for the Humanities, 1974.

Schur, Susan. "Library/Conservation Profile: The Newberry Library." *Technology and Conservation* 6:22-31 (Summer 1981).

Smith, Richard D. "Paper Impermanence as a Consequence of pH and Storage Conditions." *Library Quarterly* 39:153-95 (April 1969).

Spaulding, Carl M. "Kicking the Siver Habit: Confessions of a Former Addict." *American Libraries* 9:653-56, 665-69 (December 1978).

Stannard, Trevor. "An Introduction to the Photographic Recording of Archive Material During Conservation." *The Paper Conservator* 4:45-51 (1980).

Stern, Arthur E., ed. *Air Pollution.* 3rd ed. New York: Academic Press, 1976.

Stolow, Nathan. "The Action of Environment on Museum Objects, Part I: Humidity, Temperature, Atmospheric Pollution. Part II: Light." *Curator* 9:175-85, 298-306 (September 1966, December 1966).

Stolow, Nathan. *Conservation Standards for Works of Art in Transit and on Exhibition.* Paris: UNESCO, 1979.

Streit, Samuel and Roberta Sautter. "Brown Renovation for Preservation." *Conservation Administration News* 10:1-4 (July 1982).

Stuhrke, R.A. "The Development of Permanent Paper." In Williams, John C., ed., *Preservation of Paper and Textiles of Historic and Artistic Value I.* Washington, DC: American Chemical Society, 1977, pp. 24-36. (Advances in Chemistry Series 164).

Swan, Alice. "Conservation of Photographic Print Collections." *Library Trends* 30:267-96 (Fall 1981).

Tanselle, G. Thomas. "Bibliographers and the Library." *Library Trends* 25:745-62 (April 1977).

Thomson, Garry. *The Museum Environment.* London: Butterworths and Co. Ltd., 1978 (The Butterworth Series on Conservation in the Arts, Archaeology and Architecture).

Timmons, S., ed. *Preservation and Conservation: Principles and Practices.* Washington, DC: National Trust for Historic Preservation in the U.S., Preservation Press, 1976.

Veaner, Allen. *The Evaluation of Micropublications: A Handbook for Librarians.* Chicago: American Library Association, 1971. (Library Technology Program Publication No. 17).

Veaner, Allen. "Permanence: A View From and To the Long Range." *Microform Review* 8:75-77 (Spring 1979).

Walker, Gay. "Library Binding as a Conservation Measure." *Collection Management* 4:55-71 (Spring-Summer 1982).

Walker, Gay. "Preservation at Yale." *Conservation Administration News* 1:1,6,8 (June 1979).

Waters, Peter. "Archival Methods of Treatment for Library Documents." In Williams, John C., ed., *Preservation of Paper and Textiles of Historic and Artistic Value II.* Washington, DC: American Chemical Society, 1981. pp. 13-23. (Advances in Chemistry Series 193).

Waters, Peter. *Procedures for Salvage of Water-Damaged Library Materials.* Washington, DC: Library of Congress, 1975 (LC Publications on Conservation of Library Materials).

Weinstein, Robert A. and Larry Booth. *Collection, Use, and Care of Historical Photographs.* Nashville, TN: American Association for State and Local History, 1977.

Weiss, Dana. "Book Theft and Book Mutilation in a Large Urban University Library." *College and Research Libraries* 42:341-47 (July 1981).

Weiss, Susan E. "Proper Exhibition Lighting." *Technology and Conservation* 1:20-25 (Spring 1977).

Welch, Walter L. "Preservation and Restoration of Authenticity in Sound Recordings." *Library Trends* 21:83-100 (July 1972).

Wessel, Carl J. "Deterioration of Library Materials." In Kent, A. and H. Lancour, eds. *Encyclopedia of Library and Information Science, Volume 7.* New York: Marcel Dekker, 1972, pp. 69-120.

White-Zeigler, Merry. "Marriott Library's Preservation Program." *Conservation Administration News* 2:4-5 (September 1979).

Wilhelm, Henry. "Color Print Instability." *Modern Photography* 43:92 (February 1979).

Williams, Gordon R. *The Preservation of Deteriorating Books: An Examination of the Problem with Recommendations for a Solution.* Washington, DC: Association of Research Libraries, 1964. Reprinted in revised form in *Library Journal* 91:51-56, 189-94 (January 1 and 15, 1966).

Yale University Libraries. "Guidelines for the Handling of Microforms in the Yale University Libraries." *Microform Review* 9:11-20, 72-85 (Winter, Spring 1980).

Yale University Libraries, Conservation Department. "Simple Repairs for Library Materials Educational Package." New Haven, CT: Yale University Libraries, 1981. (Includes 74 slides, cassette tape, script, and 6 pamphlets).

Index

ABOUT THE AUTHORS

Carolyn Clark Morrow is conservation librarian/assistant professor at the Morris Library, Southern Illinois University at Carbondale. She is also project director of the Illinois Cooperative Conservation Program (ICCP). Previous positions include conservator, Department of Rare Books and Special Collections, Washington University Libraries, and head, bindery section at the Morris Library. Ms. Morrow has been active as a consultant, speaker and writer of many articles and reports. She is the author of *Conservation Treatment Procedures: A Manual of Step-by-Step Procedures for the Maintenance and Repair of Library Materials* and coauthor of *A Conservation Bibliography for Librarians, Archivists and Administrators*. Ms. Morrow is an executive committee member of the American Library Association, Resources and Technical Services Division, Preservation of Library Materials Section and currently chairs PLMS' Policy and Research Committee.

Gay Walker is librarian, Yale University Library, where she is also head, preservation and preparations department and curator, Arts of the Book Collection. Ms. Walker has published articles in several professional journals. She is a member of the Council on Library Resources Committee for Production Guidelines for Book Longevity.

Pamela W. Darling is lecturer in library service, Columbia University, School of Library Service. She was formerly preservation specialist for the Association of Research Libraries. Earlier, Ms. Darling was head of the preservation department, Columbia University Libraries. She is the author of *Preservation Planning Program: An Assisted Self-study Manual for Libraries* and has written numerous articles for professional journals.